Reforming
OPEN AND
DISTANCE
Education

Reforming
OPEN AND
DISTANCE
Education

Critical Reflections from
Practice

EDITED BY
Terry Evans and Daryl Nation

KOGAN
PAGE

20164 7 104566 120

Published in Great Britain in 1993 by:
Kogan Page Limited
120 Pentonville Road
London N1 9JN

© Terry Evans, Daryl Nation and named contributors, 1993

British Library Cataloguing in Publication Data

A CIP record for this book is available from the British Library.

ISBN 0 7494 0822 7

Typeset by DP Photosetting, Aylesbury, Bucks
Printed and bound in Great Britain by
Biddles Ltd., Guildford and King's Lynn

Contents

1 Introduction: reformations in open and distance education

Terry Evans & Daryl Nation

The contexts of open and distance education

As the Earth enters the last decade of the twentieth century it endures considerable social, political and economic turbulence. Recent changes to political systems and ideologies are profound and remarkable. There has been a global economy for centuries, but recent information and communications technologies have made instant international transactions feasible and, thus, global economic command very efficient. Cultural exchange has also been transnational for centuries, but global cultural industries are now controlling these exchanges. In these circumstances politicians, policy-makers and citizens are making demands upon education systems to reform.

Open learning and distance education are at the forefront of educational responses to the changes that are taking place locally, regionally, nationally and internationally. Arguably, the people who work in these forms of education are directing some of this response to achieve their own ends – they are not merely passive respondents to the dictates of government and bureaucracy. The contributors to this book can be so described, although they would argue that the ends they have in mind are concerned with the quality of education for all, not just themselves. This book is concerned with the reponses of its contributors to particular challenges in the contexts of open and distance education in the relatively stable nations of Australia, Canada, the United Kingdom and the United States of America. However, their experiences have significance for people in open and distance education further afield, and for those in education more generally. It is worth dwelling on the broader connections and implications of the international rise of open and distance education because they provide a context within which this book can be read. Distance education has developed significantly in recent decades. In most countries it has emerged to provide education at all levels for people who were removed in space and/or time from the major sites of education in towns or cities. The education provided was typically external or extension studies modifications of the existing curriculum offered by institutions to their on-campus students. These external or extension students were often teachers in rural areas, military personnel posted overseas and children in isolated communities. No matter how successful these programmes were in their own terms, they were usually regarded as marginal forms of education. More recently, open education institutions have been created, not as modifications of established educational practices but, ostensibly, as reformed practices with new values, approaches and students. However, open education has emerged internationally and historically under various promotional catch-phrases: equal opportunity, industrial and economic restructuring, efficiency and effectiveness, work-based training, independent learning and experiential learning. If distance education represented marginal education for marginal students, then open learning represented reformed educational practices for more varied economic, political and social purposes.

A separation of distance education and open learning, together with the representations of their different interests noted above, cannot be sustained beyond the domain of theoretical argument. Arguably, distance education is characterized by the use of educational technologies which assist teachers to span the distances between themselves and their students; and open learning is characterized by teachers' frames of mind, which lead them to teach courses in ways which reflect the needs, circumstances and interests of their students.

In practice, the relationships between distance education and open education have been multiple and fundamental. Probably, open learning emerged because distance education was already institutionalizing itself within the core of educational practice at post-secondary level. The UK Open University (OU) can be seen as an important landmark in (or even catalyst for) these interrelated developments. The term 'open' in its title signified enrolment policies which allowed entry to those who had not completed secondary schooling and teaching methods which catered for students who could not attend campus-based programmes on a regular basis. Its educational practices were essentially grounded in distance education; its students had to conform to a timetabled curriculum similar to those of conventional universities. In some respects, the 'open learning' push, at least in the UK, was partly a reaction to the entrenched educational practices and values of all educational institutions dealing with adults. These entrenched values and practices were not sufficiently congruent with the Conservative government's push for economic (and social and political) restructuring and so the government espoused an open learning ideology which defined new forms of education (or training) which were to be 'delivered flexibly' often to, and in conjunction with, industry.

A detailed discussion of the relationships and distinctions between distance education and open learning are offered in the final chapter, in the context of a discussion of the practical and theoretical developments in educational technology that have been of fundamental importance in both fields. As human societies sweep towards an ever more integrated global economy and polity, it will be argued, institutional education may be mutating towards structural changes of comparable significance to the birth of the academy in the wake of the literacy and the growth of mass schooling in conjunction with the industrial revolution. Although well-informed practitioners usually have a good grasp of the immediate nature of these changes, the historical and deeper theoretical connections are often less understood.

. The global market, or to use the terms of the phenomenon itself, global marketing, assaults and seduces international consumers daily. 'Coke is it!'. A few French names sell perfumes all over the world. When the Foster brothers brought their beer brewing arts from America to Melbourne in the early 1900s, possibly they dreamed of producing a global brew. Eventually, they went bust and sold out to the company which, numerous take-overs later, is Fosterizing the world.

The global media brew 'infotainment' for international consumers. We saw the Gulf War televised with all the hype of a postmodern Olympics. As the oilwell fires were slowly extinguished, viewers of a post-war documentary learn that the desert trenches may have been the front line for the Iraqi army, but the Allied front line was a series of video display terminals: command and control.

What do such changes to our contemporary world mean for education, especially for forms of open and distance education? The Pilgrims took the Protestant concept of a university with them to Massachusetts and created Harvard College. Countless other university models were exported by colonial regimes. Prestigious universities in the cultural heartlands of empires have attracted students internationally for two centuries. The managements of contemporary universities are planning campuses (branches) in other countries. The open universities have been in the vanguard of internationalizing their operations. For example, the Open Learning Institute of Hong Kong uses teaching materials from open universities of various countries on a franchise basis to teach its 'own' degrees. Rival open universities have established partnerships with colleges and universities in Hong Kong to teach their degrees in the Territory. Government agencies fund exhibitions in foreign countries for their nation's institutions to show-off their educational wares. University emissaries travel the globe, often to developing nations, to sell their courses. Open university teachers work at 'internationalizing' their courses for the global market and others work at 'localizing' the courses that they have bought in.

The technologies employed in open learning and distance education enable them to encompass anything from mass to 'boutique' education for areas such as basic literacy, agricultural or health education in developing nations, mid-career professional development for the burgeoning middle classes, school subjects for children, and workplace education for specific industries and occupational skills. Within and beyond these examples, distance education and open learning are often expected to provide more equitable forms of access to education for clients whose circumstances or disabilities have made other forms of education difficult or impossible. In any specific local context in which distance education and open learning are practised it is possible to identify the particular ideologies which frame their history, administration and approaches. Some of these ideologies will be reflected in government or other agencies' establishment and control of the institution; others will be reflected in the values of the people who work in the institution and give it educational life through technological means.

In the course of global and national changes there is a continuing reconfiguring of open learning and distance education through the interplay between governments and their agencies and the actions of people in local contexts. Education has always been under challenge for change; the reformations facing open learning and distance education in the future will require creative and critical thinking on the part of everyone involved. An implosion in education can be envisaged as all institutions reform within the emerging circumstances using technologies and approaches to teaching and learning which have come from other education sectors to their own. This could lead to the border between, for example, open learning and distance education becoming ever more permeable. New borders could be drawn around different aggregations of educational practice and student populations. Within the borders people and institutions will continue their efforts with a mixture of conservative and reforming interests.

Creating this book

All contributors to this book share a commitment to openness as a principle and a dedication to enhancing the autonomy and independence of the learners with whom they work as teachers. The book originates from a critical community convened for the purpose of reviewing the practices of its participants. Some readers may be familiar with this process from our earlier book *Critical Reflections on Distance Education* (Evans and Nation, 1989b); however, the process has been modified somewhat as the following description makes clear.

The book departs from the conventional methods employed in the production of edited collections. As for *Critical Reflections on Distance Education*, we invited contributions from people involved with a variety of interesting work in open or distance education. Where possible, contributors were encouraged to work with at least one other author to enable a process of critical reflection to occur within the writing team. A condition of being involved was that at least one of the authors of each chapter should attend one of the two contributors' seminars at which draft chapters would be reviewed. Unlike *Critical Reflections on Distance Education*, which was based entirely on Australian contributions, *Reforming Open and Distance Education* has an international authorship. Therefore, we organized one contributors' seminar in Cambridge during September 1991 – with important help from Alistair Morgan, Greville Rumble and Alan Tait – to precede a conference run by the Open University, Empire State College and the International Council of Distance Education. We organized the other in Melbourne during November 1991 to precede the Research in Distance Education (RIDE '91) seminar held at Deakin University. It was probably an indication of the contributors' enthusiasm and commitment for the project that, with one reluctant exception, every contributor attended a seminar and four, including the editors, attended both.

Prior to the contributors' seminars the authors had been encouraged, through various means, to communicate with each other directly if they wished to do so. At the seminars other forms of contact were established as people identified common interests and exchanged contact details. As some distance educators know, it is difficult to sustain a critical community at a distance. However, we knew from *Critical Reflections on Distance Education* that it was possible to make significant steps toward this goal by employing approaches common in effective conferencing and by using a variety of communication technologies. The process would have been nigh impossible without jet air transport and telecommunications!

The contributors' seminars had several purposes. The first seminar was an important deadline for all contributors to submit their first drafts. This was reinforced by the knowledge that all chapters were to be discussed whether or not there was an author present at that seminar. All discussions were tape recorded, thus giving all contributors access to a recording of the entire discussion at each seminar.

The seminars were designed to develop a community of scholars. For practical and scholarly reasons the seminars were held at educational venues: at the East Anglia Regional Office of the Open University in Cambridge and at Queen's College in the University of Melbourne. The venues provided opportunities for scholarly dining and drinking which induced conviviality. Each seminar was held over two days, commencing mid-afternoon on the first day. Although many contributors had met previously, everyone was meeting at least one 'stranger'. Some were meeting people whom they had known through their publications. Given that people were to be discussing each others' writing critically, it was important to provide a convivial context in which to meet together. In this sense we remained true to campus traditions.

The first session of each seminar was presented by the editors to establish the approach to be followed thereafter as each of the chapters was discussed in sequence. The seminar adjourned in the early evening on the first day and reconvened the following morning and continued through to its closure at mid-afternoon. However, in an informal sense the seminar continued through dinner on the first day held at a local restaurant in each case. In a more limited sense, the seminar continued at the associated conferences, as some contributors met together to discuss aspects of their writing before dispersing to their respective corners of the globe.

This book represents a sequence of events spanning more than a year during which the contributors wrote about and discussed their critical reflections on an aspect of their work. In a sense the book is a frozen text of these events, which readers may thaw to enable the various stories, images, facts and interpretations to flow into their own educational experiences. These scholarly practices are in no sense unique: much collective scholarship is nurtured in similar collegial circumstances. Many individual writers can also draw upon similar systems of social support. Indeed, all we have done is run an international seminar. However, very few of the edited collections which are such an important part of academic publications are produced through similar processes. We urge others to consider adopting and adapting the approach. The irony that distance educators need to meet face-to-face has been obvious to the contributors. We would point out that occasional face-to-face meetings are a common practice in distance education. On the other hand, we are considering computer conferencing as a basis for a future project, although it will be hard-pressed to match the scholarly dining and drinking! While the important judgement about effectiveness is ultimately with our readers, the contributors to this volume believe that it has improved our intellectual processes and product. It has fostered a spirit of critical reflection and created an enduring, if dispersed, community.

It is not always easy to reflect on one's practice in a critical way. Quite apart from the uncertainty of writing for an unknown and diverse readership, there are also the known readers who reside within one's own institutional context. For some contributors, the known readers, usually in the form of powerful figures in their institutions, prompted them to remove or dilute aspects of their critiques so as to minimize the risk of retribution. This is a sad fact of academic life which highlights the potential of critical reflection to challenge established practices and power structures. This exemplifies the political potential of critical reflection; however, our somewhat eclectic interpretation of the process of critical reflection, as it was espoused in *Critical Reflections on Distance Education* (Evans and Nation, 1989b, pp.10–11) was not 'political' enough for some readers and was doubtless 'too political' for others. We remain confirmed in our view that the process of critical reflection is a means for humans to analyse elements of their lives, as individuals or members of small groups, against a broader theoretical framework created collectively. The theoretical and practical implications of critical reflection in distance education have been pressed further in the *Beyond the Text* collection (Evans and King, 1991, see especially, pp. 7–18, 227–9). Simply, this was what we invited the contributors to do in relation to an aspect of their work within open or distance education. The project provided the contributors with circumstances in which they could do this and share their critiques within a community of similarly involved persons. Arguably, it is empowering for individuals to be involved in such forms of critical reflection because it enables them to create knowledge about their practices, and also obtain knowledge from sharing in the work of others, which enables them to act more powerfully in the future.

We hope that by sharing in the various critical reflections in this book, readers will also be inspired further to reflect critically on their own practices and contexts. Clearly, the reformation processes which surround us all in education, especially in open and distance education, call for creative and critical thinking and action. The following chapters cover a variety of different aspects of open and distance education which the authors want to share with others. We have sequenced the chapters on the basis of their common themes and resonances; however, they can be read also as separate entities which readers may take in any order they wish.

2 Open Learning and the Media: transformation of education in times of change

Rob Walker

Throughout the world a major contemporary issue in education revolves around the question: how to provide for the development of intellectual skills in the community and in the workforce? Particularly in the industrialised west, and elsewhere as governments see in education and training a mechanism for accelerating the speed of economic change, the problem of how to increase the effectiveness of professional, managerial and technical workers looms large. As economic change bites, this is often followed by the related problems of how to secure communal action, social participation, the basis for a common culture and personal safety in what has come to be called a 'post-industrial' society.

There are myriad facets and dimensions to each of the many questions that arise from this general concern but what I want to discuss here is one aspect of the central contemporary educational problem, namely the use of the media as a means of delivering open learning to the home.

Fordism and the industrial model of distance education

Open learning is currently a significant issue on the political agenda and its first appeal to politicians and planners lies not so much in its capacity to escape the 'tyranny of distance', but in its low unit cost and ready accessibility. At first sight, distance education appears to provide a solution to the current dilemma of reducing public spending while maintaining a sense of government investment in education without jeopardizing 'quality'.

In the last few years, however, as experience of distance programmes has accumulated, we appear to have moved beyond this assumption to seeing the capacity of open learning to provide a flexible and adaptable response to the kinds of changes required by rapidly fragmenting and fast moving markets, and the workforce demands that follow, as its key value to policy-makers and planners. The current claims for distance education are less about its low unit cost and more that it offers the promise of advancing the implementation of an advanced service economy and extending the scope of social justice, without the commitments, institutional costs and long-term inertia associated with the expansion of conventional educational programmes.

In the current debates about educational change, economic factors provide not just the primary motives but also the dominant motif. In metaphorical terms, distance education has often adopted an industrial model of a kind often referred to as 'Fordist' (see Campion, 1991; Campion and Renner, 1992); Evans and Nation (1987; 1989a; 1989c) have also discussed this as a model of 'instructional industrialism'. That is to say, it has been assumed that distance education – like the car production procedures instigated by Henry Ford – requires a mass audience, long-term planning, high development costs and a relatively stable product. This model also assumes the need for a range of necessary ancillary services: research and development, advertising and promotion, maintenance and quality control as well as a highly developed infrastructure.

In recent years the assumptions of 'Fordism' in education (and in industry) have reformed in terms of commitments to limited-run programmes, rather than semi-permanent organizations, to splitting training functions off from established institutions and re-locating them in temporary programmes, to valuing technical expertise and the capacity to deliver on time and to valuing independent or critical capabilities.

All this might be interpreted as a move to a post-Fordist model, though often such programmes are only possible in the short-run against a wider commitment to complex and extensive schooling and tertiary education systems (and, in the case of distance education, to a broadcasting system) which are of a different character. So, for the moment we appear to have Fordist and post-Fordist systems running alongside one another in parallel, or even in close interconnection with one another, rather than one replacing the other.

Distance education and the media

Despite the existence of better examples elsewhere, the UK Open University is usually taken to be the paradigm case of the Fordist model of distance education. Until a recent decision to revise its contract with the BBC, the OU was locked into a set of assumptions and a pattern of media use which emphasized broadcast media, when what may be more appropriate in its current context is 'narrowcasting' or what Brand (1988) calls, 'broadcatching'.

Current changes in the structure of broadcast media are interesting because they raise significant questions for distance educators. The Fordist image which lies behind the original OU model fitted well with the broadcast assumptions of the BBC when the need was for a mass audience and economies of scale at a national level. However, the BBC now appears to see its future in the worldwide satellite TV market, where it is in direct competition with CNN, rather than more narrowly with national educational broadcasting. At the same time, the emergence of Channel 4 has demonstrated the viability of an alternative set of assumptions. The underlying model here is not Fordist but closer to the assumptions of the fashion clothing market, where the aim is to respond quickly to a wide range of changing demands through the use of dispersed production with integration achieved by effective communication.

Channel 4 is commercially sponsored but its material is independently produced; it broadcasts nationally but attempts to identify minority segments of the audience. In this sense it is like a modern shopping mall or perhaps like a primary school classroom created as a set of 'learning centres'. The key assumption that Channel 4 makes about the audience is that, rather than it being a 'mass' audience it is a series of specialist audiences for which it becomes increasingly difficult to find common ground or a common culture. The image of the media that narrowcasting suggests is culturally plural, politically critical, relatively low-cost in production terms, segmented, interactive and innovative; an image in many ways closer to the current demands for open learning than the mass audience, broadcast model.

Beyond narrowcasting, the notion of 'broadcatching' looks forward to the implementation of emerging technologies which provide for a great variety of incoming broadcast sources, many of which are geared to specialist interests and which require the viewer to act in the roles traditionally assigned to editors and producers. To give an illustration, Stewart Brand describes a project under development in the Media Lab at Massachusetts Institute of

Technology which involves displaying images from multiple channels on to one screen from which a computerized system detects the viewer's gaze and selects channels for screening. Having selected one channel the viewer can then branch out into hypermedia options, for instance moving from a news presentation to background information or previous reports. This kind of technological development gives video the responsiveness to gaze we have come to expect of books and presents obvious challenges to the notions of instructional design and programming we have conventionally built-in to most distance education courses. In particular it challenges the notions we have adopted in distance education about the nature of learning, the necessary structure of courses and, more fundamentally, the relations between knowledge and control.[1]

The intersection of publishing, computing, the media and education

In his account of the work of the Media Lab at MIT, Brand (1988) uses an iconic device borrowed from the director of the lab, Nicholas Negroponte. Negroponte conceptualizes the work of the lab by depicting the realms of publishing, electronic media and computing as institutionally separate but set on a course leading to convergence as a result of technological development. The convergence occurs in home entertainment, he argues, as CD players, television monitors and receivers become more closely integrated, to be followed soon by computers, CD recorders, digital tape and modems. It is this level of integration of the technology that opens up the possibilities of 'broadcatching' as opposed to 'broadcasting', for it provides the basis for systems which place the receiver in roles that conventionally belong to programmers, editors and even producers.

The notion of the viewer as editor is exemplified by the idea of a news service that allows viewers to treat the conventional broadcast news as hypertext, moving out to background information, historical records, past news items on related topics or more detailed accounts of particular facets of a story. It should be noted that there are also developments that work to mechanize this same programming and editing process, as in the idea of the fully electronic office or the programmed television receiver that automatically records broadcasts it 'thinks' you might want to see, based on its memory of past requests.

Underlying this chapter is the assumption that, if we add 'education' as a further realm to Negroponte's diagram (Figure 2.1), what we are beginning to see, and will become a more marked

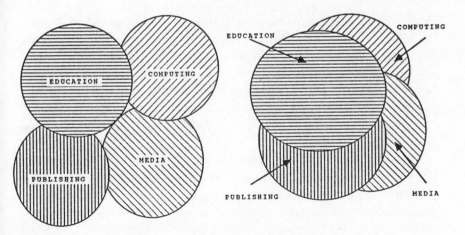

Figure 2.1   *The growing convergence between education, computing, publishing and the media (after Negroponte)*

trend in the next five years, is an increasing convergence between institutions that have previously remained separate. The change will not just be technical but organizational, economic and cultural. We will need to rethink the separations we have come to accept between education and entertainment (Brand talks of 'infotainment'), between high culture and vernacular culture, between private and public enterprise, between the word and the image and the sound.

It is, of course, important not to let the rhetoric run away with itself. It is no accident that Negroponte and the Media Lab get most of their funding from the military-industrial complex, and particularly from the communications corporations and from defence contracts. Brian Winston, one-time researcher with the Glasgow Media Group[2] sees this and warns:

> The information revolution is an illusion, a rhetorical gambit, an expression of profound ignorance, a movement dedicated to purveying misunderstanding and disseminating disinformation . . . It is my contention that far from a revolution we have business, and I mean business, as usual (Winston, 1986, pp. 363–4).

But, whoever has controlling interests at stake, it seems clear that change is imminent, and certain to have effects for education. Brian Winston's warning is important and reminds us that, in dramatically changing circumstances, we should not lose sight of the issues of equity and access, and knowledge and power.

Education and the limits of rational planning

In discussing education and the media it is easy to become seduced by the rhetoric of the post-modern. It would be a mistake to dismiss the Fordist assumptions which were previously used to underwrite distance education just because policy is shifting and some academics have found new ways of thinking about the issues. Fordist models and the rational planning models, including instructional design, management by objectives and programme budgeting, which make it possible are still in active use even if their rhetoric has been eclipsed.

Since the Second World War, and in the USA particularly during the period following the Korean War, we have seen a dramatic growth in application of rational planning models in the public sector and especially in education. Curriculum, instruction, administration, evaluation, assessment and training have all been drawn into the ambit of state, bureaucratic and organizational control via management by objectives, programme budgeting and performance review (see Chapter 7). The application of such methods has been reforming education in the past four decades. The paradox is that such methods assume a stable substrate: they fail when objectives change faster than the process can be developed and implemented (as the turmoil in many educational bureaucracies exemplifies). I suggest that we are reaching the point where social change is outpacing the capacity of rational planning models to respond adequately. The assumptions of the rational planning model which are embedded in government and administration dissolve in the face of the need to innovate rapidly.

Twenty years ago it was pointed out by the Swedish geographer, Gunnar Olsen, that planning models are not objectively responsive and value-neutral, but create realities of their own. On the basis of his experience in attempting to use regional planning models to engineer social equality, he wrote:

I have gradually and rather painfully come to the conclusion that if we continue along the methodological and manipulative path we have been following thus far, then we run the risk of *in*creasing those social, economic and regional inequalities, which the planning initially was designed to *de*crease; our good natured attempts to rectify current injustices will be self-defeating, not because some vicious bureaucrat designed them that way, but because we have failed to understand the deep structure of social research and action ... by employing analytical techniques and social engineering devices which are founded on rather peculiar assumptions about categorisation and linearisation, ... we have in effect come close to creating a society for human beings who themselves are peculiarly categorical and linear. If regional planning in Sweden, the Soviet Union and the United States have nothing else in common, it is exactly this simplified and dehumanising conception of man [sic]. Instead of creating a world for becoming, we are creating thingified man ... (Olsen, 1978, p.353–61).

What Olsen identified as a consequence of applying rational planning models to regional planning problems is even more critical when they are applied to education, where the transmission of social and cultural values is at stake. His challenge is that we cannot merely re-apply the methods, techniques and procedures we have used in the past, because they embody social values and ideologies suited to the past.

Educational technology, educational change and the state

I take it for granted that educational technologies have changed more rapidly than the capacity of institutions to reform their structures and practices. Likewise, it is important to recognize that educational institutions are not free to follow technological change. In Australia, there appears to be a prototype for a 'university of the air' patched together on the basis of a 1960s, Fordist distance education model, not for prior educational reasons, but to cope with the shift of schools' television from broadcast to video and the consequential spare production capacity, and the likely emergence of pay-TV (see Moodie, 1991b). Such policy-making, while it creates some limited opportunities, leaves unchallenged the assumptions underlying educational reform in relation to the future potential of the media. It acts to reinforce those very values and practices which need to be challenged by treating them as technical means for the delivery of existing programmes.

It is important to recognize that the need for rational planning implied by the industrial model is framed after political compromise has been secured. Behind the surface presentation of rational plans, the scale of operation of the tertiary education sector ensures a degree of state control, and relationships between education and the state are everywhere increasingly marked by conflict. Any institution which requires large scale investment is likely to be slow to change and increasingly to be vulnerable to government control[3]. Rhetoric may focus on innovation and change, but the processes ensure that conservatism dominates, and especially when concerns for accountability predominate. Education is particularly vulnerable to conservatism because its cultural role, as Willard Waller pointed out 60 years ago, is to act 'as a museum of virtue' (Waller, 1965, p.34).

Expressed another way, educational reform involves challenging values and established practice, and it therefore involves risks. The size of educational institutions and bureaucracies is such that the prevailing political concern is to reduce risk-taking, while wider, unpredicted and uncontrolled changes constantly create new problems and new opportunities, virtually with every news bulletin. We sometimes choose to act as though education were apart from politics but the truth is education is always concerned with values and its inherent dialectic lies in its simultaneous commitment to both conserving the culture and to changing it.

Two transformations

Two social transformations are critically important to educational reform in these fast-moving times. One is the institutional transformation from the campus to the workplace and the home; the second is the media transformation inherent in the shift from broadcast to recorded sources. It might be thought that the second transformation is not social but technical, but the term 'media' is necessarily social as it includes the concepts of audience, production and meaning (see Chapter 4). These transformations are two aspects of the previous discussion upon which this chapter will focus, hence there are significant questions that will remain unanswered: questions about the need to protect risk, about the desirable scale of educational institutions, about the nature and conditions of intellectual freedom. The fact that in this chapter these questions are left untouched does not mean that they are unimportant.

I should also add that my own concerns as a distance educator are defined by working largely with the problems of providing professional development programmes for teachers and other educators. I believe though, that none of us should let the scope of our activities become too closely defined, since this traps us in a limited frame of reference. So, here I have attempted to retain the problems of professional development for teachers as a point of reference rather than as a restrictive frame. What remains unstated is not necessarily neglected nor forgotten.

School and home
One aspect of distance education neglected in the haste to establish programmes is the need to think about what is involved in changing the location of study from school to home. Distance educators usually assume that their students are mature students for whom study is but one facet of their lives. This often leads them to see curriculum and learning as constants and to see the significance of the shift to home study to lie in the need to 'individualize instruction'. This limited view of the significance of context is perhaps a reflection of the fact that 'professional distance educators'

have been strongly influenced by educational psychology and instructional design. A significant consequence is the separation of curriculum from pedagogy, production from delivery, course development from research. These separations are not simply abstract or distant from the action; they have serious consequences for students.

As a way of unravelling some of these complexities, it is necessary to develop a student perspective: what looks to be rational to the planner may appear confusing and even irrational to the planned. As a way of beginning to do this we have asked students on distance courses what images they have of themselves studying.[4]

A dominant image is one of silence, stillness and of being alone. The themes that recur are of 'study' being the time, late at night, when the children are settled, the husband is watching TV in another room (many of our students are women), it is dark outside, there may be a dog or cat close by, the kitchen is clean and tidy, the lunches are ready in the refrigerator for tomorrow and the student has cleared a space at the end of the table, minimally disturbing the table set for breakfast. The books are opened and 'study' can begin.

I am intrigued, even obsessed, by this image, not least because it is at odds with many of the images I hold as the 'teacher'. It is an image in which education is seen as marginal, both socially and within the domestic economy; an image of education as contained by strong brackets, and of learning as passive, receptive and intensely personal.

It is also an image that challenges many of my assumptions, for I have tried to design courses that are activity-based and socially interactive and which build on conceptions of knowledge as communal. In our courses we require people to take photographs and talk to people, to watch their children at play, to take note of what their children say when they come out of school, to engage those they work and live with in games and puzzles and to listen to meal-time conversations with a new ear; all activities which overlap as much as possible with the demands of everyday life. But, while some students leap at this opportunity to engage in a course that is seen to be 'different', many are disturbed by the conflict that is created between the view of learning encoded in these activities and the common view of 'study' that is seen as synonymous with isolation, quiet and their transient space at the end of the kitchen table.

Whichever way we look at it, it is clear that 'individualizing instruction' is not just a matter of allowing students to make their own pace as they work through the materials. Taken seriously, it can also involve some negotiation over what constitutes the curriculum and how it is to be assessed. For instance, in the tension that exists between the students and myself there are differences in what is valued, in the assumptions we each make about what constitutes academic work, in the status of course materials as against personal experience, in the educational value of cooperative as against individual work and in the role of assessment. Gender issues are never far from the surface. These are, I believe, creative tensions of the kind that make the course 'educational' in a deep sense, at least on those occasions when the tensions themselves become the curriculum. They are not assumptions that make it easy to think about the course in the simple language of 'delivery' and they are not assumptions that make it easy to separate out the roles of course developer, teacher and assessor, or even student.

Some distance educators would see these problems as essentially technical, that is to say they believe that they could be solved with faster and more efficient communication. New advances in educational technology may offer some solutions, but I believe it is too easy to see in computer-based interactive video, or electronic mail networking, solutions to problems that only exist for the planner and not for the student. The new technologies offer planners visions for the future, but in the present world that teachers and students inhabit, they often only make things worse, encouraging us to retain separations between course development and delivery, for example, which are counter-educative. Discussions about educational technology frequently assume a plasticity in the student that is misplaced, and particularly misplaced when our audience consists of adults. Whether you sit at the kitchen table with a pencil and a book or with a personal computer does not make much difference. The real problems are primarily educational and they demand an educational, not simply a technical, response.

The image of 'the space at the end of the kitchen table' as part of a definition of what it means to be 'learning' is a particular image that appears to fit my teaching. I am sure there are other images, even within this same course. Then there are the images students have of what it means to teach and of me, the teacher. We sometimes assume that placing course materials in a nicely designed binder in itself obliterates the image of the teacher, placing the student in direct contact with the curriculum. But, as I mentioned earlier, the fact that curriculum is necessarily mediated means that teaching and learning are never the naked contact of minds and ideas, the ideal 'teacher-proof' curriculum. The curriculum is always mediated. The media are not simply contextual but a necessary part of the content.

Some might see the image of the 'space at the end of the kitchen table' as peripheral to the distance education enterprise, but to do so is to adopt the blinkered perspective of the rational planner. From a student perspective, the programme may look very different, and different in ways we cannot fully know or predict. It is also true that what is important is not just the content of the image but the fact of its existence. The point is that such images are not simply a consequence of a curriculum model: they are not noise in the system, but part of the system itself. They are fact, not artefact. They may even become the content of the course itself. For example, for teachers, to consider the images they hold of what it means to study, to teach or to learn can in itself be educationally significant and an intrinsic aim of the course.

I am intrigued by the idea of creating courses that are about themselves. In our course we ask students to examine photographs of themselves, and of other course members, teaching. A difficulty we always encounter stems from the fact that many of our students are women on leave from primary teaching to be with their children. We encourage them to persist with the task by thinking of ways in which they might depict their parental role in educational terms. The result is often delightful pictures of mothers with children, baking, gardening, reading stories, making music, caring for animals ... Somehow though, there remains a sense of disappointment that is not 'real teaching'. Later we ask them to listen to a videotape in which David Hamilton talks about his research on the history of classrooms, using old paintings, drawings and photographs as a source of evidence. Faced with images of schooling in the seventeenth century, when 'classrooms' were of a more domestic character, class instruction did not occur and the curriculum was largely individualized and informal, those students who are parents gasp at the recognition of the parallels between their circumstances and historic situations. The fact that such classrooms are seen to be closer to the modern conception of an open primary school classroom than are some of the images of class instruction in the nineteenth century adds to the insight.

The shift from school to home as the locus for the delivery of education appears at first sight to be a relatively simple change of location, but it is much more complex, not least because it causes us to rethink what we take for granted about education in institutional settings. We too readily assume that the organizational features of schools – classroom teaching, institutional timetables, simultaneous instruction – taken together constitute what counts as education, when they are essentially means not ends. Considering alternative means, even the space at the end of the kitchen table, creates different images which undercut values and practices that we tend to take for granted. I have to keep reminding myself that placing a personal computer or a video screen on the end of the table in itself changes very little. The important questions lie in the relationship between learning and the domestic economy, in how we perceive the nature of work, in the nature of the authority implied by the idea of the university[5], all questions that I would argue are fundamentally educational.

Fieldwork, desk work and reverse ethnography

Anyone who has done laboratory research, tried to carry out sustained ethnographic fieldwork, or attempted to make a documentary film, will know about the difficulty of directly observing the concepts encountered in textbooks. Face-to-face with actuality there are no equations, kinship systems or bureaucratic structures, no relationships, authority or learning. These things are abstractions which only exist when we represent what we encounter in numbers or in words. Research workers (and film makers, journalists and writers) have developed ways of coping with the ephemeral nature of reality that make it make sense, and it is this sense that generally forms the content of curricula. What we teach is mostly at the level of concepts and theory, highly abstracted from the immediate confusion presented to us in our first-hand contacts with actuality.

The problem is that those who are learners, faced with an abstraction removed from the social context of its origin, have to reconstruct it in terms that are recognizably 'real'. Hence, a large part of what counts as teaching and learning consists of visualizing and verbalizing illustrations, models, examples, anecdotes and metaphors that bridge between abstraction and our perceptual experience. In short, learning can be thought of as reverse ethnography, for where ethnographic fieldwork forces you to move from the particular to the general, learning essentially progresses in a reverse cycle.

On a longer time scale these cycles merge, and this is important for reforming open learning because it aspires to insinuate itself into the patterns of working and social life. Unlike conventional undergraduate education, the aim of open learning is much less concerned with indoctrination and more with reflection on experience. This raises important questions for those assembling, delivering and assessing curricula because it implies that we need to build in the full cycle into the way we think about course construction. At some times it may be important to present concepts, theories and ideas in the way that they are conventionally presented in university courses, and to value students' competence in assimilation, information recall and analysis. However, it is equally important to build in tasks which call for judgement, synthesis and collaboration. This may mean providing tasks that simulate the pre-world of the textbook, providing students with the vicarious experience of doing research.

Broadcast and recording
The second transformation I want to consider is a media issue and concerns the shift away from broadcast sources to the use of recordings. Current Australian Broadcasting Corporation (ABC) policy, following recent changes in the Australian Copyright Act, is to encourage educational institutions to use video and audio taped programmes rather than make use of direct broadcasting. In other countries, where copyright practice has been less constrained (in the UK, for example), video and audio recording have been used more extensively in schools and in open education.

There are many reasons why moving from broadcast to recorded sources is a sensible idea: it fits timetables, it allows teachers to preview material and students to use programmes as a source rather than as a course. It seems, though, that we have not thought through the educational impact of relying on tape as opposed to broadcast sources, which I believe should cause us to rethink the way in which we programme audio-visual material. In particular, research suggests that the use of television in school is qualitatively different to its use in the home[6], the differences being not merely differences in context but in the nature of the medium.

The production of broadcast TV and radio requires the adoption of a number of conventions which can be summarized as being the conventions of 'programme-making', that is, all those techniques and skills that producers and others use to make broadcast radio and television. Programme-making has a long and honourable tradition, it involves years of professional training and despite its basis in technique there is a certain magic to it when it works well. It is celebrated by film critics and deeply incised in the culture of institutions like the ABC, being encapsulated in the phrase 'production values'.

From the point of view of the programme maker, broadcast production values are often not appropriate to open learning video. In using video the essential values that underlie programme-making are dissolved. We no longer need to think of standard time slots, we no longer need to 'hold attention', indeed we may no longer need to edit. It is true that some of the magic of the medium may be lost, but there is considerable potential for educational gain in the complexity that can be built into the medium and in the control that the learner can have over replay. In the shift from broadcast to recorded sources, the need for authoritative narration, perhaps the definitive feature of educational programme-making, disappears.

The overall planning rationale appears to be that the shift from broadcast to recorded sources is essentially organizational. Thus, decisions are made on the basis of costs and availability, with few implications for programme organization, use or content. For the educator, however, there is more involved. Shifting from broadcast to tape is not simply an organizational and technical decision, but one that has significant educational implications, many of which are not fully understood. From the viewpoint of a young audience, sitting close to the screen with a group of friends sharing a bean bag, a packet of crisps, the family cat and the remote control[7], the world of the recorded image and/or sound is very different to the world of broadcast, not least because it can be retrieved, manipulated, discussed, dissected and deconstructed. In the process the nature of time changes, ceasing to be linear and metric, progressing from determinacy to uncertainty and instead becoming fragmented, branching and polychronic. This has consequences for the domestic economy and also for the programme-makers, not least in that it implies very different models of learning. Central to the repercussions it creates for production values in educational television is that it raises a large question mark over the need for narrative and for narration.

More than broadcast television, video has the capacity to develop a sophisticated, critical audience, more conscious of the grammar of film. In the case of children's favourite video clips, children may approach the point where they have a complete, 'frame-by-frame' memory. What they come to understand is the deep (generative) structure rather than just responding to the surface effects of the film. Perhaps perversely, television, often popularly decried as responsible for falling educational standards, can achieve a long-held aspiration of educators: to take students inside structures of knowledge rather than leaving them with the notion of learning as the rote learning of surface effects.

In one example of an alternative to the conventional programme structure, we have replaced a course that occupied 400 pages of print by one that occupies 200 pages and a 3-hour videotape (how these equivalencies are calculated is probably best left as a mystery). While some of the video is programme-like, as it includes documentary-style segments, other parts resemble observational cinema in that they aim to provide 'ethnographic' records; some are didactic; some tutorial-like; some are very short, running for less than two minutes, but requiring students to view them repeatedly in order to understand, for example, the speed and subtlety of non-verbal communication associated with conversation. Overall, the 3-hour video makes little sense without the print, which is closely integrated with it. What we have, we believe, is a course which, contrary to the conventional model, has strong aims but weak objectives and which integrates the media (we also use audio and photographs) in a way which is difficult to achieve with broadcast sources.

The implicit educational model is of the student as editor, for students are given a range of different kinds of material from which they have to recreate a text that makes sense for them. Educationally, if not technologically, the course simulates the 'broadcatching' notion mentioned earlier.

On campus – off campus

Discussions of distance education frequently start from an inherent deficit model. 'Real' education is taken to be proximal and the problem for distance educators is seen to lie in doing the best we can to approximate it (see Chapter 11). In this view the central transformation that we are concerned with is that of translating materials from on-campus to off-campus use. Starting from this point of view the problem becomes one of taking the educational assumptions of on-campus teaching and finding distance substitutes; instead of giving lectures and holding tutorials, distance educators invest their efforts in written texts, telephone conferencing, audio and video tape.

It is true that much effort goes into rethinking what we teach in terms of the demands of these formats and this is not a simple or trivial process; it demands knowledge, experience, skill, imagination and teamwork. Behind this accumulated craft knowledge, in the general direction we have taken research, development and practice, lies an error of judgement. In educational planning it is always tempting to begin in the wrong place, that is, with organizational means rather than educational ends. Curriculum, teaching and learning too easily become icons to move around on timetables, schedules and year planners and in the process whatever is human in the process becomes virtually defined out of existence.

One way of recovering other options is through historical analysis. Historical analysis has recently located the 'invention' of terms like 'curriculum' and suggests that a key term in the social process of evolving language use is 'class instruction', that is to say, simultaneously teaching numbers of students the same thing (Bartlett, 1989b; Hamilton, 1987, 1989a, 1989b). Class instruction is a relatively recent phenomenon, closely related to the development of the industrial revolution. As Hamilton points out, the classroom is in itself a technology. The very idea of 'classroom teaching', which constitutes the reference point for the use of media in education, may be transitional. The contemporary power of the media may be that we can dispense with the classroom rather than looking to replicate or supplement it. This leaves us with the interesting educational question of what education might look like if classrooms did not exist.

Open campus – open classroom?
This suggests that one of the keys to the unlocking of the classroom door lies, not in the obvious dimension of space, but in the dimension of time. It is not the walls but the timetable which constrains classroom teaching, so it is not distance which constrains distance education but course deadlines. While many distance courses allow freedom to students in the ways they programme their work between units, when it comes to a particular sequence of instruction we find it more difficult to give up the notion that everyone should proceed lock-step. David Stowe's innovations of the nineteenth century live on, close to the surface of even the most technologically-rich modern educational programme (Hamilton, 1989a; 1989b). For the student to take control over the pacing of knowledge – as Bernstein stated (1977) – is to threaten conventional notions of curriculum structure. To do so has significant consequences for what and how we teach and for how we assess student progress.

We have to turn away from teaching toward learning as the organizing concept and, in this, distance and adult educators can claim some success (see Marton *et al.*, 1984) but the research literature takes a limited view of learning, creating a perspective which only takes us so far. First, available distance learning theories mostly focus on a teacher-dominated model typified by undergraduate teaching, that is to say they assume learning objectives and they see the essential problem as one of producing unambiguous texts coupled with reliable, effective and efficient tests. Things might look different if we took PhD programmes as the model and worked back. As I argued at a more general level earlier, an approach based on the objectives model can be said to work in conditions of stability and consensus but it is not well adapted to change, particularly when plural values are involved.

One response to this problem has been to create courses that seize on contemporary or emerging ideas and use these as organizing devices. However, while this style of advocacy response has had some success it is a response that invites conflict and may place students in situations they are not equipped to handle.

Restricting our vision and our efforts to refocusing on 'learning' as an organizing principle is not sufficient for real reform. To focus solely on 'learning' is to ignore the current state of chaos in many curriculum areas and, more important, the significance of the material, social, cultural and biographic, working and family contexts within which students learn. Taking the wider view, learning objectives are unimportant and subsidiary to learning. In times of unpredictable and fast-moving change, what is important is only that students learn from the programmes we provide and develop the capacity to reflect on that learning; it should not be our primary concern to specify curriculum outcomes or to measure their efforts against performance criteria.

It does not require too deterministic a view of history to suggest that the current context is one in which we should think about moving away from the Fordist notion of uniform mass production, which has been built-in to much of our thinking about education in the last 30 years. Instead, we can begin thinking about education systems that are 'individualized' in that they incorporate within them a wide variety of designs, options and changes and are subject to constant innovation. Implicit in the notion of 'individualization', viewed this way, is not simply that the student has control over the pacing of knowledge, but also engages in the processes of its selection and evaluation. This revaluation of the relation between the student and the subject in turn raises other questions about knowledge in terms of educational purpose and the role of education in maintaining social structures and cultural continuity. Do developments in education, the media and society give us cause to redefine educational inequality? Do we need to reassess the notion of expertise and the role of the expert? What is the nature of professional judgement? What are the institutional imperatives required to secure the free development of knowledge? Such questions are essential to the universities and central to the development of open learning, for it is in open learning programmes that we have the best opportunity to reconstruct the relationship between those who learn, those who teach and what counts as learning (but also the best opportunity to close the questions).

Policy reformations

I have argued that, instead of trying to identify 'mass' audiences to whom we can deliver a highly formalized common course at low unit cost, we need to begin thinking about highly differentiated programmes through which individuals can create specialized and indeterminate routes. We need to think less about reform as creating a common culture through a common curriculum, and more about responding to individual *curricula vitae*. Educationally, this means rethinking questions of knowledge and control in relation to the roles of students and teachers, it means taking greater account of the experience students bring to programmes and it means rethinking the stance we conventionally take on the relationship between knowledge and values.

The economic assumption that distance education is characterized by high investment and low unit cost needs rethinking. Instead, one can think of spreading the cost of investment over long periods and in terms of creating generic programmes that can be tailored fast to meet the needs of emerging demands and niche markets. The 'programme funding' model needs reconceptualizing as a way of responding to fast emerging needs because courses need to be constructed around deep structures rather than surface learning. In common language, such courses need to be very clear about their philosophy, because in adapting them to different audiences and different purposes a flexibility is required which demands more than than merely updating or substituting readings.

Questions about the media are intrinsic to such reforms. It is crucial to think critically about the impact of using media other than print in open and distance education. Contemporary video and audio tape conventions of programme-making imply passive roles for the audience. The typical use of other media merely disguises the authoritarianism inherent in instructional models. There are other traditions we could draw on (as David Harris shows in Chapter 4), in community television, in documentary film making, in observational cinema, perhaps even in arcade games, and the questions are not confined to the visual media – they can be applied equally to the way we read books. As educators, our uses of language (visual and literary) tend to be unidimensional. We continue to act didactically, to teach from texts with a narrow and highly stylized view of what it means to be literate, of what it means to read, write and understand; a view which seems to ignore both the nature of contemporary culture and what many linguists and critics have to say about such things.

A central paradox for distance education

At the heart of distance education lies the problem that the ways in which we define instruction and learning – as ordered, atomistic and sequential – are in fundamental contradiction with the nature of the knowledge we seek to teach. Educators in general, and educational technologists in particular, have assumed that learning cannot be accomplished unless the teacher has a clear, unambiguous understanding of the subject to be taught. Distance education embeds instruction by objectives and strives to create texts which avoid any trace of confusion or uncertainty. But the reverse side of our acceptance of the objectives model is that we have rejected the essential values of liberal education. We have made it more difficult, not easier, for our students to learn, for 'learning' in the way that universities value the word involves the student (and the teacher) in confronting paradox, ambiguity, uncertainty and disorder. In sanitizing the concept of learning, we have deskilled both our students and ourselves, reducing our capacity to learn by reflecting on experience and so learning about learning.

Educators talk sometimes of a 'curriculum' and a 'hidden curriculum' and, hence, the discontinuity between the nature of knowledge and the restricted view of knowledge implied by our approaches to learning and teaching could represent a case of curriculum and hidden curriculum. There is some truth in this; the structure of this problem is somewhat different. The two curricula run parallel as reversed images: matter and anti-matter, chaos and order, purity and danger, each constantly destabilizing the other. As course developers and teachers, working in distance education we constantly encounter the fact that written into the script is a deep sense of irony. We find ourselves desperately trying to make sense in a world that constantly threatens to pull the ground from under our feet – and in which our best critical efforts are frequently redirected to strengthening and multiplying the forces acting to remove the rug on which we stand. The problem stems not just from a mismatch between curriculum and pedagogy, but from the realization that, while learning is difficult, teaching is fundamentally impossible.

Some concluding statements and an emerging programme of reform

1. Distance education is often treated as though it were a specialized and applied field at the margins of educational debate and educational research. The reverse is true. Classroom teaching, which is at the heart of 'proximal' education, is a highly

problematic enterprise created by historical circumstance. Distance education, in undercutting assumptions about teaching and learning in a classroom context, is a critical site for educational research.

2. Distance education, being uncluttered by accretions of organizational precedent, provides the best practical opportunity we have for disentangling accepted notions of the place of authority in education.

3. The use of media in education is not an option. All education is necessarily mediated. The important questions are about the particular characteristics of different forms, contexts and uses of media in relation to educational aims. All education and all educators are necessarily inside the media, not outside looking in. Just as goldfish are said to see everything but the water they live in, we are all users of media even though we may find this hard to acknowledge.

4. The images we hold of teaching and learning are not simply consequences of the process, or noise in the system, but a necessary part of the system. The institutional and organizational structures of education: timetables, roles for teachers and learners, textbooks, and particularly the notion of the 'classroom', have increasingly taken on a significance of their own. They can no longer be treated as a means to an end, but have become definitive of the process. While this remains an assumption of educational planning, part of the task for distance educators is to act subversively to undo it.

5. Conventional instruction by its nature creates educational disability and undermines intelligence. Any attempts we make to create curricula in which knowledge is depicted as ordered and sequential undermine the capacity of students to grasp the truth. (That knowledge is, at heart, discontinuous and fraught by paradox, ambiguity, uncertainty and contradiction.)

6. Distance education has used the visual media more for distance teaching than for open learning. Part of the challenge for distance educators is to create learning possibilities for students that creatively disrupt both the assumptions of instructional design and the conventions of media programme-making.

Notes

1. Note that the seminal book, *Knowledge and Control*, edited by Michael F D Young (1970) was very much a product of the first generation of Open University courses, but that, despite a contemporary concern with reflexivity, it

largely failed to turn its argument to distance education.

2. The work of the Glasgow Media Group has included a series of research projects into television news broadcasts which have led to a radical social analysis of news making, reporting and news broadcasting (Philo *et al.*, 1976; 1982; 1985).

3. An interesting illustration of technological inertia in the context of large programmes arises in Richard Feynman's account of the Challenger investigation (the space shuttle that exploded on take-off, killing the crew). Feynman points out that the common public perception of the space programme is one of a testing ground for leading edge technologies. Far from it, he says – the computers used in the Challenger programme were virtually antique but so much time and effort had gone into developing the software that it was impossible to change the hardware. The whole Challenger programme was built around outmoded technology (Feynman, 1990).

4. I shall draw on evaluation reports of the Deakin University course, ECT 401 *Classroom Processes* written by Herbert Altrichter, Terry Evans, Lynette James, Alastair Morgan and Chris Saville, and also by David Kember and his colleagues at Hong Kong Polytechnic (see Altrichter *et al.*, 1991). I teach this course – and another one, ETL 822 *Classroom Research*, upon which I shall also draw – with Helen Modra, Wendy Crebbin and Wendy Crouch.

5. Another facet of this argument is the way in which the very architecture of universities is constructed to impose, or at least to celebrate, particular notions of authority in relation to knowledge. At the very least, a university course which takes as its architectural facade the space at the end of the kitchen table, is required to rethink its assumptions about the location of authority in the context of learning and teaching, even if it only displaces them into the design and presentation of course materials.

6. Patricia Gillard (previously, Palmer) has pioneered the innovative use of children's drawings to investigate children's television watching, a method Susan Groundwater-Smith has adapted to the development of a comparison between watching TV at home and watching TV in school (see Palmer, 1986 and Groundwater-Smith, 1990). There seems to be a gap in the literature on how children watch video.

7. The image here is taken from Patricia Palmer's evidence (see above). The parallels with the 'kitchen table' image used earlier are not accidental.

3 Teaching towards Critical Research, Reflection and Practice in Distance Education

Terry Evans, Bruce King and Ted Nunan

This chapter represents a critical reflection on the work of planning and developing courses on distance education through distance education. While the process of writing the chapter presents, in itself, an opportunity to step back and mull over our experiences of our collaborative development for two courses, it is our intention to imbue such reflection with a critical essence. Bartlett (1989a) notes of critical reflection that it is,

> not just practitioner enquiry into practitioner practices. It is not just an individual, psychological process akin to 'thinking'. Critical reflection is action-oriented, historically embedded, and a vital part of social and political process (p.352).

Our quest for critical reflection is motivated by beliefs that critical reflection connects us, as academics, with the struggle for achieving practices which have an emancipatory intent both for ourselves and our students and, we believe, for our readers. This quest is both collective and personal and is concerned with the processes of educational reform. As we write we know that our public collective texts are really palimpsests written over our private understandings and concerns about our teaching. To reveal a glimpse of the personal we have included three 'tales' of our private concerns about teaching toward critical research, reflection and practice in distance education.

Our practical context

This chapter focuses on our experiences as teachers of two courses within the Master of Distance Education (MDEd) programme which is jointly developed and taught by Deakin University and the University of South Australia. We have been deeply involved in the development of the whole collaborative programme (see Calvert *et al.*, in press). However, the two courses (called 'units' in our universities) which we will focus on here – *Critical Issues in Distance Education* and *Research in Distance Education* – are ones which we have been responsible for developing and are teaching currently.

The MDEd programme is designed for practitioners, both present and intending. However, it is not merely about improving practice through the development of knowledge and skills, it is also about improving practice more broadly through both critical reflection and research in distance education. The MDEd staff hold the view that on completion of the programme the students should be capable of critically reflective practice and research. The MDEd is usually studied part-time at a distance. Typically, the *Issues* and the *Research* courses are studied in the first and second semesters during the second year of the programme alongside two elective courses. The first year of the programme comprises four courses which are entitled: *Introduction to Distance Education, Management of Distance Education, Distance Teaching and Learning 1 and Distance Teaching and Learning 2.* The final year of the programme consists of an individually supervised research project equivalent in study load to each of the previous years and which culminates in an examined thesis.

The arrangements agreed between the MDEd staff at both universities established the basis for the practical aspects of collaborative development and teaching of each course. Course teams involved staff from both institutions, although they varied in size and had differing levels of contribution from staff and consultants. Terry Evans worked with Bruce King on *Issues* and with Ted Nunan for *Research*. Both courses were principally developed by the authors with contributions from Australian and overseas consultants and with assistance from other MDEd staff in reviewing materials, etc. Both courses use print and audio materials, and are tutored using principally telephone, teleconferencing and computer communications.

Historical context

The historical context of the *Issues* and *Research* courses extends into the mists of the experiences of the authors. It is difficult to point to the origins, but some important landmarks can be identified. Terry Evans and Bruce King were involved in the first *Critical Reflections on Distance Education* project (Evans and Nation, 1989b). With Daryl Nation, Terry Evans had been pressing the case for critical reflection in distance education (see Evans and Nation, 1989c). Their approach was based broadly on Anthony Giddens's theorizing of critical social science (see Giddens, 1987, especially pp. 51–72). Terry Evans (1988) had also been arguing for 'gender-critical' approaches in other aspects of education and these also could be appropriately applied to distance education. Bruce King's writing on the antecedent course to the MDEd had also been within the framework of a case-study based critique (King, 1989). Ted Nunan had previously published in the history, philosophy and sociology of science and had written a critique of educational design (Nunan, 1983).

We also had colleagues in our universities who provided support for our work, either directly or indirectly. Some of these colleagues had been contributors to the first *Critical Reflections on Distance Education* project (see Cook, 1989; Fitzclarence and Kemmis, 1989; Grace, 1989; Modra, 1989; Smyth, 1989b) or are involved in the present project (see Walker, chapter 2). In addition, the approaches taken on other (in effect, previous for the students) MDEd courses were complementary and critical reflection itself was enshrined in the principles of the programme.

Developing and teaching the courses

Both the *Issues* and the *Research* courses needed to build on the previous studies of the MDEd students and to contextualize these in terms of broader educational, social, economic and political issues, and to provide the students with the opportunity to develop their capacities for critique and research. In many ways the two courses complemented each other although they differed markedly in curricula and pedagogies. The conceptualizations were common to the extent that they aimed to help students become critical scholars of distance education. This meant that they should be enabled to sustain critique of the theory and practice of distance education, to theorize their own practice critically in terms of broader theoretical traditions and to engage in research which is appropriately planned, practised and communicated in order to provide (critically) useful knowledge. Through such capabilities the students should be alive to the possibilities of reform to their educational practices and contexts.

The *Issues* course took curricular and pedagogical shape as we identified what we considered to be some of the major areas of distance education in which critical debate was warranted. Apart from Harris' *Openness and Closure in Distance Education* (1987) and the *Critical Reflections on Distance Education* book, there had been little work of this kind in distance education. Also, Faith's collection *Toward New Horizons for Women in Distance Education* (1988) represented the emergence of feminist critiques in distance education. This meant that the course needed to create a curriculum which was in itself novel in its critical approach to issues in distance education; there was also our belief that the course needed to be open pedagogically to the creativity of the students in fostering their own critiques. A concern was that we could form a course which could create (ironically) a form of critical orthodoxy. Therefore, we wanted to keep the course as open as possible to critiques of many sorts, especially to those of its students.

The course materials take the form of five books and six audio-cassettes. The first book introduces the notion of critical reflection in social science, education and distance education. This book, together with its accompanying audio-programme and supporting reading, is intended to provide a foundation for the critical analysis of issues in distance education. Four areas of such issues are then covered in each of the four remaining books with accompanying audio-programmes. Each of these books is written by two or three consultants who were selected on the basis of their previous critical contributions to such debates. Each book contains two consultants' contributions and some readings. The book titles are: *Independence, Autonomy and Dialogue in Distance Education*; *Access and Equity in Distance Education*; *Distance Education in Developing Nations*; and *Technology in Distance Education.*[1] We selected these areas because we recognized that they encompassed important debates within the field; however, as we do not want to restrict the students to our views, the course also has an 'open' area in which the students are free to write their own critical essay on an aspect of distance education as their final assignment. Each student is required to write a final assignment within one of the areas. Two previous assignments are required and these take the form of a short personal reflection on their studies of each of the books which is ungraded, and a brief critical reflection on the issue they are intending to pursue for their final assignment. The latter two assignments are graded. We offer the students participation in group tele-tutorials or in computer-based tutorials.

The *Research* course falls into three parts. The first provides an introduction to research paradigms in social science, education and distance education; this is in the form of a study guide and readings. This part of the course has an explicit pedagogy which guides the students, sometimes using a personally reflective approach on the part of the author, through the various research paradigms. The assessment is based on their reading of this material together with some exploratory reading of their own, following 'signposts' provided in the text. The second part provides a series of resources on research in distance education. This section has no explicit pedagogical structure, but comprises a book on forms of evaluative research on a distance education course (Altrichter *et al.*, 1991), four booklets with accompanying audio-tapes from researchers on their styles of research in distance education, and a reader of examples of research in distance education and open learning. The final part of the course returns to an explicit pedagogical structure which takes the students through a series of activity-based steps which culminate in a fully documented research proposal. This part of the course draws on the work of the two preceding parts and assists students to reflect critically on an actual research project which they intend to implement. This project may be the research they propose to complete for their final thesis or it can be any other project in distance education which they have the prospect of completing.

Terry's tale of the two courses

I write aware of having to bring my underlying political project to the surface. I feel it is a project which many people in education and distance education share to some degree, although they probably see it somewhat differently. As a university student in the late 1960s and early 1970s I became aware of the political nature of education and that teachers should understand the political nature of their work. This view is critical, both in nature and in process, and was founded in the 'new' sociology of education of the 1970s[2] and the various 'progressive' educational writers of that period.[3] My critical position is not one of a particular ideological stance – indeed I am captivated by many critical readings of the discourses which swirl around me.

What is the critical project underlying my teaching? It is one which recognizes that unequal distributions of power and wealth are unjust, and that education plays an important part in the construction and reconstruction of such injustices. Similarly, education can help make people aware of such injustices and help them to engage, resist and overcome them. My teaching has often taken me along paths where a curriculum contains aspects which enable me to focus on the structures and processes of inequality (which I then hope my students will see for what they are) and the pedagogical approaches I employ are usually ones which require the students to think it out/ work it out for themselves. For me this latter process is very important because, if the students do not think it out/work it out in their own way, then an 'emancipatory' stage is not possible or is without intellectual foundation. It is important to me that people are provided with the opportunities through their learning to achieve what Mezirow (1981) calls 'perspective transformation'.

I have often heard from students that they think about and see themselves differently after they have been involved in one of my courses. Partly this is connected to the curricula of those courses which have usually been within sociology or the sociology of education. Apart from my current work in distance education, I am also involved in teaching, researching and writing about the sociology of gender (see, for example, Evans, 1982, 1988, 1989a). Here my students – men and women – have expressed feelings such as anger, frustration or guilt as they struggle to do things differently (in terms of 'gender justice') for themselves and those, especially their families, with whom they relate most closely. I see that these students are transforming their perspectives and actions in ways which are emancipatory in nature, but are constrained by the discourses and structures within which they live.

In my view, through both the *Issues* and *Research* units, we have been endeavouring to provide both curricula and pedagogies which open up the possibility of the critical and the emancipatory. This is most clear in *Issues* because each book of the course has its own critical form and each of the writers has their way of constructing their critique of the problem.

I wrote the first book (*An Introduction to Critical Issues in Distance Education*) with the personal and intellectual in mind. Personal in the sense that I was trying to create space for the students to put themselves into their study of *Issues*; and intellectual in that it provided a theoretical foundation for their critical study of the course. Some of the intellectual territory of the 'critical theorists' is very hard going and so my intention was to try to take them into this terrain to see what it looked like without having to scale every peak. I also used Schön's work (1983) because it is both readable and makes obvious the illusion of the theory-practice dichotomy; hence the students may see that their thinking/theorizing about distance education is interwoven with their action/practice in distance education. Books 2–5 present several authors' critiques of issues in distance education which enable the students to read different discourses on issues in ways which will help them develop their own critical discourses of their own thinking and practice.

In teaching the course with my colleagues from the University of South Australia it has become clear that some students at both universities find the first book (and the subsequent books) very difficult to come to terms with. Other students engage with it and the rest of the course in a highly enthusiastic way and seem to revel in the possibilities they are encouraged to consider. There are also students who fall somewhere between these two positions. As a teacher I worry about the first group of students and have discussed with Bruce and other colleagues what we could do better. At this stage we have revised the assignment guides and the introductory audio-cassette to provide what we hope will be better assistance for such students. I also felt that some of our problems were similar to those experienced by David Harris in his teaching (see Chapter 4) in that a few of the students, especially at the University of South Australia in 1991, were 'innoculating' themselves against any critical approach to their work or learning.

In this context it is important to specify the meaning of 'critical' in the development of the *Critical Issues in Distance Education* course. In my work, especially with Daryl Nation, I am influenced by Anthony Giddens, whose views about what constitutes critical social science can be viewed as somewhat eclectic and broadly-based and, hence, distinguishable from the Frankfurt School of critical theorists such as Jürgen Habermas and Max Horkheimer. Schön's work on the place of reflection in professional practice provided a basis for conceptualizing the students' own reflection on practice as theorizing about practice. The potential existed to locate such a conceptualization within the approach of critical social science which would create the foundation for critical reflection on practice. Put simply, personal reflections on practice can be understood against broader theoretical frameworks which have the capacity to change, hermeneutically, both the understanding of the personal and the social. Using Giddens's approach to understanding the nature of social structure and human agency, one is then able to posit that the aforementioned understandings reform practice, that is, human action, and such action will affect the social circumstances in which it is located.

Within *Issues* I use the following quotation from Giddens to show the inescapable nature of the critical in the social sciences – in which we place distance education – and in human culture:

If the ideas and knowledge-claims of social science cannot be kept insulated from the social world itself, we reach a new appreciation of the significance of critical theory. Social science does not stand in a neutral relation to the social world, as an instrument of 'technological change'; critique cannot be limited to the criticism of false lay beliefs. The implication . . . is that social scientists cannot but be alert to the transformative effects that their concepts and theories might have upon what it is they set out to analyse. Critical theory is not an option for social science, which can either be taken up or left alone; it is inherent in its nature (Giddens, 1987, p.71).

I find this conceptualization useful because it allows me to weave various themes together in my research, writing and teaching.

The *Research* course is emancipatory and reformative in a different way to the *Issues* course. Part 1 of the course leads towards the critical research paradigm in a way which (possibly) implies its superiority and more exclusive nature than that articulated in *Issues*. The presence of a critical paradigm, including feminist research critiques, is presented through Ted's writing in a way which provides a foundation and an awareness of the critical. The nature of Ted's writing in Part 1 also has personal reflection embedded within it in a way which is somewhat similar to Book 1 of *Issues*. A substantial theme of the course is concerned with providing people with the capacity to plan, develop and implement their own research. This has both a utilitarian and an emancipatory purpose. If we see research and enquiry as important elements of the critical process, then by enabling students to develop and implement their own research, and to review critically their work and that of others, we are helping them increase their critical skills. This is especially so in the case of contributions on action research and distance education in the course.

Given Giddens's argument that all social science is critical in the sense that it provides knowledge and ideas upon which people can take action to reform their social worlds, then the *Research* course is a more practically (ie, research-work) oriented, but complementary, course to the more 'theoretically' oriented *Issues* course. I trust the complementary nature of the courses is evident to the students not just as a curricular phenomenon, but also as personal and political phenomena.

Bruce's tale

Working on *Issues* with Terry was a comparatively easy task in relation to my simultaneous involvement with the course team preparing the *Distance Teaching and Learning 1* course, which has been discussed elsewhere (Calvert *et al.*, in press). On reflection, however, I was insufficiently critical of the processes in which Terry and I were initially involved. However, having now taught that unit, it is evident that concerns which should have been aired between us were not, and the course is less satisfying to me than first seemed to be the case for that reason.

I should introduce a caveat. On the whole, *Issues* is very satisfying. I think it affords a sound opportunity for Masters students to engage with contemporary concerns of distance education and to explore aspects of their own professional experience in a reflective and empowering manner. What my teaching now suggests, however, is that greater opportunities could have been created for the students. My concern is not for any failure to achieve intended goals, rather it is in relation to issues which were either not addressed or dealt with on the assumption that they would follow as a consequence of other decisions.

My involvement in the planning of the course can be grounded in its historical and political contexts. There were two shaping considerations in my approach to *Issues*. First, I was concerned that my institution should maintain the initiative it had seized in mounting the original Graduate Diploma in Distance Education by successful involvement with Deakin University in an improved version of the course which included its upgrading to Masters level study. Second, I wished to see that aspects of the earlier course which were valuable were retained in a new programme.

In relation to the first of these, my determination was that the academic staff working on the new course from Deakin University should see the collaboration positively. To this end, I was prepared to accommodate their aspirations in my belief that the Deakin involvement was essential to the viability of the MDEd. However, there was an element of intellectual cringe in this because University of South Australia staff were not as experienced in teaching at Masters degree level, or at research and publication, as their Deakin counterparts.

There were personal uncertainties, too. I had not written for a distance education programme for several years, nor taught at Masters level, yet Deakin staff considered my involvement as essential. My work as Head of the Distance Education Centre restricted the time I could give to the collaboration. This personal reaction was highlighted by the experience of working with Terry. In a sense, I felt much more at home with my involvement in the development of the *Distance Teaching and Learning 1* (despite the difficulties involved) both because it was an area in which my involvement had been significant in the earlier Graduate Diploma and also as it drew more directly on my own research interests in academic planning and course development. With *Issues*, it was abundantly evident that both content and approach were likely to be closer to Terry's more recent experience, including his major role in the development and authorship of the prescribed text, *Critical Reflections on Distance Education.*

I was more conscious of my other concern, preserving valued aspects of the former course, as we discussed the scope and approach of *Issues.* Elsewhere I have written of the commitments (intellectual, emotional and physical) made with my colleagues to the development of the Graduate Diploma. A major personal lesson for me had been coming to understand and value,

> that if you believe that the knowledge of the field rests with the experienced practitioners, then determining what is important to study cannot be dissociated from practitioners and the context in which practice is displayed.... The test of a course like the Graduate Diploma must be the extent to which it endorses this approach to understanding through its own practice, while continuing to serve the other purposes for which it is also established (King, 1989, pp.119–20).

In this, I was closer to Schön's (1987) 'reflective practitioner' than the critical social science perspective Terry brought to our collaboration, although I subscribed both to notions of social contestation and the transformation effect of testing one's own thinking against the positions of others.

I was determined that the position I had reached as a result of working in and reflecting upon the process of developing the Graduate Diploma should not be lost in my contribution to the new course. There was little doubt that Terry could accommodate the intellectual position, but I was worried about its practical application. My sense was that the study materials from the Graduate Diploma had encouraged and facilitated the process of student reflection on practice by yielding significant control of the learning situation to students (at least, in the latter units of the programme). My difficulty was embedded in the decisions we were taking about the *Issues* course, particularly in our identification of certain key issues and the use of concentrated writing to provide the content on which the study materials would largely be based.

We were concerned that students taking *Issues* should have the opportunity to identify and handle issues in their own professional practice in a critical and empowering manner. This was to be achieved by introducing students to analyses provided by commissioned authors to issues we had identified. It was not our intention to suggest that the four areas of concern we selected were definitive; rather they were to provide both exposure to reflection on issues and model the reflective process. We wanted to provide examples for students to emulate in their own professional situations. We intended students to move beyond their present level of analysis of problems, testing their views against the understanding of others, and being able to discern in issues the potential for, and constraints upon, personal liberation.

We shared a strong view that the content of the unit should afford a model of 'how to do it' but that students should also gain some further understanding of some of the critical issues in distance education. The latter was very important to me. I was of the view that the Graduate Diploma had moved back from the position it occupied when first developed, of affording students contact with the most recent debates of the field. So there was an element of necessary engagement with what we as academics considered important, despite our recognition that these concerns were not exclusive.

It is less clear now how we expected students to make the reflective process their own. It seems in retrospect that we assumed that if we described what we understood critical reflection to be and showed some instances (more or less sophisticated) of reflection upon practice, students would understand how to do it. In terms of the educational stance outlined above, this seemed an appropriate opportunity for students to take responsibility for their own study and determine their own learning emphases. What I had real doubts about was the level of support we were providing for students to experience success in this process. How would students make meaning of the reflective process and achieve the capacity to apply it to their own situation without having been required to demonstrate that they could do this, or having had the opportunity for practising the skills involved in non-threatening situations and supported by appropriate and informed feedback on their performance?

This was something I either did not raise, or explored too indirectly with Terry. Ted Nunan has written here of his search for 'appropriate teaching for fostering research activity'. What I did not sufficiently deal with was my own indecision about what constituted appropriate teaching for Master's level students generally. My sense was that Deakin staff saw the embedded instruction and student support in the original Graduate Diploma course materials as too overt, prescriptive and inappropriate for Master's degree work. Yet previous students had valued this approach. For the reasons indicated above, the matter was insufficiently pursued. (I recognized that it could too easily be seen as commitment to an institutional perspective and that my role was to convey reasonableness and responsiveness to Deakin perspectives.) As a consequence, a number of students floundered. Perhaps another model could have been used. One of my students invoked Smyth's (1989b) approach to helping teachers reflect on their practice to structure her assignment exercise, which brought her closer to realizing the prescribed task than several of her peers.

It is difficult for me to concede that our early planning saw too much acquiescence and uncritical involvement on my part, but that now seems to have been the case. There were probably two reasons for this, one of which has been partly suggested above. The ease of the experience of collaborating with Terry was in marked contrast to the efforts required to produce *Distance Teaching and Learning 1*. The comfortable nature of the relationship predisposed me to seeing success in the collaboration and to assume a commonality of purpose and understanding which may not have withstood much testing. The ease with which decisions were taken, and our apparent close tracking on matters of substance to do with content and methodology, however, in the context of the difficulties of getting agreements on even the most fundamental aspects of course design in the other unit on which I was working, afforded little reason to challenge a process which was so relatively undemanding.

Too much should not be made of this. The second reason for my acquiescence in our collaboration derives from the similarity of our professional orientation and personal backgrounds. Terry and I share a number of values and it is probably the case that it is only on matters of detail that the different emphases we bring to bear on course development become evident. General agreements about purpose are easier to reach than those about detail, as we have discussed elsewhere (Calvert *et al.*, in press). However, as curriculum developers know only too well, there is a divergence of actuality from intention almost as soon as educational proposals begin to be implemented, and details which have not previously been considered, let alone seen as contentious, emerge to confound those initial agreements. What is important is that while the process is predictable, the specific matters which will give rise to later concern cannot necessarily be anticipated, as they occur as the result of the actual processes of development and implementation.

Ted's Tale

The starting point in reflecting upon my experiences in designing course materials for *Research* is to revisit the period just prior to writing the materials. Terry and I had already agreed upon a broad framework for the course and the contents of each section. However, underlying this framework were concerns involving philosophical and pedagogical matters which I regarded as problematic and important. I experienced uncertainties about whether my co-writer would find substance in my concerns; in addition, I was unsure that I could predict what might become our 'public view' about these and other issues.

My initial concerns were largely an undifferentiated mixture of the personal (how would I handle dealing with theoretical issues about appropriate content and could I translate the intentions of *Research* to successful teaching and learning at a distance?) and the socio-political (how would our approach embody practices which would avoid reification of research and researchers, and instead encourage and empower students to participate in research in education at a distance?). For personal reasons I felt I needed to have rehearsed my own answers to these questions yet recognize that collaborative work might well challenge my answers and set new directions and boundaries.

The notion of empowering students, even in some small way, was soon to occupy much of my thinking. While the texts that we chose, Carr and Kemmis (1986) and Evans (1990), could set a course for empowerment within the framework of a critical social science approach I felt that we should explicitly address issues of how we empowered students as researchers. Also, because I had the task of writing the first section of *Research* I felt I was faced with the problem of introducing and justifying our 'public view'.

I needed a pedagogical starting point. I can remember arriving at the conclusion that I could use the sequence chosen by Carr and Kemmis' chapters or I would have to construct an argument to arrive at an understanding of critical social science through other means. If I chose the Carr and Kemmis sequence of introducing paradigmatic positions about theory and research practice I would be employing, as my pedagogical starting point, an exploration of the values behind empiricism. I was not sure that I wanted to start at this point as such an exploration activated a peculiar set of intellectual baggage that I carried to this task.

An area that I had previously read and published in was the history, philosophy and sociology of science. Consequently, I was familiar with the works of Popper (1968), Lakatos and Musgrave (1970), Kuhn (1970), Feyerabend (1975) and Foucault (1972) regarding the nature of scientific research activity, theories of knowledge production and legitimation, and their implications for the education of scientists. It was in this context that I met Polanyi's argument that research activity, in the final analysis, cannot be formally taught (Polanyi, 1960). It was somewhat ironic that in seeking an approach that empowered students I was to revisit arguments which were essentially socially elitist and politically conservative.

The challenge of this argument was that it has a definite view about appropriate 'teaching' for fostering research activity. As I had yet to decide upon my starting point for *Research*, dealing with the argument would possibly sharpen problematic issues and perhaps bring forth clear political choices.

The argument that troubled me was that a skilled researcher knows far more about the practice of the craft than can be told. What can be told can also be formally taught. However, even if the learner received all this explicit knowledge it would be an insufficient basis for becoming a skilled researcher. Polanyi (1960) contends that explicit knowledge of maxims, rules or theories serves to guide practice only if it can be integrated into the practical knowledge of the craft. He links this act of integration with possession of tacit knowledge – explicit knowledge must rely upon being tacitly understood to achieve skilled practice.

Thus, knowing how to do research requires more than the information which can be portrayed in texts, research reports, etc. Becoming a skilled researcher requires an induction into the craft where an 'apprentice' can, through an involvement guided by a skilled practitioner, observe and experience the integration of tacit and explicit knowing within the practices of the 'expert'. Studying about research without this form of induction into the craft is a sterile activity.

The course materials for the *Research* course might be seen as providing a particularly efficient way of presenting explicit knowledge about research. In addition, there may be the charge that, despite all our best efforts to involve and engage external students in the craft of research, these efforts are likely to be focused around explicit knowing and therefore quite sterile. Thus, whatever *Research* might achieve for the learner it will be less than empowering – it will not, in Polanyi's terms, represent a genuine attempt to induct neophytes into the attitudes, skills and traditions of research in distance education in ways which enable the student to become a competent researcher. That is, the course cannot claim to lead students to skills which produce significant new knowledge. Further, if the outcomes of a course are not directed towards knowledge creation it is unlikely that it will receive a wider legitimation from those who act as 'gate-keepers' within the field of distance education. Now, while it may be unrealistic to apply such a stringent test to the

Research course, it is nevertheless the case that to lose sight of the goals of knowledge creation and legitimation is to provide an experience for students which has little value in empowering them to deal with real problems and real research.

The argument presents two challenges. How would the design of *Research* adequately address this view about research activity or should the course adopt a different view about the nature and purposes of appropriate research activity? And to what extent is an 'apprenticeship' mode necessary to enable students to undertake research activity? Hence, to what extent can course materials be expected to achieve objectives which are related to the practice of research given that they, by definition, cannot transmit tacit knowledge?

I can remember trying to change 'frames' and imagine a similar argument constructed from a view of research which saw participatory action research as the norm. Was there an alternate form of social induction in the art of collaborative activity within a 'self critical community' (McTaggart, 1989)? Could the course materials deal with the ideology and techniques of participatory action research in ways which would enable students to participate in this form of research activity? Could I, as a teacher, assist external students engaged in research activity when I would find it difficult to achieve some sort of 'participatory role' within their research study?

I was tempted to dismiss the challenges of the conservative position by claiming that the questions were ideologically biased and framed around a view of research which did not represent educational research – however, this dismissal relies upon a claim about what researchers do, or should do, when researching education and distance education. Clearly, the issue is complex and its practical resolution difficult within course materials representing one third of a semester course! In the literature within education I hoped for a solution – instead, it reflected or exacerbated matters. I found Hocking (1990) writing on 'Educational research in chaos'; Gottlieb (1989) discussing 'The discursive construction of knowledge' and Cziko (1989) debating the 'Unpredictability and indeterminism in human behaviour'. Unfortunately, the literature offered no easy introduction to the issues or a pedagogic starting point.

These issues were left unresolved – they remained undisclosed as personal uncertainties. There was the pressure of writing deadlines – I had to start drafting materials. Terry and I discussed an approach to addressing the learner in a form of dialogue that explored the teaching and learning decisions which might be made about introducing research activity within distance education – this presented a means of revealing ways in which teaching and learning environments are constructed, interact and develop. This was a precursor to employing our texts as a vehicle for describing paradigmatic positions and infusing issues from current research and writings about research in distance education.

Once writing began there was little time to grapple with previous personal uncertainties. Indeed, I found that Terry saw different issues and concerns – it was important to engage with these matters as they were wider than my previous personal uncertainties. It took me some time to recognize that Terry was operating from a wider framework – there was a potent 'driving force' already installed within the MDEd which exerted considerable influence in resolving pedagogic and theoretical concerns. This driving force was the critical reflection framework that had already been established through Bruce and Terry's work on the *Issues* course.

Because I had not been extensively involved in the *Issues* course I underestimated the effects of this critical reflection framework. First, students were expected to have engaged critical perspectives which would enable them to negotiate their way through, or deal with, whatever structure or approach that might be employed within the research course. The fundamental issue was not one of structure or pedagogical starting points, but rather to ensure that the course materials about research activity and researching in distance education themselves modelled approaches which demonstrated a critical perspective to course design, teaching and learning. *Research* could be seen as an extension and application of operating within a critical perspective which commenced in *Issues*. Second, the impact of critical reflection was to provide an epistemological framework which was saturated with education values. I had not fully understood that the purpose of *Issues* was to 'bring both critical reflection into distance education and distance education into critical reflection' (Evans, 1991, p. 15). With distance education within critical reflection there are consequent epistemological implications. As Bartlett (1989a) notes,

> critical reflection as a form of public enquiry enables the reflective practitioner's knowledge to be tested against what other practitioners know. Public debate also enables others to test the 'truth' of one setting against cumulated knowledge about teaching. The notion is not only one of shared understanding ... or of the democratization of research; public debate is also about verification and a search for the 'truth' of measuring of the educational setting (p.355).

Critical reflection aligns with a form of research *for* education which combines ideals of intellectual liberalism with a social responsibility and adds intended action through a consideration of pragmatics of political action.

The epistemological issues that I had been grappling with privately as a part of my intellectual baggage were largely irrelevant when considered against this background. Terry's writing was later to reveal ways in which *Research* provided resources which featured practitioner knowledge and encouraged critical analysis and reflection upon actual research within educational settings.

The epistemology of critical reflection has certain alignments with the nature of distance teaching and learning. First and foremost it is learner-centred; second, it represents a valued process within learning which can take place in 'isolation'; third, teaching-at-a-distance can be seen as a form of intervention which sets the conditions and provides the resources for critical reflection; fourth, critical reflection implies a necessary learner control over the learning processes. Thus, issues about the design of *Research* were always seen to extend beyond the prepared course materials – indeed, where students are able to critically reflect within their area of study it is axiomatic that the boundaries of their studies are only partially set by the intentions of the course.

Our belief in the amalgam of epistemological and pedagogic values presented in our application of critical reflection explains why mutual exploration of teaching and learning issues proceeded so smoothly. To some extent these matters were the taken-as-given, the unsaid – our points of departure for writing were the different ways that we saw the operation of these values within the parts of the course that we were developing.

Concluding comment

Some time has elapsed since we first exchanged our three stories and then shared them with our collaborators on this book. Over that period, we have each taught small numbers of students in the units described here, exchanged assessment scripts for the purposes of moderation, and been involved with our colleagues from both Deakin and South Australia in a joint review of the first year of operation of the whole MDEd course. That experience underpins this final section.

Overall, there is some reason for optimism about both units. At one level – acceptance by academic peers – the course materials appear to have been a successful undertaking. The commissioned papers from *Issues* have been published in a single volume (Evans and

King, 1991) as a result of wider interest and have been received positively by reviewers. The research unit has also been sought out by academics overseas who have entered into negotiations to include it within their own teaching programmes.

Student reaction has been mixed. In both units, some have indicated that they have encountered content and approaches which were new to them and that the experience was stimulating and worthwhile. Other students have indicated that the demands made by the two units seemed disproportionately greater than those in earlier units and this appears to have been substantiated by an increase in student attrition during 1991, particularly for *Issues* students at the University of South Australia where many of these students had enrolled with advanced standing from the former Graduate Diploma in Distance Education, which they had either completed (sometimes a few years previously) or were studying prior to the new courses being offered in 1991.

In this regard, it is noteworthy that other academics now also teaching these units but who were not involved in their development are not proposing changes to either content or approach. They do discern difficulties, however, but prefer solutions which relate more to the passage of students into these units rather than the units *per se*. What is currently proposed is that the preceding units be seen as more directly related and preparatory to the *Issues* and *Research* units. In other words, there has been some recognition that there is a disjunction between the epistemological and pedagogic values of these units and those which precede them and that this should be altered by reshaping the earlier studies, particularly the two units, *Distance Teaching and Learning 1 and 2*.

This development raises other issues, only two of which will be introduced here. First, to what extent is a professional development programme which consistently invites students to engage in critical reflection compatible with the needs of practitioners who may have no theoretical background in the processes, rather than the substantive focus, of their professional operation? For example, is the increasing commitment to critical reflection of the Masters in Distance Education likely to improve the practice of senior accountants recruited to work in business courses offered by distance education if those academics have no background in education theory?

Second, by relying so heavily on critical reflective approaches in the overall course, are we moving towards an explicable and valuable, or even simply different, construction of distance education? Can we go beyond the 'alignments' Ted has noted above?

Both these issues involve matters which need to be addressed in the future. We invite and welcome reaction to them.

Notes

1. We have since edited the original writing from the course into a single collection so that other people also have access to this work (see Evans and King, 1991).
2. Young's collection (1971) was the touchstone of the time. Since then the writing of people such as Michael Apple, Basil Bernstein, Pierre Bourdieu, Henry Giroux and Gerald Grace has been influential. Particular works such as Bowles and Gintis' (1976) *Schooling In Capitalist America*; Dale *et al.*'s (1976) *Schooling and Capitalism* and Willis' (1977) *Learning to Labour*, were influences during this period. In the early 1980s Connell *et al.*'s (1982) *Making the Difference* was a particular Australian influence.
3. The writing of Paulo Freire and John Holt springs to mind and works such as Berg's (1969) *Risinghill: The Death of A Comprehensive School*; Illich's (1970) *Deschooling Society* and Neill's (1968) *Summerhill*, Rubinstein and Stoneman's (1970) collection *Education for Democracy*, Schoenheimer's (1973) *Good Australian Schools* and Skidelsky's (1969) *English Progressive Schools*.

4 Distance Education at the Margins

David Harris

This chapter considers some recent experience gained as a tutor on the Open University's (OU) new MA in Education programme. I am a Regional Tutor on two MA modules: E812 (*Classroom Studies –* hereinafter referred to as *Classrooms*) and E814 (*Organisations and Professionals – Organisations*). Students must pass three modules to gain their MA. I have an opportunity to offer some reflections on teaching these modules (Open University 1987a; 1988a) and commenting on two others (Open University 1987b; 1988b), and to revise some of the critical comments I offered in my book about the OU (Harris, 1987). At the most obvious level, the book had not covered postgraduate work nor OU summer schools.

Happily, as well, the ground has already been cleared by the book and by subsequent work (Harris, 1991) and I can concentrate here on the substance of the critical reflection, and less on the vexed questions of how one reflects, and what apparatus one reflects with. I am happy to line up with the discussion in Evans and Nation (1989b) on these matters:

> Critical reflection is the process through which human beings use their analytical powers to assess elements of their lives against their explanatory frameworks (theories) (p. 10).

Of course, there is still much to be resolved for pedagogues in statements like these. Mostly, they turn upon issues like what happens when an assessment of this kind clashes with more formally developed explanatory frameworks. A 'critical' course for example, is one which might permit students the chance to engage in the kind of reflection upon conditions of action described by Evans and Nation, and which provides students with the material to permit reflection (beyond the immediate demands of the task in classrooms in the case of education courses). What happens when that material produces problematic, challenging or uncomfortable kinds of reflections (see Chapter 3)?

It is often argued that teachers need to know about the social or political context of their teaching, for example, and that this knowledge cannot be gained from 'consciousness-raising' alone. More generally, there is also a case that radical knowledge, knowledge that breaks with 'common-sense' or 'ideology', requires an 'epistemological break' with existing consciousness or experience, and that this break into theory must be signalled and managed in the course. Radical insight and radical reflection does require a new set of concepts with which to think, I want to argue, and this raises interesting problems for course designers and tutors in developing pedagogic strategies to teach this radical knowledge, especially at a distance.

Drawing upon some general work developed in studies of popular film and television, I shall try to argue that meanings are delivered in critical courses at three levels or moments. First, the text itself tries to construct 'subject positions' for students (and local tutors), which readers are encouraged to occupy so that they can be addressed and taught something. Second, there is a context in which texts are both produced and read and which serves as a reservoir of meanings and alternative or additional subject positions. I like the term 'reading formation' to account for reader competencies (see Bennett and Woollacott, 1987). Finally, I have used the term 'pretext', as an emergent network of meanings and subject positions into which the text is interwoven when it is discussed in places like tutorials (or in 'internal dialogues' – see Chapter 6).

A pretext is a less formal and pedagogic version of Walker's notion of a hypertext (see Chapter 2): students use the materials as a pretext to discuss other issues, in different non-educational ways. They score points, raise wider issues, talk to impress other students, and so on. Buckingham (1990) provides a good example of children talking about television programmes which show how one statement can spark off another comment, so that the talk itself generates new perceptions.

This sort of thing goes on in tutorials (or in mine at least), although the courses invite me to react rather differently when it does, as we shall see. Managing this pretextual moment is a problem faced only by face-to-face tutors, and so it is easy for us to see it as the decisive moment. It is certainly a neglected moment in distance education.

This collection also offers a chance for authors to be personally critical and reflective. I have not worried at all about the usual requirements for careful reservations about the typicality of the observations: I take it for granted that readers will see these comments not as the results of actual research (which cries out to be done), but as preliminary, limited and personal reflections.

A context: the OU MA in Education

The OU launched the MA programme at an interesting time in teacher education, in the midst of a battle over the future type of and funding for programmes for experienced teachers. In brief, there was a pressure towards 'relevance' in these courses, just as there had been one in initial teacher training (as it is now called in the UK). This pressure can be understood as part of the state's campaign against 'progressive' teachers, itself interwoven with other moral items on the neo-conservative agenda (see Dale, 1981), and there is a 'micro-political' element, involving the internal struggles for resources between parties in teacher training to be considered too. (I have suggested elsewhere that the debates about 'theory' and 'practice' in education studies in Britain are often best seen as a micro-political struggle between two parties of teacher educators, masquerading as an epistemological one – see Harris, 1989)

In these circumstances, the success of the MA programme represents something of a reversal of the trend towards shorter, more immediately 'practical' courses. The first clutch of modules also seem unusual – deliberately 'academic' and 'critical' (in different ways) modules were offered first, including *Classrooms* mentioned above, and the brilliant *Gender and Education*. Even the second wave included *Organisations* and *Language and Literacy*, with an introductory section on linguistics of a decidedly critical nature.

Recently, the modules have taken on a more 'relevant' look, with courses on *Management*, or *Curriculum, Education and Employment* (although this will almost certainly include some politically critical material), or *Child Development*. The OU is about to launch a substantial experiment in teacher training (as it is being called again in Britain) which must be under pressure to be uncritically 'relevant'. It seems set to launch its own 'in-service' courses, with the sorts of shorter, more 'professionally-based' courses already familiar in the field. With these changes, and the moves from the OU of the main authors of these critical modules, the future looks less promising.

The story of the struggles behind these policies at the OU remains to be told, but it seems clear that the 'academics' in the School of Education were the first to take advantage of the opportunity to develop MA modules, and to open what might be a final chance for critical work to occupy the central ground of education modules. The haste can be detected in the design of *Organisations* especially, as one of the authors herself has confirmed.

The reasons for students applying in large numbers are also unclear to me. From my own discussions, the familiar factors identified in the research on undergraduate courses have emerged again, like the perception that further promotion or consolidation of one's position requires a postgraduate qualification, as a kind of re-run of the credentialist anxiety that provided the OU with its first undergraduates in 1971 (one reason perhaps for the overwhelming demand for the *Management* module in 1990). There are also hints of the importance of the status side of the credential again, with students seeing an MA as an official recognition of their merit (sometimes as consolation for lack of promotion), or as a kind of parallel career where their teaching does not provide them with enough sense of intellectual stimulation or reward.

I had found in my own small-scale research on undergraduate education students in 1973, that none of them were particularly predisposed to be critical or self-critical about educational practices, and instead spent some time in deflecting or defusing the critical thrust of the course, a second-level sociology of education course *School and Society* in that case.

Experienced teachers in 1987–91 seem rather different, possibly because they have been through a lengthy series of struggles with the government about nearly every aspect of their work, from the curriculum to pay and conditions. As a tutor, I can only report that I find a much more sympathetic audience these days for Marxist analyses of the role of the state as a hegemonic agent, or for teaching as having been 'deskilled', or for critical analyses of educational organizations as arenas for the interplay of micro-politics and other power struggles. There is also considerable scepticism about attempts to define and measure educational outcomes, because of the purposes to which the government wants to put the results.

This audience might not wish to embrace the full set of political or theoretical implications of Marxist analysis, but I do not have to appeal to students to suspend their initial disbelief while I outline it! Scepticism, critical perceptions and a politicized stance towards organization, management and measurement are all part of the inter-textual resources student teachers of this generation bring to their work.

The texts: modules and strategies

The two MA modules which I know best have quite different strategies in order to foster a critical response in their students. *Classrooms* pursues a classic approach whereby students are to be provided with a set of critical concepts and, more generally, a critical perspective with which to analyse common (often famous) examples of classroom research. These concepts and perspectives (which can be operationalized as a set of questions to ask of published research) are taught both explicitly and by example, as students are invited to try out critical approaches for themselves, in self-assessed questions and in assignments. The author's own responses in the text, and the detailed notes given to tutors to guide their assessment, try to anticipate common responses by students as well as suggesting the 'correct' line. These are common ways to position a reader in OU materials, of course.

Gradually, most students accept these positions, at least for the duration of the course, establish the power and the possibilities of the critical perspectives for themselves, and can offer sophisticated critiques of selected published material as well as of their own project work. However, in the early stages of the module, I have to police student responses quite closely, as they refuse the invitations to be positioned and try to pursue alternative strategies to manage the material. This repeats the point made earlier about the possibility of 'deviant' assessments of theoretical frameworks, of course.

It is common, for example, for students to mount some sort of moral evaluation of the pieces of classroom research in question, to support 'progressive' ones and resist studies which raise doubts about the 'professionalism' of teachers. It is also common for students to wish to pursue implications for practice directly, to make the concern for practice the centre of their evaluation, and to privilege 'action research' as the only valid mode of classroom research. The module will have none of this, however, insisting that its focus is not about evaluation or practice, but about the technical validity and reliability ('descriptive' and 'explanatory validity' are the terms used in the course) of classroom research.

Classrooms argues that teachers need to know about such research so they can intervene academically in debates about policy allegedly based upon it. It highlights in particular the controversy caused by Bennett's study of 'progressive' and 'traditional' teaching (Bennett, 1976). Bennett's study became popular and often-quoted in the debates that raged in Britain in the 1970s (and it has recently reappeared in some of the latest panics about 'progressivism') but the research itself was seriously flawed, the findings have been reworked and, in a typical argument that students encounter on the course, the whole attempt to isolate the single variable of 'teaching style' has been abandoned in favour of an approach that is much more sensitive to the complexity of classroom life.

Wider implications are hard to avoid: any single variable 'technical fix' policies are likely to feature the same flaws, including those currently on offer from the government. Several students have also pointed out the implications for schemes of teacher appraisal, past and future: what methods do inspectors use when they observe classrooms and make those confident statements about the effectiveness of our teaching techniques? What measurement problems and methodological claims are inherent in the government's drive towards 'quality' or the use of 'performance indicators' for institutions? What inferences are to be drawn from annual appraisal interviews, what explanations will be available to appraisers, how will alternative explanations for an individual's performance have been eliminated? No student (or tutor!) on this module is likely to act as the cultural dope presupposed by many official data gatherers and evaluators.

This sort of argument requires a systematic induction process, both to practise the techniques, but also to avoid the quick solution. No researcher is safe from the accusation of making too easy a set of inferences from a slender base, and most students I have taught eventually come to a point when they are asked to critique their own favoured pieces or approaches: humanists, who enjoy the critique of positivist techniques like 'systematic observation' and begin to feel at home with 'ethnography' encounter perceptive critiques of techniques like 'exampling' and other forms of violence to linguistic data, or, worse, learn from Hammersley (1986) himself that ethnographers use 'weak measurements' too.

Back to Context: the readers

One student in my group last year survived all these insecurities only to find that her own preferred explanation of underachievement ('teacher expectations') stood on feet of methodological clay just like all the rest: at that point she balked, and carried on with her coursework listing carefully-assembled summaries of the findings of endless studies of 'self-fulfilling prophecies' as if nothing had happened, refusing to acknowledge any of the problems. 'Theories' in education are not held by all teachers dispassionately, nor solely within a 'structure of thought'.[1] I have met tutors who also refuse to take the course on its own terms and simply introduce their own preferences.

Push too hard, and your students become cynical about what looks like an obscure academic game, or they simply manage the course in the familiar 'instrumental' ways (including, in one case, I am fairly certain, faking an entire project). Yet taking the easy way out, coming off the central ground of the module, bowing to the current pressures for immediately relevant or politically acceptable (and largely uncritical) classroom research misses the whole rationale for the module, and means students almost never learn the point of doing all the ground clearing: in the absence of any perceptible alternative position constructed in the text, cynicism or *ad hominem* assertions about the personality defects of the author, or weary re-runs of the micro-political struggles between 'practitioners' and 'theorists' rise to the top.

Of course, even here, having decided to tough it out, one has to act initially in bad faith as a tutor, pretending that some universal or disinterested 'objective' critique is on offer, or that a 'grand narrative' 'under' the specific pieces of research being discussed can be developed and applied without contradiction or dogmatism: at the end of the day, we know it is a game or a narrative, but if we told students that right from the start, they would probably never bother. If they did not take the module, though, they would still be open to persuasion by plausible-looking research or opinions which concealed their flaws altogether. The trick seems to be to try to hold a 'line' strongly enough to see off 'common sense', then to signal to students that criticisms of that line are possible and welcome. It is not at all easy to hold constantly to the progressive sides of this strategy of closure followed by openness.

There are ways for students and tutors to manage the course, despite its strong 'party line', the apparatus of tutor notes and tutor monitoring and the rest. Students can choose issues to focus upon and simply avoid others: many 'get through' by focusing on an early debate between systematic and ethnographic forms of observation, for example. Tutors can set agendas in tutorials that give students a hard or easy time – and students do not need to come anyway.

The module has a summer school (the MA was the first education course to have such) which offers a chance for the central authors to reassert direction, however, and activities are tightly specified. Informally, a kind of moral career can take place at summer school too (see Chapter 5), as students find themselves stripped of their previous identities and audiences, isolated on a university campus for eight-hour days in a long week and immersed in the activities, tasks and techniques of classroom research. Some students have told me that they grasped the issues for the first time at summer school, that they can see that course writers are not ogres, and that the activities really do demonstrate the pros and cons of different techniques.

I have been in groups that have been wonderfully therapeutic and students have gained confidence and practised that necessary temporary 'distance' from the immediate issues that the rather abstract focus of the module requires, often after having seen one or two fellow students demonstrate the critical perspective in a calm, skilled, ironic and charming manner. Finding students able to do this for other students is one of the great benefits of tutoring teachers, of course.

In one nightmare of a group (one out of five) members disliked each other and me, however. No one wanted to do the activities, and a large contingent from one region had become irrevocably cynical and defensive (and would introduce their comments with horribly contagious sarcastic remarks like 'I know I'm only a teacher and not a bloody researcher, but...'). I decided on that occasion to abandon the set activities myself, since they only served as occasions for some middle-class cultural deviancy. Summer school, and the intensive interactions it offered, only taught those students more sophisticated immunization strategies to preserve their world views against the arguments of the course, rather as a spell in prison teaches some inmates better house-breaking techniques.

Pretexts in *Classrooms*...
As indicated, in tutorials and in summer schools, the preferred role of the tutor is to police the discussion pretty carefully and to seize opportunities to refer to the privileged discourse in the text. To give a clumsy example, one might intervene in discussions about new contracts for teachers by asking how speakers would design a research project to test out the various predictions about teachers' reactions, and thus drag the conversation back to the central ground. At summer school, this sort of thing can ruin your social life, though, as your contributions to small talk in the bar afterwards are anxiously scanned by students for deep pedagogic meanings.

There was often a struggle over this hierarchy, though. The process seemed to involve students attempting to reverse the approved relation between text and discussion, so that the text became 'strange', and the discussions among experienced practitioners the approved version of reality, that which 'we all really know schools are like'. I have met tutors who were also prepared to abandon the course's strategy and use their pretextual moments like this to rehearse students in reasons for not taking the arguments seriously.

The text of *Organisations...*

Organisation's strategy was quite different and far less dependent upon a careful induction into a particular specialist perspective in the classic sense. One obvious (and attractive) feature, for example, was its light assessment burden – six assignments, only three of them 'summative' (ie, counting towards the overall grade for the module), no summer school, no project, one end-of-module examination (like all the others). The design of the assignments was novel too – they appeared in pairs and the first one (which did not 'count') was deliberately designed to focus on the student's own experience in education. The second of the pair invited students to consider that experience in the light of the reading on the module.

The organizing framework for the arguments in the first half of the module was a 'British Gramscian' one, with its characteristic blend of Euro-Marxism, feminism, liberalism and activism. Enlightenment would follow the possession and deployment of concepts like 'hegemony' (to describe the twists and turns of state intervention in education in Britain), or 'proletarianization' (to describe the struggles over skill and local power, as well as a hope for a 'correct' political identification for teachers). En route to the emergence of these concepts, the module considered some ethnographic or life-history work on the dilemmas, tensions, strains and rewards of teaching, not all of it recognizably Marxist or feminist. It seems that material like this can be used most effectively to 'reconstruct teachers' practices' (see Smyth, 1989b).

The second half of the module was differently structured, with much less of an attempt to weave all the different elements into some overall account. Instead, a number of debates were offered to students, grounded in the more concrete work on organizational theory. This work can be summarized as offering students a number of current models of organization – schools as bureaucracies, as machines, organisms, etc. – and then developing some of the criticisms of these formal models involving an acknowledgement of the subjective or political life of organizational personnel. The module comes up to date with a consideration of a number of models that openly embrace the 'loose-coupling', 'structural looseness' or dualism in organizations that this discovery implies, and finishes with a discussion of micropolitical strategies that can be found in educational organizations as managers and underdogs alike struggle to impose some kind of order and direction.

As with *Classrooms* there is a relentless discussion offered in this second half of all the models and approaches discussed. Many of these are the fashionable models familiar to students of modern educational management, including 'human relations' or 'cultural leadership' approaches. To mention my own favourite, the module is calmly analytic of and deeply sceptical about the attempt to foster a 'sense of mission' via a suitable 'organizational culture', and I read the critique at about the same time as attending a staff meeting in my own organization where our management revealed its sudden and suspiciously enthusiastic conversion to precisely that approach! (See Chapter 7 in this volume for a discussion of how to develop practice more sensitively.)

In place of such ideologies (to use the old terms), the latter half of the module offers an embryonic science of power and its deployment, via Ball and (briefly) Foucault. Despite the latter, the break with 'juridical' conceptions is not complete and so a tendency to see power as merely manipulation remains: nevertheless, students are offered a very detailed list of manipulative techniques (including the use of 'unobtrusive power', to cite another favourite concept).

Organisations in practice

I must confess to an initial scepticism about the overall strategy to engage student experience with academic arguments in assignments, since I have seen several conventional undergraduate courses that claim to do this but fail. Students adopt an instrumental approach, keep their own views quiet, and produce whatever is required to gain the grade on the 'summative' parts. I was interested to see exactly how the assignments were to be graded – would they feature a hidden agenda of necessary points after all, that had to be covered whatever conclusions students had come to in their reviews of their own experiences? If not, how could comparability be maintained? I was rather alarmed to discover that the course team simply passed this problem over to tutors and provided us with the barest minimum of tutor notes.

Some students felt insecure about their assessment too, for similar reasons – was there a catch, did they have to trot out a party line after all? When I got to know some *Organisations* students really well, it was clear that some were expecting to have to import a technique from their own undergraduate training days and develop highly stylized examples of how their actual practice somehow directly 'reflected' or validated the 'theory'.

At our first meeting, we discussed assessment (inevitably) and I suggested we adopt our own group conventions for assignments. I promised I would modify the approach if it proved incompatible with any hidden course policy (revealed through tutor monitoring) or assessment practice (such as in the centrally organized examination). I wanted students to feel they really could describe their own experiences in their own ways in the formative assignments, that I had no specific personal or pedagogic axe to grind (more tutor bad faith here), that I would respect their confidence in terms of any personal or organizational details they wanted to provide, and confine my comments to 'technical' matters to help them write the next summative assignment.

For summative assignments, I thought it might be useful to disclose and discuss a homegrown grading procedure. 'Experience' and 'theory' could be linked in a number of ways:

1. Via 'recognition', a process of simply recognizing, somehow, a link between one's own account of difficulties with colleagues, say, and Ball's account of typical micro-political struggles for resources.
2. Via 'exploration', a hunt for implications, in the spirit of my earlier work on the *School and Society* students. If there is a link of recognition with Ball's work, do any of the more general implications in Ball apply back to experience, as it were? (The earlier study tried to specify types of change in a teacher's 'constructs' that might be detectable after such a flow of implications – these days I am inclined to think of the process as involving exploring chains of signifiers in the texts, pausing to attach a signified from experience to one signifier, going back to the chain of signifiers, and then inviting students to attach signifieds further down the chain.)
3. Via a 'critical discussion' openly comparing experience and theory: did Ball's work need to be modified in the light of personal experience of teachers who seemed not to fit any of his categories or to offer mixtures of his categories, for example? Again in the spirit of the earlier work, I was interested to see how any differences would be reconciled, and wanted to encourage students to avoid the usual stale immunization strategies ('When was Ball last in a classroom?').

In grading terms, these levels could even be ranked, with Level 1 gaining grades up to the middle of the range and with students having to demonstrate evidence of operating at Levels 2 or 3 to gain better grades. Most students (and their tutor!) had technical objections to this cheerful operationalism, but we agreed to work it as a solution to our dilemmas: it did not seem any more arbitrary than any alternative and at least they could see where they stood.

When the first assignments arrived, perhaps 10 out of the initial 18 (and roughly the same proportions with other groups since) did feel they could offer a detailed and 'unofficial' account of their careers to date (the usual opening assignment). Although they were asked to provide a 'naïve' account before having done much reading, many of these accounts anticipated course material very closely. Most writers suggested they had been only weakly committed to teaching as a career initially, for example. This could be a self-deprecating occupational ideology, or some additional evidence for what Ball and Goodson (1985a) point to as the uneven growth of commitment experienced by teachers, quite unlike the official view of the immediately and totally dedicated professional. Some writers had anticipated the course material on 'life-cycles' and had charted changes in their career expectations and orientations as they matured.

Quite the most powerful material was provided by some women who wrote of the close intertwining of their occupational and personal lives. There were many examples of women being expected to have to consider their families in career interviews, being channelled into 'female' careers and roles, finding ways to resist and manage these pressures (eg, by instrumentally conforming to the perceived image of the woman teacher in particular schools, or trying to balance the levels of submissiveness and ambition in the image of a 'proper woman') and managing their work against a background of a variety of relationships with men including extra-marital affairs with colleagues. Some of these affairs had a direct relationship to career for one student, who was asked to leave her school when an affair became public (the male was allowed to remain), while another wrote of the relief to be found in work when emotional matters became too intense (which I had always thought to be a male reaction until then!).

Indeed, subsequent discussions in pretextual moments prompted a number of additional thoughts about careers, flowing indistinguishably from student comments, course material and my own interests. It was clear that males often considered their careers in the context of their lives as a whole too, even the most apparently dedicated and compartmentalized careerists. They too consider the impact on their wives' careers and on their families of origin in choosing where to work, or in making the difficult decision whether to accept promotion to managerial positions or 'spend more time with their families' (to cite a notorious phrase).

Many students had 'parallel careers' far beyond the types suggested for art teachers by Bennett, and worked in a range of areas from self-employed antiques dealer to training consultant. Language skills as well as artistic ones opened up a range of opportunities for one student to withdraw from a particular school and live abroad for a while, quite confident of being able to return to a job in Britain when ready: he wrote his account as one making a choice between a solid career or a more adventurous and fulfilling life.

The discovery of parallel careers for teachers introduces an intriguing possibility for other studies of work, since an individual might experience quite different social and work relations as they go from being, say, a basic grade teacher in a small rural primary school, to being the manager of a small textiles business, and back again in the course of a long weekend.

As an example of the curious way in which *Organisations* could produce unintended critical insights, it was often this apparently 'neutral' material on careers, intended as a preliminary, that had an effect upon students' perceptions of themselves as professionals, rather than the later material specifically designed to focus on the concept. As indicated above, this later material featured a specifically Marxist line on professionalism, seeing it, briefly, as a device used by the state to win consent for its policies (as in 'legitimated professionalism'), or, more generally, as dangerously within the gift of the state to bestow or withhold as conditions demanded (Grace, 1987). A 'labour process' approach was introduced as an alternative.

Student difficulties with this material were soon apparent and took a familiar form. As suggested above, student sympathies were much more readily extended to this kind of analysis, but getting students to go beyond the stage of 'recognition' proved as difficult as usual. Thus students could readily identify with the empirical examples in Riseborough's account of pupil resistance and rebellion (Riseborough, 1985), but found it obscure to try to trace the argument to the more general points about pupil resistance and its effects on teachers as an aspect of a wider hegemonic (inevitably) class struggle in the Marxist sense.

Similarly, critical accounts of the history of the relations between the state and teachers' work were ably summarized and often read with relish, but again the general framework was less appealing. In debates about proletarianization or deskilling of teachers' work, there was often recognition of the symptoms, but little reference to the underlying arguments about the long-term necessity of deskilling to capitalist accumulation, or a tendency to run together Marxist and Weberian accounts of the new managerialism in schools.

With the feminist work, recognition proved relatively easy for many students, albeit of a rather wary and tentative kind on the part of some of the males, but having identified the problem as located in 'patriarchy', little else developed. It was rare for students to be able to account for discrimination against females in terms of combinations of factors like personal prejudice by males, gender as a micropolitical strategy with no particular personal prejudice, and various institutional pressures like managerialism, the moves towards a 'market-based' system, the impact of deskilling upon females specifically, and so on. Enthusiasts for the feminist work tended to clutch at it as a quick answer for everything (with one or two superb exceptions). This arises with any powerful general framework, of course.

Even if you have the audience's sympathy for the concrete points in the works in question, it requires quite a different level of commitment on the part of students, and quite a different pedagogy, to move on to the terrain of theory, methods and arguments. Critical 'activist' approaches are like uncritical 'practitioner' stances in this respect, since both are particularly unsuitable in encouraging this move towards a relatively detached consideration of 'theory'.

Unfortunately, the structure of the course and its assessment patterns permitted students to miss out much of the second half of the course altogether (this situation is to be rectified in the final year of operation). Those that did tackle the issues here were often the successful or the aspirational who approached the sections from the point of view of wanting to learn about 'management'. One or two students, especially in the first intakes, also realized that the material provided a brilliant critique of 'management'. This material lent itself very well to 'pretextual' discussions, and the group sometimes spent a good deal of time in therapeutic and critical discussions of the strategies pursued by their various managers, although these rarely developed any theoretical insight.

Even the assignments from this part of the course were often memorable. One consisted of a straight-faced account of recent managerial changes in an establishment, followed by a superb and relentless analysis, locating the current 'management philosophy' in a tradition of alternations between models of control and induced consensus, and pointing to the real micro-political advantages at stake, as competing parties formed up around the different approaches. Another student wrote a penetrating account of the techniques used by his senior managers to rig agendas, stifle dissenting voices, produce a managed consensus and ruthlessly witch-hunt any remaining opponents.

Other accounts did the same from within, as it were, looking back over a successful career and reconstructing it in terms of micro-political manoeuverings and the pursuit of tactical advantage. Again and again, the need to 'fit in', to be 'the right sort of person', to 'look the part' came to the forefront of these accounts. Personal sponsorship from an existing member of the élite seemed crucial too. What these accounts were doing was undermining forever the claim to cool professional authority: I was reading material that reminded me very much of the backstage world of the professional, the one the public or the underdogs never see, in the classic work of Goffman or Hughes.[2]

With these accounts too, we are much closer to notions of class as a phenomenon of 'closure', as in neo-Weberian approaches like Parkin's (1974). The absence of any systematic discussion of Weberian approaches in *Organisations* (although some are demonstrated on the module), the lack of any reference back to the Marxist work in the first half of the module, and the usual problems with pushing on into the theoretical background of work like Ball's all make it difficult to develop these very promising implicit notions, though. Weber is still seen by many British activists as a conservative, too, of course.

Here too, the dilemma of the regional tutor is heightened – whether to stick to the agenda set by the module and help students cope with it, or to break away from the agenda and introduce new material to already busy students (see Murgatroyd, 1980).

As a result of taking *Organisations*, and discussing it in the pretextual moments, I learned a lot about management in my own sector, although it was not highlighted on the course. I found myself able to critique my own institution on its own terms (as indicated above). The recent flood of material on 'quality assurance' in particular emanating from the latest government funding body for Colleges and Polytechnics in Britain (the PCFC) offers a rich hunting ground for the *Organisations* enthusiast. For that matter, the empirical proposals to measure 'quality' provide further objects for an *Organisations*-type critique as well (see Gorbutt *et al.*, 1991).

Conclusion

Teachers are able to grasp and use critical material taught at a distance, and these modules found a receptive audience. The audience at this level is a most competent one, capable of following the critical implications of the material and developing a sense of critical relevance for themselves, in ways unanticipated by the course designers. Both modules I have discussed have generated very effective strategies to engage with the views of existing teachers and to provide materials for critique, while staying within the very tight 'academic' conventions and political constraints of course production at the Open University.

At the local level, it has been possible to use the materials critically. There have been constraints here too, set by the OU contract, including OU monitoring on the one hand and by the demands and expectations of the customers on the other. The main factor here has been the very low-key assessment scheme, with as little strain as possible placed on students (the MA is pass/fail only), and with a wide variety of choice and encouragement to try out the ideas in formative assignments (especially on *Organisations*). However, many of the answers in the *Organisations* final examination I marked one year (about half of the total taking the paper) were dreadfully banal and descriptive: this can clearly be interpreted in several ways.

The positive outcomes are not simply the result of good course design (including assessment design, although this helps especially). The current struggles over teacher education in Britain have had an important effect on both the provision and reception of critical courses for teachers. That struggle seems to be tipping in the direction of providing uncritical courses and modules. Although the older generations of teachers can compare their current conditions with more favourable ones prevailing not too long ago and become predisposed to critique as a result, this experience of 'colonization' will be less available to the new generations. The same changes will affect local tutors' interests in critique too, no doubt.

As I have tried to argue before, critical courses like these do not lie at the centre of institutions like the OU, nor indeed anywhere else in higher education these days. Even the writing of such courses seems to have to be done with some micro-political skill, almost to thwart the institution and to offer a respectable front to the public. Within modules, it seems almost impossible to advance beyond what I have described above as the first level, 'recognition' of links between experience and critical material. Students wishing to advance more deeply into critical theories find very little to guide them explicitly. There are allusions to more general frameworks, references to further work, footnotes – but also much verbal camouflage and euphemism, transparent to the competent reader, but mysterious for many beginners. The justification aspects of argumentation are as minimal as ever in OU 'effective communication'.

There is some apology for explicit theory too, since writers in the 'Gramscian' tradition have long relied upon a 'false consciousness' approach to critique, whereby 'true' perceptions come not from lengthy theoretical labour, but from some sudden flash of insight, often engendered by a piece of popular rhetorical writing or a 'roots'-type evocation of a glorious past of struggle. Other theorists are offering a tactical withdrawal of explicit theory from teacher education, perhaps knowing they have lost their organizational and political bases in educational institutions: 'recognition' and micro-politics are, perhaps, the only form in which critical thought and action can find a place at present.

Notes

1. This is a term used by Evans and Nation in discussing Gibson's work (itself based on the work of the pre-Gramscian R Williams). See Evans and Nation (1989c).
2. For an excellent account of this tradition and the critical purposes to which it can be put in reflecting on teaching, see an earlier OU Education third-level course, Open University (1973) Block 6.

5 Residential Schools in Open and Distance Education: quality time for quality learning?

Alistair Morgan and Mary Thorpe

Introduction

In reviewing the role of residential schools in open and distance education, it is relevant to examine the status of such schools in the theoretical writings of the field. What role and function do they take? Are residential schools a residue from conventional teaching and learning? Or, alternatively, do they provide a unique dimension to the experience of being a student, without which the quality of learning would diminish? These are the key questions which this chapter sets out to address. Although the detail focuses on our work on Open University (OU) summer schools, the issues discussed are of general concern in open and distance education, as Gavin Moodie and Daryl Nation exemplify in Chapter 8.

In developing a theoretical framework for distance education, Keegan (1986) refers to the 'teaching and learning act' as the essence of the work of educational institutions:

> I believe that a theoretical justification of distance education can be found. It is to be found in the attempt to re-integrate the act of teaching which is divided by the nature of distance education. The intersubjectivity of teacher and learner has to be artificially recreated. Over space and time the system seeks to re-construct the moment in which the teaching learning interaction occurs (p. 110).

In looking at residential schools in open and distance education, it is crucial to see them as just part of an overall teaching system, in which they provide a particularly rich dimension to student support. There is nothing taken for granted or sacrosanct about residential schools.

Clearly, residential schools locate the teaching-learning interaction directly in the face-to-face context. However, this should not presuppose that the nature of this interaction is derived from traditional teaching. Throughout this chapter we want to raise fundamental questions about the purpose and nature of residential schools.

The OU provides a useful starting point for this analysis as it is an autonomous university set up specifically to teach students at a distance. In the early history of the OU there were no 'single-mode' distance teaching universities (that is, with no on-campus students like their 'dual-mode' counterparts), hence it is relevant to examine how the OU developed the experiences of distance education out of that of other institutions. Here is how the first vice-chancellor, Walter Perry, expressed the rationale for the residential (summer) schools:

> From the beginning I regarded the summer school less as an integral part of a multi-disciplinary multi-media course than as a necessary extra – a learning experience that the student could not otherwise undergo and a chance to taste the flavour of an on-campus situation in contact with many other students. Here students would learn for the first time that many other students were having just the same difficulties as they were and would discover how other undergraduates worked. It would be an intensely motivating experience which would reinforce students halfway through their course with the determination necessary to carry them through to the end (Perry, 1976, p. 117).

In reviewing residential schools in distance education it seems appropriate to commence with Perry's views; his vision of the role of residential schools as providing 'a learning experience that students could not otherwise undergo' has had a major influence in the OU. In promoting the idea of summer schools, Perry acknowledged the influence of the experience of external studies in Australia:

> My initial commitment to these [summer schools], as a requirement for all students proceeding to a degree, stemmed from my association with Howard Sheath, who had for many years been Director of External Studies in the University of New England in New South Wales. On his prolonged visit to us in early 1969, he laid great stress on the advantages of summer schools in motivating and holding the interest of scattered students studying by correspondence in the Australian outback. He advised against making summer schools voluntary, maintaining that they were critical to the success of students. I was impressed by his arguments and determined that we should follow the same pattern (p. 117).

It is interesting to note that this early commitment in the OU to residential schools, which usually take the form of a one-week summer school, was derived from a dual-mode university in Australia (see Evans and Nation, 1989c).

In the OU, residential schools are one key part of its multi-media teaching system which is less amenable to achieving the economies of scale of a mass education system. It could be regarded as an aspect of the system which counters the criticism of 'instructional industrialism' (Evans and Nation, 1989c). Residential schools bring distance education 'alive' both for students and the teachers – they provide a unique part of the 'human dimension' in distance education. Besides any specialist equipment or laboratories, for example, the process of intense 'immersion' in the culture of learning and teaching in a residential setting provides a major learning experience for any course. (OU residential schools are designed to encourage student participation and active learning – formal lectures occupy a very small part.)

The role of residential schools is a topic which raises issues common to the discussion of the role of any form of face-to-face teaching in distance learning institutions. It has been suggested, for example, that the necessity of tutorials and local tuition at the OU was an admission of defeat within a distance teaching system. While such an argument has been effectively countered by Sewart (1981) and others, there has probably been less debate over the necessity of residential periods for study, as part of distance learning. This chapter lays out the grounds for such a debate and looks at some of the issues which have arisen concerning residential study.

Residential schools within distance learning entail considerable costs both for the institution and for the learners. It has always been necessary to provide arguments for their importance, for their necessity even – in the OU, attendance at residential schools is always compulsory on the one third of undergraduate courses which have them. Although each course has reasons particular to its own curriculum for having a residential school, it is possible to identify a number of general arguments which can be used to justify residence on a campus, following an intensive programme of study for a weekend, or more usually, a week. These are reviewed below.

Transforming the learner's understanding

The first argument concerns the nature of change which it is felt that the course requires of the learner. This may be seen as purely cognitive, to do with the learner's conceptual grasp of a body of knowledge, or it may also include attitudes. Higher education, particularly, asks the learner to consider and to use different ways of looking at the world and different ways of constructing meanings for experience than those of everyday social interaction. Changes of this order require the learner to transform existing knowledge, to re-order and to re-value taken-for-granted attitudes and experience. Research and practice with both 18–21 year olds and much older adult students confirm that this process is not an automatic outcome of successful study, and may prove painful and difficult once begun (Marton and Säljö, 1984; Northedge, 1991; Perry, 1968). A residential school offers a number of features which, in theory, enable and support this transforming process – to enable students to adopt a 'deep approach' to their studies.

First, the learners give themselves time devoted solely to the activities and thinking required by their course, without, as is normally the case, trying to 'fit the course into' the daily round of responsibilities which take priority for virtually all adults. This allows time for the realization that major changes of perspective or attitude are required, and for the consequent deconstruction of old ideas and reconstruction and development of new ones. This process needs to incorporate understanding of how the new ideas come about and of the relationship for the learner between old and new, between knowledge in use and course-based knowledge, 'new' to the learner. However, reflection alone is not the only issue for many learners. Contact with other students studying the subject is also necessary – both as stimulus to making deep-seated changes in thinking and attitude and as support during the process.

The second point is that residential learning brings together people whose only ostensible purpose for being together is their wish to learn the subject, and thus 'the subject' in some shape or form is never far from being the overt topic of all the dialogues taking place throughout the period of residence. This provides significant – in distance learning – opportunities for informal conversation during which learners can voice uncertainties and fears which they might never choose to express to tutors, or within formal learning groups, because they fear to reveal too much about their level of understanding. There is a widespread apprehension of 'sounding stupid' and displaying lack of understanding.

The reflection required for change to occur is stimulated by exposure to an extended period of 'immersion' in the subject or area of learning. Instead of short bursts of learning crammed into the small spaces of busy lives, the learner suddenly has full days and evenings exposed to activities and discussion focused in one way or another on the content of the course. This generates many opportunities for learners to talk through their own insights, check out understandings and generally come to terms with what there is to learn. Learning which is challenging to existing conceptions of the individual and views about society tend to be resisted. Change takes time and is more likely to be facilitated in a residential setting with the extended opportunity for dialogue with student peers and with tutors.

Access to specialized teaching facilities

A major rationale for campus-based residence arises in the case of subjects which require facilities otherwise unavailable to learners locally – laboratories, computing resources, archives, specialist library facilities, simulation equipment and so on. Much learning can be undertaken effectively with print and, where necessary, with home experiment kits, but many things cannot be accomplished in this way. Extensive supervision of laboratory work and other 'hands-on' learning is also required to help those who are struggling, as well as to extend the learners who have coped with course demands thus far. Indeed this area has marked off the curricular boundaries of distance learning. No reputable institution has yet claimed to provide qualifying programmes in a whole range of areas requiring complex behavioural, cognitive and physical skills – in medical or dental practice, for example – using distance learning, although the simulation and 'virtual reality' technologies may be leading in this direction.

Access to particular forms of learning experience

Although many forms of distance learning are multi-media, there are nonetheless inevitable limits on the form of learning activity these allow – much distance learning is largely encompassed by reading, thinking, writing, listening/watching a video or audio cassette. Residential schools offer many more possibilities: large-scale group events, allowing for role plays and simulations, as well as the more conventional lecture or presentation, performances by poets, actors and musicians, amateur performances of plays, poetry and music by learners themselves, and a whole range of social events bringing together learners from different courses and backgrounds. In the context of particular courses, any one of these learning experiences could be the basis of a very strong argument for a residential school.

There is no completely effective substitute for live performance, for example, especially where the performer is able to explain or comment and discuss with learners about their performance and its meaning. Such an argument can be made for the necessity of residential study on courses addressing issues in, or histories of, the theatre or music. It has also been a powerful component of the case for a residential school for the OU's course in *Third World Studies*. Here not only is it vital to hear and see productions by Third World artists, but to listen to their perspective on the work they do, in the context of their country's history and political situation. A particularly forceful example of this point occurred in relation to the residential school for the course *Popular Culture* which used the seaside resort of Blackpool (in the north-west of England) as a form of large-scale performance in its own right. Blackpool's amenities and entertainments for a wide variety of ages and (largely working-class) interests, were analysed, tasted, heard, seen and in every way possible experienced 'in the round' by each year's school of students, resident nearby at the University of Lancaster. They needed this direct experience in order to develop their grasp (in every sense of the word) of the theoretical and subjective dimensions of *Popular Culture*.

Access to specialized tuition

It is often difficult to appoint tutors local to students, who have expertise in the content of all areas of a course. Where courses are interdisciplinary, sometimes inter-faculty in approach, it is recognized that the nature of help available will be generalist rather than specialist. Courses of this kind at the OU are the product of a team of authors and developers, and it would be unreasonable to expect every tutor appointed to mirror this range of abilities in supporting students through their course study. In some courses this is sufficiently important that a residential school is required where specialists can be brought together so that students have access to specialist knowledge and understanding in areas different from the expertise of their local tutor. Courses with projects carried out by students themselves are another case in point. Where there is freedom for the student to choose their topic, specialized advice is often difficult to provide unless there is a residential school, where a range of expertise can be made available. There may also be intellectual 'economies of scale' in offering residential schools where specialist help can be provided in the techniques of project work (survey design, interview analysis and so on) at a time when all the students have similar problems, even if they are working on very different issues in different contexts.

Many course teams at the OU have based their bids for resources to mount annual summer schools on some particular combination of these general arguments. Whilst the validity of their claims is not in question, there are, nonetheless, problems and issues presented by such commitments to residential study. Issues of equality and access have always existed as a 'negative feature' of residential schools, creating problems for certain students. Recently in the OU the operational problems have prompted a review of residential schools. These issues and problems are discussed in the next section.

Issues of equality and access

It is known that a substantial proportion of OU students find extreme difficulty in making arrangements for alternative care for dependants and in paying for the costs of attendance at a site remote from their homes. Typically, residential schools present considerable barriers to many women students and to unemployed students and those on very low incomes. Although the financial assistance schemes run by the OU do cover the University's fee for a school, the assessment is based on family income and disadvantages those women who do not have easy access to the income of the family.

The OU's ruling on compulsory attendance causes considerable resentment among some of its students. There is a feeling, for example, that academics value campus residence for reasons which, whatever their overt rationale, draw too much on irrelevant parallels with conventional undergraduate study. During 1991 a pilot scheme was tried on the *Social Science* foundation course whereby places in the crèche of host universities were made available to OU students. Prior to this, no large-scale facilities had been offered, but it remains to be seen whether these can be provided at a cost that will not prove prohibitive to the very students it is intended to help.

It is not only the parent with difficulties in arranging child-care who questions the compulsory nature of residential study. Many older students may find the stress of long journeys, uncomfortable student accommodation and unfamiliar social requirements leads them to question the validity of compulsory attendance.

In the early 1970s when the University was being established, the emphasis was on ensuring that OU students had study experience of equivalent quality and status to that of the dominant campus-based model, and residential schools contribute to this 'university experience'. Since then, however, institutions of higher education have increased the number of mature and part-time students they admit, and made a number of changes to the way they teach, such as modular courses and the combination of learning through work experience with institution-based study. This means that there is now much more diversity in the form of provision of so called 'conventional' higher education, and perhaps less reason to take for granted the necessity of campus-based study. In parts of the UK there is also a degree of competition for mature students which did not exist during the 1970s, and the student as client is a much more established approach in British higher education generally. Institutions which make unwelcome demands on their students can certainly expect criticism and may well lose students as a result.

Operational difficulties and costs

Distance teaching institutions are usually dependent on the facilities of other institutions of further and higher education and thus considerable planning resources are required for the scheduling of both teaching and living accommodation to cover the very different demands of different courses. In the UK, where there were levels of student attendance of 45,000 in 1991, projected to rise close to 60,000 by 1993 (Open University, 1991), it is easy to see that there are constraints on expansion simply in terms of the limited number of appropriate sites available.

The rapid and large increase in demand for computing facilities is also posing considerable problems. Both the *Mathematics* and *Social Science* foundation summer schools now require direct access to computers, and there are increasing pressures from the *Arts* foundation course and others. The importance of computers for learning in a great many discipline areas, and the pressures for skill-based learning, where computer literacy is increasingly seen as an essential outcome of almost any higher education experience, mean that there are sharp increases in costs of provision which have consequential effects on the costs to students and therefore the accessibility of OU study. These may be to some extent within the control of the University, but increases in the charges of host universities are not, and these rise regularly. In 1991 there was a demand for a 40 per cent increase in *per capita* charges for basic residential services, and it is unlikely that such increases can be avoided, thus leading to regular increases in the costs to students.

Staffing

The OU is also realizing constraints on staffing, in terms both of internal staff to provide management, and of part-time tutorial and counselling staff who provide the immediate support for students. A recent report on quality tuition in the OU highlighted the need for more staff development to improve the tuition at residential schools. The intensive nature of the residential schools is well known, and requires skills and personal qualities which cannot be assumed of staff who may otherwise be well qualified. Thus far the OU has not provided for more than a few hours preparation prior to teaching at residential school, and any expansion of the demands of this area of teaching will bring added costs.

Expansion into Europe

By 1993 it will be possible for virtually anyone resident in continental Europe to register to study an OU course. In the past, the limited schemes in Europe did not present a major challenge; such students made their own arrangements to attend UK residential schools, many of them being UK nationals with several reasons for wanting to travel 'back to base'. If the projected numbers of tens of thousands of Europeans registering for OU courses is achieved, this will present another occasion for reviewing the legitimacy of residential study. The present policy is to support residential schools outside the UK, 'only where the student numbers, costs and operational capacities allowed them to be viable' (Open University, 1991). The closer integration of Europe is also manifested in the potential movement out of the UK of OU students whose study obviously calls for direct experience of continental European, culture, language and people. The Centre for Modern Languages argues that there should be week-long residential schools in France for those studying French in 1994 and thereafter.

Although we have focused the discussion on problems and issues in the OU, it seems likely that these will be of general concern. However, the size of the OU and the lack of its own residential accommodation, in contrast to the dual-mode distance education universities in Australia, New Zealand, North America and elsewhere, make some of the operational problems specific to the OU and the other single-mode universities in other countries.

The analysis in this chapter so far has concentrated on elaborating various rationales for residential schools and key problems which are raised. To highlight some of the issues and to bring our personal experiences more to the forefront in this chapter, we shall now look at one OU summer school which we have both been involved with very closely: *Third World Studies*. This course ran from 1983–91 and was replaced in 1992 by a new course, *Third World Development*.

The *Third World Studies* summer school

In this section we provide some personal reflections on our course team involvement in the excitement and creativity of developing a new broad interdisciplinary course which also had a summer school. We have tutored summer school for the *Third World Studies* course every year from 1983 to 1991. We have also acted occasionally as course director, a role which provides an overview of the progress and experience of all tutor groups in any one week. At summer school we have experienced the human dimension of study, which enlivens it in a manner which course materials cannot. We have also experienced the strains and problems of intense residential schools which course materials avoid.

We established a residential school in the belief that students of *Third World Studies* ought to have a direct experience of the culture of the Third World. Naturally, it was not feasible to arrange to visit a Third World country, but at least we would have a good second best, through simulation, role play, games, theatre, poetry reading and lectures drawing in people from the Third World. The University of East Anglia (UEA) in Norwich was chosen as the site to simulate a Third World experience for our students. This was done partly because we could add our course to the existing OU summer school held there (OU summer schools typically have several course summer schools running concurrently at each site) and also because UEA has a School of Development Studies, which seemed to offer an excellent opportunity for collaboration.

We wanted summer school to be fun, to be a setting for opening avenues for debate and exploration and for the exchange of ideas – we had a commitment to 'opening up the discourse' for students. However, such great ambitions have to be put into practice! In the OU, developing summer school activities does not have the same kudos attached to it as producing the course materials. Hence, it was quite difficult to maintain the commitment of staff to work on summer school. In spite of these problems a small core of staff developed the summer school activities. Within this group, broadly speaking, there were shared values about teaching and learning – essentially, a student-centred approach to learning, derived at least for some members of the group, from the work of Rogers (1983) and Mezirow (1981).

The first week of summer school in 1983 was an exciting period. On our first encounter with the students we had questions in our minds. How was the course going? How was the summer school going to be received? Most of the academic staff who had contributed to the course wanted to be at summer school to gain a first-hand experience. OU academic staff are required to teach for two weeks at summer school, so we ended up with a large number of full-time staff in the first and second weeks. What an excellent idea – full time staff very closely involved at the start! A good idea, but one which proved to have unduly problematic 'side-effects'.

We had not really anticipated the level of conflict and contestation which would surface, in what was rather like having a residential course-team meeting of one week's duration, while at the same time teaching a new summer school for about 120 students! The intense pressure of summer school brought differences of content, political differences and differences of teaching styles into the foreground. Members of staff who had not been directly involved in designing the summer school suddenly declared an immediate interest in redesigning activities when they were asked to run them! Traditional didactic views of teaching and learning were being challenged by the student-centred approaches we had planned. And, of course, some of the activities did not work particularly well in the first week. Some extremely critical comments from our colleagues, which challenged the basis of some of the teaching-learning activities, did not help our students. The students were there for one week and they needed and wanted to make the most of it.

In spite of these difficulties, those first weeks of summer school were very positive and exciting. Students were tolerant of those activities which did not work as planned. In some ways each week was a formative evaluation or a form of action research. In each week we had N' Gugi Wa Thiongo, the Kenyan writer, as guest speaker, for the final session of the school. The intensity of this session is difficult to convey; it included readings from his work, an explanation of how he changed from writing in English to writing in Kikuyu and was subsequently imprisoned in Kenya, his exile in the UK, and a view of development as personal empowerment. Students and staff hold vivid recollections of these guest lectures by N' Gugi as the highpoint of the summer school.

Another aspect of OU summer schools is that the intense nature of the week demands that the schedule should run reasonably efficiently. This is not an argument for bureaucratic efficiency with extremes of punctuality, but students do need to know what they are expected to do, where it is likely to occur and that tutors are reasonably clear about what they are supposed to be doing. In the *Third World Studies* summer school, the activities are very tutor- and student-dependent. Therefore, the level of specificity in the tutor notes is far less detailed than is often the case in other forms of residential school. Also, the programme involves tutors working on a wide range of topics, rather than teaching a specialism or single module repeated a number of times throughout the week.

These features of the school present a number of crucial issues for the course director. First, obtaining agreement for tutors to do things; second, briefing tutors and supporting them in their work; and third, communicating the programme and its expectations to the students. These may seem very obvious issues, but in practice they can prove to be difficult. The time pressures for everyone – students and tutors – seem to increase the importance and urgency of these issues. A small amount of 'slippage' or a few administrative mix-ups over rooms or student groupings, which would be almost irrelevant in the context of a full term or semester, becomes magnified in importance at summer school. So communicating timetable and activity changes to 120 students is quite a challenge.

How can a course director allocate various teaching tasks? Although the management style or milieu of the tutor group is democratic, there are still tasks to be allocated to individuals. In the early 1980s in the UK, to have three or four one-week residential schools on the Third World and Development Studies was quite an important academic event nationally. Certainly we attracted high quality tutors, many with national and international reputations in the field. This introduces another quite complex issue of how best to handle *prima donnas* in the tutor group. Obtaining tutors' agreement to do particular tasks is a subtle combination of management style and authority, legitimated through appropriate knowledge of the subject material. There are certain contradictions in maintaining a delicate balance between a democratic/charismatic style of management, and at the same time keeping a 'firm' grip on the programme.

In spite of these contradictions and problems, the *Third World Studies* residential schools have proved to be extremely stimulating for both students and tutors. The residential schools appear to be an important factor in the popularity of the course. After the first year's school, a student association was established by ex-*Third World Studies* students with a programme of regular local meetings.

Critical issues for residential schools

The previous reflection on the positive aspects of residential schools and then on the difficulties they create shows that characterizing the debate about residential schools as one of traditional versus distance learning is an oversimplification. However, asking fundamental questions about teaching and learning and the possible ways to use intensive face-to-face contact in a residential school raises critical issues for distance education. Also, as the debate is specifically about face-to-face teaching, the insights are particularly relevant to the theme of reformation in open and distance education more generally.

What happens at OU residential schools is certainly not a 'mini-version' of conventional face-to-face teaching in higher education, compressed into the space of (usually) one week. The programme begins on a Saturday afternoon and finishes the following Friday, with an intensive academic programme of work on each day and with plenty of opportunity for social activities. Many tutors only teach one week at a time and the majority of tutors are not full-time OU staff. They teach elsewhere and choose to tutor on courses which interest them. The pay is not a major attraction, especially for the long hours. Tutors are attracted to working with highly motivated adult students, developing their teaching experience and engaging with a group of colleagues away from their normal duties. The 'play hard-work hard' ethic is often strong at summer school, and it can be invigorating to concentrate on learning and meeting students and tutors away from one's other daily routines.

Policy-makers who think that the domestic and social aspects can be easily separated from the academic aspects should think again. Distance education policy-makers, especially those dealing with single-mode institutions, perhaps need to be reminded of this. So much of their time is completely remote from the physical presence of students that they forget problems of which campus-based staff need no reminder: poor food, unhelpful porters, noisy rooms or unsatisfactory social provision all lead to dissatisfaction which spills over to the classroom. These matters suddenly loom large at summer school. This is particularly so for the administrative and management staff of a school. For the course directors (responsible for the academic programme of a particular course) and the school director (responsible for the overall administration of a summer school with several courses), much of their attention is oriented to ensuring people are reasonably happy and are able to participate as planned. For example, from 1991, new procedures for handling harassment at residential school have been in operation. These procedures are oriented to any form of harassment and provide a framework within which we can take appropriate action on complaints from staff or students. These procedures are publicized and have been used and found necessary. They have a vital role to play in ensuring the rights of students at residential school.

There is one significant difference between OU summer schools and teaching in the conventional university term. Whereas conventional university teaching still tends to be dominated by large lecture rooms and a degree of impersonality, OU residential schools are highly interactive and oriented to small group work. As the rationale emphasizes encouraging students to take a 'deep approach to learning', students are less able to hide behind the passivity of being an audience for the performance of the traditional lecture. The majority of time at residential school is designed for student participation and active learning.

As already pointed out, residential schools are the one major area in the OU least amenable to operation on a mass scale. For the 'champions' of summer schools the residential requirement is crucial to maintaining the quality of the learning outcomes. In contrast, the OU's mandatory residential requirement (with limited health and other exemptions) on courses with summer schools has been described as the 'greatest barrier' to major expansion of student numbers. The role of residential schools during the 1990s is likely to be highly contested within the OU in much the same way as Moodie and Nation show is occurring for weekend schools at Monash University College Gippsland in Australia (see Chapter 8). This is likely to be one of the contested areas in reforming open and distance education, especially as the new information technologies become further implanted in education and the home.

There may be pressure in the OU, for example, to implement a gradual reduction in summer school lines to the absolute minimum, say foundation courses and a few laboratory-based schools. There may also be a move toward voluntary attendance. Together these would make way for massive expansion. Residential schools are a 'cottage industry' in a mass distance education system – essentially a Fordist model of knowledge production and distribution. Some staff and students have strategically instrumental approaches to learning. However, for many students residential school is the occasion when a course starts to make sense in the midst of all the new information which they have received throughout the year. As we start to scrutinize the rationales for residential schools, there is a temptation (or trap) to consider educational provision in reductionist terms and to ignore that there is a significant argument about the holism of the learning experience at a residential school, which does not easily fit into this rationalist analysis. Residential schools have to be understood more widely than merely as curriculum 'delivery systems'.

The arguments about how residential schools restrict access and flexibility in the context of open learning need to be looked at carefully. To what extent does a 'streamlining' of a course in distance education (by removing residential schools) deny students the opportunity to participate in the discourse of the subject area with student peers and tutors? Edwards (1991) suggests that open learning provision provides an appearance of opportunity and that arguments about the multi-skilling of a workforce have an ideological dimension to conceal the differentiated nature of work in a post-Fordist society:

> What I am suggesting is that discourses are not neutral descriptions of reality, that they are also productive and integral of the exercise of power in social relations. Discourses are therefore strategic to the ongoing and continuous power struggles in the social formation. The fact that discourses are not generally articulated this way is itself a manifestation of power, as 'neutral' descriptions of 'reality' have a power in themselves in making the contingent appear unchallengeable. Thus, notions of 'openness', 'access' and 'flexibility' become technical fixes to the 'problem' of non-participation, reinforcing the ideologically constructed inadequacies of individuals insofar as they continue to fail to make use of the new opportunities for learning.
>
> Within this context, discourses about open learning can be articulated as another aspect of post-Fordism, strategically ranged to 'normalise' a view of the future of work based in structural unemployment and underemployment – as not only inevitable, but also preferred. As a result of these discourses and practices they reflect and reproduce, persons will be disciplined into certain forms of behaviour and more easily managed within a social formation of structural inequality.... We may discuss how best to produce the flexible worker of the future, but who that person will be is left unquestioned (p. 41).

Residential schools, like face-to-face tuition, provide a unique feeling of 'connectedness' with the organization, in contrast to one of alienation – they make a unique contribution to the human dimension of student experience in distance education and the quality of learning (Student Research Centre, 1986).

This quality in learning is concerned with the empowerment of students, to allow them access to the power which is manifested in academic discourse and debate. Residential schools are a unique forum for such dialogue and debate in a liberal democracy. However, the provision of residential schools is likely to be an area of intense contestation between competing groups within organizations which hold ideologically different views on the aims of education and approaches to teaching and learning.

Evans and Nation (1989c), drawing on the work of Freire, comment on the bureaucratic and dehumanizing trends in distance education. Their argument is in accord with our views. It sets the role of residential schools in a wider arena which is crucial to their quality:

For many distance educators the process of critical reflection in the teaching-learning process may seem fanciful. Indeed, Freire himself, who constructed his forms of adult education in difficult circumstances, argues that his ideas about teaching are utopian. He declared that, 'if we are not utopian we will easily become bureaucratic and dehumanizing'; we would argue that this is precisely what is happening in distance education: it is becoming bureaucratic and dehumanizing. In Freire's terms we need to make distance education 'liberating' not 'dominating' (p. 252).

Residential schools can play a powerful role in the 'humanizing' of distance education and make a significant contribution to the quality of learning. We are not suggesting that any practice of residential schools in distance education should be accepted uncritically. An untheorized acceptance of the status quo, whether it is a residential school in distance education or a series of lectures in a conventional university, is unlikely to lead to quality in the learning outcomes. What we are arguing is that an appraisal of the teaching and learning can lead to a theorizing of practice, so as to ensure that students' learning experiences are likely to encourage them to engage in a deep approach to learning. Quality time should lead to quality learning.

6 Transformative Learning in Reflective Practice

Liz Burge and Margaret Haughey

Much of the literature on open or distance education is concerned with the relationship between the learner and the teacher and the absence of learning in a group. Writers vary in their support of these assumptions, some suggesting that since adults are autonomous learners it is not difficult for them to learn on their own, others encouraging the linking of learners to override the loneliness of the long-distance learner. Other writers point out the importance of clear objectives, logical instructions, realistic expectations and self-contained materials. These factors have been identified by students as the most effective ways to help them study. To summarize these positions would be to advocate that all distance education materials include a clear set of instructions which follow logically from objective to assignment and which can be completed without undue reference to outside sources. Opportunities for group involvement should be optional but students should have ready access to a tutor to solve any queries which might arise in the course of their studies.

While these suggestions seem to be based on the pragmatic realities of the lives of working adults, they avoid what is a more essential question: the model of teaching to which they subscribe. Although they are not tied to one point of view, a more careful perusal of the writing from which they were taken would raise questions about the epistemology espoused. Where knowledge is considered to be external to individuals and is viewed as a coherent body of ideas, some proven and hence factual, the major intent of teaching is to transfer this knowledge from the teacher to the student. From such a perspective it is crucial that the major building blocks, the concepts and theories, are explained clearly and in proper sequence so that the student can reproduce this structure internally. The intention is to have the student explore ideas and connections within that framework of ideas. Obviously, well-organized distance education materials can make this task much easier for the student.

In one alternative view of epistemology, knowledge is considered to be internal rather than external to the learner. The particular linkages among ideas and theories are constructed by learners from what is learned and from previous experiences. What is already known influences what is to be learned and what is learned is different for each learner. From this perspective, it is also important to present ideas and theories clearly recognizing that the particular epistemological perspective of the course writer influences which theories and concepts are chosen and how they are presented.

A third view of epistemology accepts the influence of past experiences on the individuality of the knowing we call learning and highlights the importance of a transformative rather than passive construction of knowledge. In this view, unless learners consider the implications of the ideas for themselves in their own lives and decide to act, know and believe in new ways, they are likely to adopt a passive acquiescence to the teacher's knowledge structure. Ultimately, this passive learning has not made a difference. It has not been transformative. At best, it may have resulted in some accretion of knowledge. From the transformation perspective, which seeks the emancipation of learners from the paradigm which has dominated teaching over the last century, learners have to be engaged in discovering the meaning of the learning for their own lives.

The advent of widespread interactive communication technologies provides us with further stimulus for critical reflection. The new technologies can allow us to adapt our existing models uncritically, or they can provoke us into confronting our existing methods, beliefs and strategies, especially those concerning dialogue and relationships in learning. If we continue to apply old models to new contexts without the benefit of reflection, we may create a negative result, that is, under the guise of our rhetoric about the possibilities and freedoms created by the new interactive technologies, we may in fact create more stress and dependence for learners because we are reducing their choices. Distance education is currently experiencing great growth in new applications of interactive technologies, but we have no guarantees that, without critical reflection on our practice, we will produce any significant growth toward transformative learning, toward the development of personal empowerment and critical abilities to question rather than to accept assumptions, beliefs and expectations about one's role in the world.

Additionally, our belief in the generic processes of reflection on professional practice leads us to value both reflection-in-action and reflection-on-action, ie, the periods of attention during and after teaching (Schön, 1983; 1987). Such thinking and feeling helps us to understand the complex and often apparently conflicting events and outcomes that characterize human behaviour. Our reflections here are based on our experiences and we have provided contextual material to make broader links to open and distance education.

When we began to create this chapter, we knew that we wanted to write about dialogue in distance education. Furthermore, we were agreed that such interaction should be the ground and process for transformative learning leading to emancipation. Following our initial discussions, we spent seven weeks as visiting professors at different universities teaching summer school. Liz taught two undergraduate courses in adult education to students who were generally full-time adult educators who were using the summer session to speed the completion of their degrees. Margaret taught the foundational graduate course in educational administration to students who were full-time educators returning to summer school for the first time. As we reviewed our stories we identified five major themes which captured the essence of the experience for us: developing the community of learners, establishing trust, accepting the challenge, encouraging their practice, and possible transformations.

When we continued our discussions by email, since we live about 2500 km apart, we decided to use these teaching experiences to explore our understandings about dialogue in learning. We wrote the narrative then tried to distance ourselves from it in order to 'organize the transformative potential of [that narrative]' (Rehm, 1989, p. 120). This chapter is in three parts. First, we explore the notion of transformative learning; then we use our stories to explore the teaching-learning process. Finally, we draw together our ideas about transformative learning and the implications for open and distance education.

Transformative Learning

Transformative learning involves empowerment of the individual. The concept of empowerment has received increased attention in various literature bases, including distance education. Values, explanations and strategies have been offered by those developing theories of critical pedagogy (Ellsworth, 1989; Giroux, 1986; Liston and Zeichner, 1987; Simon, 1987); in discussing helping relationships (Rappaport, 1986); in teaching and curriculum design (Grundy, 1987; Smyth, 1989a, 1989b); in literacy education (Freire, 1970; Freire and Macedo, 1987); and in cross-cultural education (Delgado-Gaitan and Trueba, 1991). Other terms such as voice, dialogue, radical pedagogy, emancipatory education (Hart, 1985), transforming knowledge (Minnich, 1990), and transformative education (Boyd and Meyers, 1988) also have been used to refer to a generic process of critical consciousness-raising about the sources and impacts of various oppressions, exclusions and limited perceptions; to the development of knowledge and skills for critique; and to the planning of new action as a result of that critique. 'Emancipation lies in the possibility of taking action autonomously. That action may be informed by certain theoretical insights, but it is not prescribed by them' (Grundy, 1987, p. 113). The distance education literature has espoused the field of critical reflection with the collections edited by Evans (1990), Evans and King (1991) and Evans and Nation (1989b), and pioneered to a large extent by Harris' critique of the UK Open University (1987). Definitions of empowerment involve three major ideas: the notions of choice, of control of one's life, and of emancipation from ways of thinking which for the particular individual have limited both choice and control.

> [Empowerment] suggests a sense of control over one's life in personality, cognition and motivation. It expresses itself at the level of feelings, at the level of ideas about self-worth, and at the level of being able to make a difference in the world around us, even at the spiritual level. It is an ability we have, but that needs to be released, in much the same way our bodies can be self-healing when endorphins are released. We all have the potential (Rappaport, 1986, p. 69).

Key strategies for facilitating empowerment have also been discussed at length in the critical pedagogy literature, although not without some trenchant criticism (Ellsworth, 1989; Modra, 1991). For example, Giroux's (1987) strategies focus on examination of people's social and political influences, attention to the internal and sometimes contradictory nature of their voices and experience, and the questioning of the ideologies inherent in curriculum materials.

We use the term 'transformative learning' to refer to both the outcomes and the process itself through which learners experience such significant changes in beliefs, attitudes and knowledge that they transform their ways of thinking. Transformative learning contributes to empowerment as a process of being one's own mature and autonomous person.

Transformative learning and adult education

Writers on adult education have begun to address the issue of helping learners to engage in critical reflection and to develop the skills and attitudes necessary for empowerment (Boud and Griffin, 1987; Brookfield, 1987; Daloz, 1986; Hart, 1985, 1990; Mezirow, 1989, 1991; Mezirow & Associates, 1990; Shor, 1990). As Hart points out:

> Adult education literature operates mostly on the basis of implicit assumptions about what comprises democratic forms of education and learning, placing its main emphasis on methods and strategies which assume a clear sense of achieved autonomy and independence in adults. Structures of communication and interaction among adults which reveal the continued existence of unfreedom and dependence are not acknowledged as problems or research priorities; at the same time, unrecognized power relations are carried into, as well as being reflected by, educational situations involving adults (Hart, 1985, p. 120).

Mezirow has developed a theory concerning transformative learning which explains how adults may develop by challenging their old assumptions and creating new meaning perspectives that are 'more inclusive, integrative, discriminating, and open to alternative points of view' (Mezirow, 1991, p. 224). The assumptions underlying his theory are distinguishable from the current emphasis on stimulus-response mechanisms or on cognitive science and information-processing theories which, he argues, are of limited use in the facilitation of significant learning in adults (1991, p. 7).

Much that is positive in facilitating adult learning is already concerned with empowerment in the sense of consciousness-raising; critical analyses of existing knowledge traditions, constructions and applications; and the development of new knowledge structures and applications. Facilitation strategies and their underlying principles have been discussed at length in the adult education literature (Boud and Griffin, 1987; Brookfield, 1987; Freire, 1970; Merriam and Caffarella, 1991; Mezirow & Associates 1990; Shor and Freire, 1987; Taylor, 1986); in feminist pedagogy literature (Bunch and Pollack, 1983; Culley and Portuges, 1985; Hooks, 1988; Lather, 1991; Minnich, 1990; Shrewsbury, 1987); and with increasing attention in the distance education literature (Burge, 1988; Burge and Lenskyj, 1990; Haughey, 1989, 1991; Taylor and Kaye, 1986).

Transformation in learning, then, is not about mere additions to existing knowledge schemata, or about faster performance, nor is it about tacking on ideas that are discrepant to one's basic knowledge, nor is it the alleged restorative approach decried in the feminist literature as the 'add women and stir' recipe (Bunch, 1987, p. 140).

Rather, it is about the challenge, creativity and risk (Gore, 1989, p. 2) that are necessary and inevitable for confronting the strength of the traditional or taken-for-granted.

> We are challenged to immerse ourselves again in what we are studying, to suspend judgment for a while, to learn to hear new voices, and hence to emerge with new definitions and concepts and judgments that are, again, finer, more complex, more subtle, and much more adequate to the interrelated world in which we must, now, live (Minnich, 1990, p. 185).

We believe that if we are to encourage transformative learning and critical self-reflection in our learners, then we had better do the same for ourselves. This chapter, then, shows how we two practitioners used narrative reflections about our teaching to disclose our 'personal practical knowledge', to challenge assumptions and to make explicit our personal philosophy, our images and metaphors and the rhythms in our teaching (Connelly and Clandinin, 1988, p. 59–78).

Using reflections for part of our in-class decision-making and after-class review was a complex, sometimes conflicting and often uncertain process that had outcomes as much discomforting as satisfying. Schön (1987) describes the costs of reflection-in-practice:

> we must give up the rewards of unquestioned authority, the freedom to practice without challenge to our competence, the comfort of relative invulnerability, the gratification of deference (p. 299).

Hunt (1991) also describes what we must confront during reflection-from-practice:

> we experience not only the convenient and the congenial, the predictable and the generalizable, but we also encounter noise, contingency, and chaos; the resilience of reality, the continual surprise that dealing with the wealth of the world affords (p. viii).

Most important for us are the insights gained about ourselves from the understandings of our students.

Developing the community of learners

Empowerment of learners includes both providing the conditions under which they can learn best and helping them realize the constraints to which they have become so accustomed that they have become taken-for-granted. Such a complex process involves both the teacher and learners in developing a community which supports inquiry, exploration and choice, legitimates discomfort and conflict and celebrates insights. One basic strategy for empowerment is to replace the bureaucratic conditions considered to be the accepted way to 'deliver' instruction with the communitarian conditions which foster and facilitate the learning of all participants.

> My 16 students were a very mixed group, in terms of age, life experience, education and motivation. Ages ranged from early 20s to mid-50s, but most were in the 30–36 age group. All were either working full- or part-time. Some had very clear ideas about why they were taking the course – for immediate application to work; others needed to bank a university credit or two. They came into these two courses after considerable experience with the banking model of education and the lecture mode of delivery of information. They were expecting more of the same.
>
> ... I was able ... to transfer our classes to a more adult-oriented ergonomic environment – from wood and metal desks to comfortable chairs and tables in a cosier, better equipped classroom – and into more humane and productive time periods of two and a half hours twice a week. (Liz)

Developing a sense of community has to be deliberate on the teacher's part. Seven weeks is too short for this to happen among a group of strangers unless specific strategies are used. The changes in class location and time together were one such strategy. Unless students saw a relationship between what they were learning about adults' needs for an appropriate milieu for learning, and their own experience of the influence of a comfortable environment, they were unlikely to sense that they were being cared for or about. Developing community means not only setting-up situations where students are more comfortable, but also developing strategies which will encourage the development of myths and symbols and the sharing of norms, values, and beliefs.

> Because I was living on my own and missed the noise and companionship of my family, I began to eat breakfast in the university cafeteria. The students found out and a number began to join me at breakfast after their morning jog. As we ate together, we shared stories and information about ourselves.
>
> That first morning, however, we were all strangers. We began class by introducing ourselves to a companion through an interview format. I chose this strategy to highlight the importance of learning style in group work. Each person was to discover the preferred learning style of their companion. These were shared among the class, and then they were asked to form themselves into learning groups. The ensuing discussion led to the development of a myth, or generally accepted assumption, that for this class, learning could happen anywhere and by any means. One group 'golfed' as part of the group experience; another always introduced their major concept or topic in choral song. Myths about learning developed, myths which stressed the importance of learning as living. (Margaret)

Developing community also means publicly taking account of the particular characteristics of the group. These students were expecting to be together in classes but to compete with each other in class discussions and to pursue individual topics for their major paper. In order to be open to others' ideas it was important to discover the advantages of group work and the opportunities it provides for challenging ideas in a more supportive and private environment.

Establishing trust

Usually, adults are unwilling to disclose how they feel in situations where they are not sure that their opinions will be accepted (Brundage and MacKeracher, 1980). An essential aspect of critical reflection is to be able to stand apart from one's ideas and listen to others' reactions. This detachment can be difficult for us since, as adults, we have invested much time in developing our self-concept and self-esteem, both of which act as powerful filters to reactions from others. Our knowledge of ourselves comes in large part from our interpretation of others' attitudes towards us. Hence, it is essential to develop a climate of trust among the learners.

> In the first class, while students were shopping around to select courses and assess the professor, I made explicit my personal philosophy concerning teaching and learning. I talked about wanting to work with them rather than to talk at them; to provide them with resources and guiding questions for their analysis; that we would use our life experience and accept our intuitive and affective reactions as resources additional to the cognitive ones. I tried to explain why I valued critical application and assessment of others' knowledge, and not its uncritical acceptance. I outlined my difficulties with having to grade them, why I wanted to work with them as collaboratively as possible, and their accepting my responsibility to establish certain standards of academic work. I explained how my in-class actions would centre not on information transmission but on connecting them to resources, confirming or correcting their learning as appropriate, and challenging them to more elaborate and critical thinking. (Liz)

Stating one's own views and concerns at the beginning of a session is supposed to develop a sense of rapport and trust. It also modelled our belief that adults should know the why as well as the what, the philosophical underpinnings of the content and process. We also must consider that, when what is proposed is not the norm, we may be raising students' anxiety levels. When Liz discussed her own anxiety over the issue of grading and her desire to be considered a colleague rather than a marker, she broke the taboo of the 'all powerful' omniscient teacher and established the right of students to discuss not only their cognitive but also their affective reactions to the course outline. Rapport ought to develop also if one is authentic and willing to acknowledge the authority relations that exist. Balancing the closeness of authenticity with the distance of authority was not easy: it demanded answering questions directly, relating to each student differently, using names immediately and, when it was appropriate, Liz talking about her own life and work.

Three factors operated to help Liz create some dialogue and critical awareness about both course content and process. First, as a visitor, she had no obvious allegiance to the prevailing 'transmission of information via 50-minute lectures' mode. Second, the content of the two courses, adult maturation and course design, was such that she could steer the students to assess critically its relevance to their own lives, learning needs and styles. The third factor was the relocation of the class to a setting more appropriate for adult learning. Making students aware of the process to be followed allowed them to make choices. Not unexpectedly, some students chose more traditional courses.

Accepting the challenge

Our proposed process for learning, and our own definition of knowledge, was not familiar to our students and we had to describe the format and assumptions in some detail. Likewise, the fact that these were courses taught by visiting professors meant that students had no previous knowledge to draw upon. We began by being honest about our own assumptions but we also tried to encourage students to see beyond the number of required assignments to accepting responsibility for their own learning. We wanted them to accept this challenge.

I handed out the course outline and began to describe the philosophy behind the course. I wanted them to know that while I would introduce them to the theories and concepts in the mainstream of educational administration, I, personally, did not subscribe to them and that, therefore, they had to accept critical examination of ideas as an essential aspect of the course. I explained that, for me, each person had to develop a theory about administration in schools which would make sense to them so I would not mandate which perspective they should adopt. I wanted them to be able to be consistent in their thinking and acting so I emphasized the importance of using their experience as a grounding for their own theories and a touchstone for others. I tried to stress that the ways they approached problems and ideas in their working life in schools had to have a place in any theory of educational administration.

Then I explained how I had proposed to structure the course. I suggested that we would meet as a total group only once or twice a week. On the intervening days they could meet in groups where and when they chose. The early morning sun had already begun to heat our narrow classroom, and our alternatives were to draw the curtains and put on the overhead light, or gradually roast over the course of the morning: the class was delighted to be out of the room. They were less sure about what was to happen when they were on their own.

To aid their explorations in the two required texts, I gave them the distance education materials for the course. These included questions and case studies which built on one another over the length of the course. I suggested that they discuss the case studies together. When we reconvened as a full class, I explained I would spend part of the class exploring and discussing their ideas and, for part of the time, I would introduce a different way of looking at that particular concept. Finally, I announced that I would be on-campus every day and available for consultation and that I would welcome being asked to participate in their group work. (Margaret)

For students expecting to be challenged to absorb a new body of literature, these were difficult words. First was the notion that there were differing strands of thought in a field which they thought was synonymous with management; second, was the challenge to be able to explore their own theory positions based on their previous school experiences. The first challenge meant that they had to re-examine how they thought about knowledge and also how they measured their own success. The second challenge meant that they had to go beyond telling stories about what happened in their schools to exploring what the story said about them and their beliefs about the ways to act towards others.

Because we were excited about the possibilities for learning which we envisaged, we were not always as aware as we might have been of the stresses which new ways of learning put on the students.

I did not see often enough that their initial anxieties about being removed from the traditional mode of affiliation with their teacher were creating stress and apparent amnesia. The latter was evidenced in my having to repeat information, especially in regard to my own expectations. Had I not 'seen' that they were not ready to 'hear'? Had I received too many polite signals that fooled me into assuming that they 'really' understood? Assignments were a frequent topic of this repetitive and dependent activity: 'Tell me what you want and I'll do it.' (Liz)

Students in traditional education are used to reading, but it is reading for repetition. Liz asked students to critique what they read and to be prepared to present and defend their views in class. Because this demanded a different kind of reading and the ability to present and argue ideas logically and fluently, some students expressed concerns about the 'heavy' reading requirements for the course. These concerns had to be acknowledged, named and discussed as learning issues.

Stress was evident in feelings of being overwhelmed by the reading load. I considered the load to be reasonable for seven intensive weeks and eventually the students did too; I think their initial anxieties had more to do with them having to assume responsibility for preparatory work at home or in the library. I did not, regrettably, create a 'rest and recuperate' period in the middle of the course that would have given students the freedom to step back and assess their achievements before plunging into the next topic.

It should have come as no surprise to me but it was: the students seemed to need large quantities of two very different kinds of resources. One kind was guidance in how to work critically and productively with their readings in order to prepare for class. The other kind was continual legitimation of their feelings of uncertainty and inadequacy in this new mode of 'being' a learner and my stated trust in them that they would make it. A major concern for many students was their awareness of their own lack of knowledge and how to acquire it, despite having been given directions for doing the readings. (Liz)

For adults who consider themselves successful at what they do, the challenge of returning to school is often more traumatic than we realize (Boud and Griffin, 1987; Brundage and MacKeracher, 1980). This reaction has to be legitimized quickly and consistently. Coupled with what our learners considered to be 'new' content, was the requirement that they be able to read it critically, be able to discuss and critique it in class, and use their own 'personal practical knowledge' for their analyses. Working towards transformative learning involves recognizing and teaching those skills which are necessary for the student to be competent in these processes. Sometimes, as with Liz's students, the problem is not so much technical, such as in following the required steps to a good critique, as it was experiential in that it takes a lot of practice to be able to differentiate the essential from the non-essential in readings. When we are in the process of developing a framework for the ideas and theories we are reading about, we find it difficult to feel independent enough to be able to differentiate the essential from the superfluous, or to critique flaws in arguments; instead we tend to accept everything because it absolves us from the uncertainty of not knowing.

Encouraging their practice

Empowerment is not academic irresponsibility to the point where learners are supported in doing anything. Instead, recognition of learners' choices about the content and process of learning has to be reconciled with teachers' responsibilities for challenging learners to re-examine their taken-for-granted assumptions and to develop alternatives for self-control of their lives. The teacher has the additional responsibilities of providing guidance and encouragement to enhance the learners' likelihood of success and of assessing the quality of scholarship obtained.

There are two more tasks included in this theme. The first task is to pay close attention to group development processes – the maturation vehicle for the class journey over the seven weeks. When group-level difficulties were perceived, we would 'surface' them, provide information on the expected (and well-documented) stages of group evolution and alert students to the need to re-examine their assumptions once again. The second task for us as teachers was to wait in watchful, nurturing anticipation as the learners lived through the inevitable discomfort and pain of significant learning. That waiting meant not rescuing, and here trust enters again as a process issue. If we had intervened to rescue them and not let them take control of and work through their discomfort, we would have sent two messages: with the message of encouragement would have been another about our lack of trust in their ability to solve the situation. 'The truth will set you free but first it will make you miserable' became a reassuring reminder that feelings of uncertainty were to be expected and had to be lived through.

These tasks may be easier to put into practice when working singly with learners but involvement in a community of learners highlights the communitarian aspect of learning. It is not the self in competition with others, or even with past performance; it is the self helping self and others to grow. Providing a safe forum for students to explore ideas and at the same time challenging students to re-examine their assumptions in that same forum is quite a balancing act. Several questions arose. What exactly did we mean by empowerment – empowerment for what? If it is emancipation, emancipation from what? We had our own content- and process-empowering goals for our courses, but what did our students want? How would the contexts of our classes help and hinder the empowerment process? How did we help the learners to reconcile any of their emerging empowered actions with the external context of entrenched institutional customs that we had helped them to see were disempowering procedures? Were we setting up the students for a crushing sense of disempowerment once they left the contexts of our classes?

In Margaret's course, the case studies provided a ready catalyst for questions of philosophy. Students were asked to write and then analyse cases based on actual events in their professional lives. In their analysis, they were asked to identify the beliefs of each of the participants and then to suggest a possible outcome and identify its underlying rationale. All of them chose to bring their work to their learning group to obtain the benefits of others' ideas. This exercise helped them uncover their own beliefs about education and administration.

What these students valued was hearing themselves and others think out loud and claim learnings. They were not concerned with taking turns to tell their stories but in adding snatches of personal reflection to stories told or questions posed by others, snatches they added to or re-worked as the discussion evolved. Having opportunities to compare, to test, to match and to reshape their own thoughts in relation to others' ideas reinforced the importance of this oral process for students. It seemed to be a necessary step before they were able to articulate clearly their personal viewpoints on paper.

One necessary condition for this process was that students have respect for and interest in others' personal practical knowledge, but we could not take that for granted. However, we were aware that some students did not value their own knowledge, let alone that of others. Helping them to accept and use that knowledge became another specific task.

Possible transformations

Like anxious parents, we sought signs of transformation: we knew that these would probably be tentative and subtle since our classes were of such short duration, but they were there.

> Half-way through the courses, some of the students were visibly beginning to relax and talk more openly and challenge some of their conventional wisdoms. No longer were they showing so much uncertainty about the new class process; some bold confrontations with each other and myself were beginning, together with some exclamations of great insights. Some seemed genuinely pleased that they could claim ownership for an insight after struggling for days. Some showed signs of being more tolerant of the ambiguity in others' ideas and of a lessening desire to display their own expertise as learners. Others tentatively expressed feelings of a significant transition: 'I'm not sure where I was, and that's ok; and I'm not sure where I am, but I think I'll manage.' (Liz)

Transformative learning was not only evident in relation to the subject matter of the course. Transformations also took place in the ways people related to each other. For Margaret's students the importance of the group was mentioned frequently in their assessments of their own learning. For example, one mentioned the 'caring, reassurance, encouragement, trust and friendship that developed', another that 'openness in communication is critical particularly in allowing dissenting views and alternative approaches. Listening skills were very important to establishing shared meanings'. Liz's students had similar comments. One said, 'I found collaboration among group members very helpful in reducing stress', while another wrote, 'Instead of just sitting and listening, I enjoyed the interactions with other learners. I learned not only from the professor but from the other learners' experiences as well'.

At the same time, we were conscious that while some students seemed to have grown a great deal, we had not been able to enfranchise other students' learning to the same extent.

> I don't think I recognized often enough that the process of empowerment is fraught with self-doubt and blindness to achievements, and that reinforcement of even small progress is needed as much as is legitimation of associated negative feelings. I can recall several occasions when my concern for academic rigour in critical thinking made me challenge students to continue critical reflection without either receiving the benefit of confirming feedback or pausing to recognize insights gained. (Liz)

A teacher who did not want the challenge of examining her ideas posed a similar difficulty for Margaret. Although she felt much better about the course process, the student still did not think that 'she had learned as much as in a regular format class'. Although the information was available in the written materials, she wanted more guidance through direct instruction than Margaret had given her. She wrote, 'I would have preferred to have had an overview of the major concepts and theories before I did my readings'.

Transformative learning characteristics

What is essential in facilitating student empowerment? What signs were we looking for in trying to determine whether our students were engaged in transformative learning? We identified seven characteristics from our reflections.

Learners are engaged in transformative learning when they can express a new ability to do two things: to act with some personal and critical power in their world, and to take charge of their learning. They can use correctly new theoretical principles and concepts to label their existing practice and what they may have only intuited; they are having their own knowledge authenticated (Grundy, 1987). They can confidently express opinions about life that disagree with others' opinions and are able to respect and learn from that difference. They are able to recognize and identify how societal structures and forces had limited their choices. They have the following conditions under which to explore critical discourse:

(a) accurate and complete information about the topic discussed; (b) freedom from coercion; (c) ability to reason argumentatively about competing validity claims and to argue logically from evidence; (d) ability to be critically reflective about assumptions and premises; (e) openness to consideration of the validity of other meaning perspectives and paradigms; (f) self-knowledge sufficient to assure participation free from distortion, inhibitions, compensatory mechanisms or other forms of self-deception; (g) role reciprocity – equal opportunity to interpret, explain, challenge, refute and take other roles in dialogue; and (h) a mutual goal of arriving at a consensus based upon evidence and the cogency of argument alone (Mezirow, 1989, p. 171).

They trust themselves enough that their self-concept and self-esteem will not be shattered upon feeling the inevitable pain and loss of old cognitive anchors as new learnings are recognized. They are able to provide helpful critiques of others' ideas and point out discrepancies in logic, or indicate incongruencies. They can articulate how their habitual expectations and ways of interpreting the world were created and can express, albeit in halting terms, a new perspective that is experienced as 'more inclusive, discriminating, permeable, and integrative' (Mezirow and Associates, 1990, p. 4). In summary, in Giroux's terms, learners are engaged in transformative learning when they can produce and critique meanings, make existing knowledge problematic, make connections within an holistic framework, dig into and clarify their own belief systems and life experience, and identify the structural and ideological forces that affect their lives (Giroux, 1983, cited in Rehm, 1989, p. 118).

Dialogue and transformative learning

Dialogue as a concept and a process runs, as a leitmotif, through all our reflections, so we have chosen to highlight it in connection with our major themes because it is particularly important to us.

Developing a community of learners
Learning communities need time to develop and work through various stages of introduction, growth, conflict resolution, performance and closure. Such maturation needs the vehicle of dialogue, especially when differences in the members of the community become very obvious, and when there are wide variations in the maturity and critical appreciation of the students, yet all need to have their learning recognized and their ideas challenged. We experienced these competing demands in our classes and sought to find ways to

celebrate each student's learning without allowing others to feel left out or abandoned, disconnected from the ideas that enabled their colleagues who were at a different level of understanding to gain insight.

Dialogue for critical thinking requires two processes – the making of meaning that accompanies the use of language, and the public recognition of that meaning. Berthoff (1987) says this very clearly:

> When we speak, the discursive power of language – its tendency toward syntax – brings thought along with it. We don't think our thoughts and then put them into words; we say and mean simultaneously ... an active exchange from which meanings emerge and are seen to emerge (p. xiv).

Full understandings often lagged behind these emerging meanings:

> I have several clear memories of seeing some surprise on the faces of some class members as they spoke and heard this new learning; similar to the 'how do I know what I think 'til I see what I say?' process. One difficulty in handling this discursive element lies in coping with any dismissive reactions of peers; I sometimes had to signal to the rest of the class that something of significance was 'in the air'. (Liz)
>
> What intrigued me, was that as the term progressed the students were able to sustain a four-part dialogue: on one hand they took what they heard others say and used these ideas to augment, expand and explore their own experiences and understandings; yet they also participated in the discussion by providing these reflections for others to react to and by commenting on and extending the experiences of others. It was both an internal and external dialogue and a personal and group dialogue. (Margaret)

The circular nature of the dialogue in our classes continued beyond the formal bounds of the classroom but it took students some time to come to grips with the lack of closure to which they were accustomed. Brookfield (1983) notes that there is a danger when teachers skilfully and unobtrusively bring closure to a class discussion by providing a coherent summary, that 'the unanswered question, the points of genuine dissension and the inconvenient facts are all ignored' (p. 197). Similarly, he warns against 'benevolent misrepresentation' when the teacher rephrases incoherent responses on behalf of the group, ('What I think you are really getting at is ...'), and frequently paraphrases others' contributions. For our students, the class dialogues were both energizing and exhausting: exciting in the insights they gained and frustrating in their incompleteness.

Establishing trust
For us, it became clear that there had been too much emphasis in the

empowerment literature on the reasoning, rational discourse of critique, and too little on the affective, interpersonal and intuitive contexts and processes in learning. As we observed our less-vocal students in class and talked with them individually, we were reminded that dialogue is both external and internal and that it is not time-specific. Dialogue, as it pertains to learners 'playing' with and assessing information from their own and others' experiences, has to be an ever-present process in learning; we disagree with the suggestion (in Modra, 1991, p. 99) that it may be more helpful to regard dialogue as 'the goal of pedagogy rather than as process' because we believe that dialogue has to be present in some form from the beginning of a course. It will become more thoughtful and enabling as the course proceeds. Dialogue that allows for the emergence of meaning is the medium for learning.

Within a group setting, class peers and the facilitator have to be supportive of the inherently contradictory nature of individual students' 'voices' (Ellsworth, 1989). A student who is uncertain about speaking in front of peers will be less inclined to admit dilemmas or paradoxes in thinking or life experiences. These dilemmas are even more crucial when the students are not able to name or do not recognize the existence of these contradictions.

Maintenance of dialogue is always a balance between the free flow of talk and the need to redress imbalances of various discriminations. To point out occasions when class members appeared to be neither listening to each other, nor hearing with respect, nor building on existing contributions but instead talking past each other is a tricky strategy at any time. But, whether loquacious or silent, students had to be taught to recognize their mutual responsibility for the learning of others. When they didn't allow or invite others' participation, they effectively denied their peers a voice. Our students rarely needed reminders about the covert effects of gender socialization, but when they did the air was electric. Many women have been socialized to attend to and support the speech of men, and many men have been socialized to expect that women and other men will attend to their speech; it can be quite a shock to otherwise articulate and assertive women or genuinely caring and supportive men to realize how they have acted out socialized attitudes.

Accepting the challenge

Part of our challenge was to encourage students to engage in dialogue about the ideas in the course beyond the assigned class times.

One way in which students were encouraged to enrich their learning was to share rough drafts of their assignments among the members of their learning group. All spoke about how much that process both reduced their anxiety and enhanced their learning. As well, I met individually with each student and we went through the submitted assignment together. As much as possible I wanted to encourage dialogue about the ideas presented rather than focus on the technicalities of presentation. (Margaret)

Another challenge for us was to avoid reverting to the routine of lecturing and our monopolization of class discussion. One revolution in thinking that the students had to work through was changing from using class time for taking lecture notes to using it more proactively for applying and assessing information from their readings and deciding whether they had learned anything of significance. One of Liz's students expressed it thus: 'No lectures to elicit the "pearls" that we were to regurgitate in an effort to show that we had learned what had been set to be learned'.

Encouraging their practice

Terminology is an associated issue for dialogue. We used words such as 'reflection', 'transformation' and 'collaboration' to help students name their practice. We also tried to model rather than talk about 'critical' thinking. Use of language is of particular importance since it is the substance and process of most meaning and communication.

Sometimes, there has to be no spoken dialogue but a comfortable, creative silence or space before students can take responsibility for their own discussion.

I have learned that it is dysfunctional for the students' development of self-responsibility if I crowd the audio space with a rescuing, silence-breaking intervention. The real problem is how to not rescue without being perceived as irresponsible or mean. (Liz)

The silences also heightened our awareness of what we said. We wanted to model a collaborative critical process but we were cognizant that some students had a difficult time accepting that what we said was a contribution to the discussion rather than a means of controlling their thinking by providing the 'right' answer. We also learned that providing time for class discussion was only one form of dialogue.

Besides their involvement in their learning groups and their participation in class discussions, I also structured two activities which I hoped would allow students to have a dialogue in a different format. These were leading the class for a session and presenting briefs to a mock school board. In keeping with our initial discussion on learning style, students chose a variety of experiences to engage us in discussion. The presentation of briefs by each group was an opportunity for students to recognize the very specific language used to propose and defend a point of view. (Margaret)

While it was our preference to have the students be the architects of their own learning, we realized that for some students this style would need to unfold gradually. Each student has a context – a history – about learning, about their responsibilities and those of the teacher, and a context of the course content. The teacher has to listen carefully to catch the influence of these histories and contexts and surface them for discussion.

Possible transformations

For us the experience of reflecting in some detail on our experiences with transformative learning has heightened our interest in dialogue. So much of what we now know was shaped by the conversations we participated in over those seven weeks and during the process of this book and our chapter.

The term 'dialogue' now operates for Liz as a much more integrative concept than it has in the past. It connotes more of movement and process and less of outcomes; it helps Liz to focus on what makes dialogue happen, and how it may mature over time. What makes dialogue happen are the dynamics that affect people and knowledge configurations.

People can be configured to relate to one another in different learning contexts. Also each learner has her/his own internal organizations of self-esteem and self-concept. For Margaret, the notion of dialogue is about conversation, about talk that is at once immediate and ephemeral. When the voices cease, what remains are individual understandings, some shared, much still unique, which each conversationalist has made of the others' words. These understandings both construct reality and are constrained by previous constructions of the learner.

People relationships and knowledge constructions are driven or stalled by two key dynamics of expression – style and pacing. Style of expression refers to how people talk to each other eg, in negotiating, debating, collaborating, supporting, narrating, confirming, or challenging styles. Pacing refers to the natural ebbs and flows of dialogue such as the quantum leaps in energy and speed as insights are claimed, the pauses for reflection, or the silences of uncertainty or withdrawal.

In addition to being affected by configurations and dynamics, dialogue may mature or regress along several dimensions. The key ones appear to be content and process. Content maturity in dialogue can refer to evidence of advanced levels of cognitive or affective processing that may lead to transformative learning. Process maturity in dialogue refers to evidence of behaviours that promote achievement and affiliation within and between individuals. An alert and reflective teacher has to be aware of the probable effects of gender socialization and the current stage of group development; what are less easy to assess here are the stages reached in each of the sequences of individual ego, cognitive and psychosocial maturity and skills of interpersonal behaviour.

Dialogue is not neutral; the floor is always given to the other (Buber, 1970) and despite Habermas's (1984) contention that it provides for the ultimate rational act, it is in a constant process of forming and reforming. Dialogue which moves beyond the asking and answering of questions requires reflection. Reflection is that aspect of thought where we fold our thinking back on itself and one layer of thinking is enmeshed in the other. Equally, reflection requires dialogue, either the internal dialogue with the self or vocal conversations with others. But is it essential for dialogue to involve the actual presence of the speaker? When we take part in dialogue, we tend to separate the spoken voice from the speaker and find it difficult to understand the speaker as more than 'other'. This is where the interweaving of different voices during discussions seemed to make sense as students listened to others and then wove those stories and experiences into their own reflections. Listening, then, is an essential aspect of dialogue. For Bohm (cited in Senge, 1990), the major purpose of dialogue is to reveal the incoherence of our thoughts; incoherences which he identified as non-participative thought, where the constructive and constraining influence of thought is denied; programmed thought where routines disengage reality; and self-referential thought where the criteria for the solution are those which have already contributed to the creation of the problem (p. 240). To overcome these incoherences, our task is to ensure that dialogue sustains a critical edge; that through reflection, it folds back on itself, requiring re-examination of the taken-for-granted. It is dialectical in that within the general conversation are individual conversations, partly voiced, mostly internal. Taken together, they form the web of dialogue. 'In non-epistemological language we must say that dialogue is hope and uncertainty braided together' (Maranhao, 1991, p. 237).

Reforming open and distance education

At a meta level, we believe that the process of reflection in and reflection on practice is valuable in itself, and we hope to see more distance educators using the ideas and strategies that already exist in related disciplines.

We believe that what we would learn from our classroom experience would be relevant for tutoring, course design and theory-building in open and distance education. Our reflections on our summer school experience were, in part, to discover how to advance our understanding of the concept of dialogue in distance education. We believe that its current understandings need their own transformations, their liberation from their entrapment in the familiar conceptual network of autonomy, independence and support. The transformatory process will have to come also from critical and celebratory reflections-on-practice, on the warmth and colours from phenomenological experiences of dialogue-in-use. We also believe that dialogue as a goal and a process does have the potential to be a defining characteristic of distance learning and teaching (Evans and Nation, 1989a, p. 38), but only if we engage in critical assessment of its functions (eg, Modra, 1991) and reformulate guiding questions for practice. Those questions must start with fundamental cognitive and affective issues before they deal with issues of technologies and techniques.

Reading through our accounts, it would be easy to see ourselves as central to those summer experiences for our students: such was not the case. As a postmodernist critique would disclose, the crucial 'still point of the turning world' (Eliot, 1944) is the learner's moment of transformation. Even the teacher-student relationship is secondary. In the end, such moments are individual and unique even when they happen in a learning community.

We have identified five themes of transformative learning that have helped us understand the process of empowerment. Can these characteristics be realized in open and distance education? We believe so. The community of learners can come together in different configurations using various vehicles; as George (1990) has observed, the differences between teaching in classrooms and in distance education lie in the means not the ends. Our classes used readings, critique, role models and discussion in a variety of configurations. Such variety produces 'noise, contingency and chaos of events and feelings' (Hunt, 1991, p. viii) so course designers and tutors have to feel comfortable in acknowledging this creative unpredictability and surrendering control without loss of appropriate authority.

In distance education contexts, we can provide a repertoire of learning activities and facilitation options, and rely on learners and tutors to make the most appropriate decisions throughout the course. Margaret's groups were given distance education materials which in themselves contained a number of possible topics and strategies. This meant that her students' learning processes were more invisible, that she did more informal discussion with individual students and left much of the initiative for discussion to the groups themselves. While some groups did most of the work together, others worked through the materials singly and only came together to discuss the case study questions. This seemed to be a factor of group cohesiveness – the groups which enjoyed being together met most frequently, the group which lacked consensus on most issues met least often – and of geography and time as the group whose members lived off-campus met less frequently. In many ways, this format is not untypical of a distance education class. Community building is possible in distance courses where there is enough pacing of progress to enable peer learning and teaching. The fundamental issue is the extent to which the model of learner goals and actions used in the course design helps learners to share responsibility for a challenging learning community.

Trust can be established in different ways. Too often, the still point in distance education is considered to be the student-teacher relationship. Inherently hierarchical, such relations inhibit the 'role reciprocity' identified by Mezirow (1989, p. 171) as essential if students are to feel free to challenge and refute the teacher's contribution to the discussion. As Margaret found, the hearing of their thoughts woven with the reflections of others was an essential part of the students' thinking processes. Students are free to accept such searching only when they see themselves in control of their own learning. The course designer's and tutor's conceptions of learners shapes the control the learners have over their learning and the extent of recognition given to the learners' needs for growth and past life experiences.

Accepting the challenge, the third theme, relates to both learner and educator. The challenges for the learner are based in the seven characteristics of transformative learning. Whether they were learning in small and large group sessions within a classroom format, or more or less independently, students were able to act with personal and critical power to take charge of their world and their learning. In Liz's class, the twice weekly, three-hour sessions included critique and analysis of the readings. In Margaret's class, the full class session every third day at the end of a unit served to provide the opportunity for critique and questions about what they had learned. By the third such session, students themselves were able to ask these questions of the textual materials. Such questions and analysis could be included in a textual paper or computer disk format but the text must go beyond exposition and include opportunities for reflection and comparison, for exploration of a variety of viewpoints and for the integration of past experiences. It must provide for openness rather than closure, for making the implied explicit, and for experiential as well as expository learning resources.

Where our students sought discussion was in the telling of their stories and the confirmation of their understandings; particularly, in the clarification of their belief systems and life experience and the identification of the ideological structuration that has constrained their thinking and action. Although some students will seek out colleagues and friends to be their sounding boards, the complexity of the ideas involved means that they have to first orientate the people they wish to talk with before dialogue can begin (Beauchamp *et al.*, in press). We have to continue to encourage distance students to form learning groups as part of the course work and we have to find opportunities where students can come together frequently enough and develop sufficient comfort and trust with each other to enjoy genuine dialogue and cope with the discomforts of learning. Analysis of evaluation data from audio-conferenced graduate classes at the Ontario Institute for Studies in Education (OISE) has indicated a strong preference by students for dialogue and connection with their peers, and not always with the omnipresent teacher (Burge and Snow, 1990). Computer conferencing provides continuous opportunities for discussion with peers (Davie and Wells, 1991). The technology to connect learners is available but our field requires wider recognition and application of the skills and assumptions needed to use those connections for the dialogues and silences of transformative learning. We have to learn to make the hardware transparent, and to refocus our facilitation techniques on listening and responding rather than talking and directing. In such interactive and flexible contexts, course designs will have to act more as drafts than as blueprints, and tutors will have to learn to 'let go'. To some educators, that surrender of omniscience and power is unthinkable.

The major challenge for us as distance educators is for us to render explicit our implicit knowledge and attitudes about teaching and learning (Haughey, 1989). From these renderings we will be able to judge where and how we act as inhibitors of options, or where we have not carried through from thought to action. It is more a question of reducing how we demotivate learners than it is a question of how to motivate them. We may be unconsciously resisting the costs of reflection-in-practice that Newman (1991) selected from Schön's work, ie, giving up 'the rewards of unquestioned authority ... the comfort of relative invulnerability, the gratification of deference' (p.356). Similarly, we have to be sensitive to the disparate views of students, many of whom have never considered any alternative pedagogy. The shocks experienced by our students should alert us to the need to provide both pathways and guidance for the start of the journey. We could recognize the maturity of our learners by explaining these cognitive and affective processes to them rather than presuming that the content structure, reflected in the number and placement of assignments, is sufficient.

Encouraging their practice, the fourth theme, was an holistic venture. We tried to balance our understandings of the personal and professional lives of our students, their learning style preferences, and their need for constructive guidance, confirmation of learning and legitimization of their anxieties. We also tried to make ourselves invisible by encouraging students to recognize their own gifts and to recognize the gifts of others, by trying to eradicate competition and replacing it with collaboration, and by trusting students to make good decisions about their learning. We received many more cues about our students' feelings that helped us make decisions about our own interventions. To some extent, because we were actually present, students did not have to exercise a great deal of personal responsibility to let us know how they were feeling and what we should do to help them. In open and distance education, students have to shoulder more of the responsibility for sharing their needs, feelings and learnings with others. In many cases, they will have to be guided in developing the skills for this responsibility. When a community spirit is developed, that responsibility is easier to attain.

Transformation, the fifth and final theme, happened for us and our students. We experienced a renewed appreciation of the integration of the affective and the cognitive, for each has an impact on learning. We now re-vision the complex interplay between independent and interdependent learning. We take greater critical care with the language we use, for in language are our values and assumptions made manifest. We have renewed respect for the importance of dialogue because we have seen its complexities. We continue to try to model our own decentering and the repositioning of the learner in the turning world of transformative learning. In seeing our learning, we see our need for growth, and we need our own community of reflective peers to promote and sustain our growth. Transformation is seldom an epiphany; most often it is a long-term and iterative struggle toward new perspectives, toward personal authenticity and empowerment.

7 Putting the Student First: management for quality in distance education

Roger Mills and Ross Paul

The 'total quality' movement

Over the past decade or more, the corporate sector in the Western world has been preoccupied with the issue of quality – quality of production, quality of management and, most recently, quality of service. Spurred initially by American reactions to Japanese success in such markets as automobiles, computers, stereo equipment and even pianos, the notion of 'total quality management' has been advanced as an effective response to regaining markets which are purported to have been lost because of the inferior nature of both products and services.

Even governments have recently jumped on the service quality bandwagon. In July 1991, UK Prime Minister John Major published the Citizen's Charter which covers transport, trade and industry, education, environment, health and social security. It even considers an individual's right to get compensation from British Rail when a train is late!

The gestation of the Charter was not easy for, as reported in *The Guardian* (Travis and Hencke, 1991), it involved 'the whole of the Whitehall machine, resulting in open warfare with several competing departments each trying to promote some initiatives and block others'. It is interesting to note that during the initial exchange of ideas between the Prime Minister's Office and Whitehall, the Department of Education and Science failed to contribute anything at all.

One of the main planks of the Charter relates to quality, with the government upholding the central principle that all essential services such as education and health must be available to all, irrespective of means, and its consistent aim is to extend choice, increase competition and thereby improve the quality of all services. The only specific reference to education in the Citizen's Charter is to a 'Charter for Parents'.

Total quality management may be summarized as looking at the quality of the activity in every part of the service, constantly searching for small percentage improvements and striving to provide that service or product better than anyone else. In education, the quality of what we provide to students includes both breadth and depth of provision. Fundamentally, it is about the quality of the learning experience (both content and process) and the support services necessary to assist students to become both independent and interdependent learners. It must also be future-oriented to anticipate learning needs that students will confront on completion and as they return, when appropriate, at various stages of their lives.

This chapter provides a critical perspective on the application of service quality concepts to the management of open learning and distance education through two case studies – the UK Open University and Athabasca University in Canada.

The quality movement in education

It is only very recently that the quality movement has really begun to have an impact on educational reform, at least in its application to teaching and educational services (it can be argued that peer review processes have ensured much more control of research). On both sides of the Atlantic (and, indeed, across the Pacific), it has been one of the most frequent topics for discussion at conferences and seminars on further and higher education. 'Total quality' plans are advanced as the solution to declining or threatened enrolments or to growing public pressures for accountability for the deployment of taxpayers' resources, especially as education competes for such resources with health and other services.

In the UK, the recent White Paper on higher education stresses the importance of quality assurance in teaching and proposes external quality assessment of institutions of higher education from 1994 onwards. The White Paper (1991) states that:

> ... the prime responsibility for maintaining and enhancing the quality of teaching and learning rests with each individual institution. At the same time there is need for proper accountability for the substantial public funds invested in higher education. As part of this, students and employers need improved information about the quality if the full benefit of increased competition is to be obtained (para 58).

A recent research project entitled 'Identifying and developing a quality ethos for teaching in higher education' was conducted by Gareth Williams of London University's Centre for Higher Education Studies. According to MacGregor (1991), he suggests that '... maintaining standards during higher education's expansion from an elite to a mass system, *without additional resources*, is a major task for academics and administrators'. He also points out that 'there has been an enormous amount of talk about quality in higher education over the past year or so, but we believe that very little effort has been made to find out what people on the ground perceive it to be' (Williams, 1991).

In May, 1991, the Committee of Vice-Chancellors and Principals Academic Audit Unit produced the leaflet, *Quality Assurance in Universities* which sets out how each university will be audited for its quality assurance mechanisms in terms of the provision and design of course and degree programmes and in teaching and communication methods. In addition, mechanisms for monitoring and assessing staff and providing on-going staff development programmes will be examined as will the way in which students' views on courses are collected.

The UK Open University has its first audit under this new system in 1992 and it will be interesting to see how the criteria based on 'conventional' institutions relate to an open and distance teaching university.

The demise of the binary system of higher education and the common funding methodology for universities and polytechnics in the UK will add impetus to the debate on quality and quantity. Polytechnics have increased their student intake by over 20 per cent in the academic year 1991–2, while the increase in numbers of university students has been around 5 per cent, with the latter restricting their intakes in the name of 'quality'. New funding mechanisms for the sector will stimulate a further movement towards mass higher education at the same time that a new quality assurance system is being planned for the whole of higher education.

The trend in Canada has similarly been for increasing public accountability in education, although compared to the UK, Australia and New Zealand, decisions have almost certainly been moderated by strong provincial resistance to federal involvement and centralized control over education: a fundamental area of provincial jurisdiction in the Canadian Constitution. This makes even more remarkable the recent agreement among all ten provincial governments to establish national standards for elementary and secondary school performance, which may be seen as an indicator of the degree of national concern about the quality of its educational systems.

Almost every Canadian university now has a formal review process for its programmes and services whereby external experts are the dominant force on evaluative teams which operate independently of those they are reviewing. In some provinces, such as Ontario, this is formalized and standardized on a province-wide basis under the direction of an independent body, the Ontario Council on University Affairs. In every Canadian province, 'accountability' and educational 'audits' are catchwords for increased governmental interest in what taxpayers receive for their investment in higher education and there is much talk of 'value for money' in assessing educational 'outputs'. While demand for university places currently far exceeds the supply, changing demographics may soon breed a more competitive climate where the quality of services offered will be an important factor in a student's choice of university.

The Association of Universities and Colleges of Canada (AUCC) has a high profile task-force of university presidents and others seeking ways to improve the public accountability of universities, working from the premise that the universities must take the initiative, otherwise others may do so. Two recent public inquiries, that by The Royal Society of Canada (into research) and the 'Smith Commission' on university teaching sponsored by the AUCC have received considerable attention in the media, although this bifurcation of teaching and research has been viewed as highly inappropriate by many.

Canada's ability to improve the quality of its universities is seriously compromised by its decentralized system of provincial control over education. This helps explain why, in comparison with the much more diverse and entrepreneurial American system, Canadian universities are usually ranked fairly highly but none of them is ranked at the very top by world standards. Most Canadian universities have strong regional mandates and, hence, are less specialized than many of their international counterparts.

Hospitals, schools and municipalities are also provincially funded and in an environment where resources are increasingly scarce, universities may be seriously disadvantaged. They are misunderstood, seen as relatively well-off and are suffering from past tendencies to 'hide behind' academic freedom as a reason to avoid more open public scrutiny. It will not be enough for the universities to ensure the quality of their programmes and services – they will also have to do a much better job of explaining their missions and potential impact on the future of the nation if they are to continue to attract their share of public resources.

The challenge to institutions: value-driven leadership

It is one thing to talk about reforming quality of service and quite another to bring it about. Expectations for leadership from the top are increasing as growing recognition of the importance of universities in the 'knowledge age' yields concomitant concerns about how they are deploying their resources. In assessing the complexities of corporate and educational management, Badaracco and Ellsworth (1989) write convincingly of the merits of 'value-driven leadership', the essence of which is to lead by example:

> A leader must be an exemplar to the organization, demanding the highest standards of integrity, and be doggedly consistent in word and deed in all matters affecting the company's values (p. 74).

Paul (1990) has adapted this to the management of open learning systems with the simple premise that the style of management must reflect the values inherent in the organization or, more to the point, that an institution dedicated to the values of open learning must be led in an 'open management' style (p. 72). More than any other, an institution of higher education must be, in Senge's (1992) terms, a 'learning organization' with concomitant implications for its management style.

In this context, a total quality programme must start at the top. It must be more than the latest device to motivate staff to provide better service, but a fundamental value which is both espoused and exemplified by the senior management. Themes such as 'putting the student first', student-centred learning, customer orientation or total quality management have been prevalent at many recent educational conferences, but examples of their effective implementation have been much more difficult to discern. As such, a total quality management programme should not be embarked upon until its implications are carefully considered. Experience has underlined the importance of strong leadership from the chief executive officer.

Perry (1991), a polytechnic director in the UK, distinguished quality 'assurance' – a broad concept implying structures to 'guarantee to the consumer that the produce or process is all that it should be' and which is suited to a national inspectorate, from quality 'control' – which applies to 'day-to-day controls that check the performance of every aspect of an organization against required specifications' and is the responsibility of each organisation and each unit within it. She goes on to outline four conditions necessary for effective quality assurance:

- inspection should not be seen as a policing function and a duplication of quality control;
- inspection must be independent – 'the inspector has no friends other than the client, consumer or stakeholder';
- there should be a legal framework. Such a framework should define the consumers' rights and entitlement; set the standards against which the service is judged; and lay down sanctions as well as rewards;
- the findings of an inspection should be published openly.

In practice, this approach acknowledges that those best placed to carry out the processes of quality control, evaluation and review are those directly responsible for the provision of services to students.

How quality is defined and measured are major issues for education today. If one accepts that 'higher education is shifting from a system of producer ideas of quality, where academic criteria determine what is perceived to be good quality, to a system where consumer perceptions are far more important' (MacGregor, 1991) it may be easier to deal with these within open and distance education which purport to have a more direct commitment to the needs of the learner than does traditional education. Simultaneously, this value system may be depicted as confronting traditional academic culture and, hence, engender strong resistance from academic staff, especially if it is implemented superficially without dealing more fundamentally with the quality of the whole process of research, scholarship, teaching and learning.

The effectiveness of attempts to 'put the student first' will now be assessed within two case studies – the UK Open University and Athabasca University.

Applications to open and distance education

The Open University

Over the past 20 years, staff in the Open University have prided themselves on their commitment to its institutional mission and to its students. Students are also committed to the institutional ideals and the recent development of an equal opportunity policy and a statement of the university's policy on access are examples of the way in which this long-term commitment is now being formalized (see Chapter 9). Both aspects are essential components of the OU's commitment to quality, as is the development of the University's Strategic Plan.

Since 1982, much work has been done on various aspects of

quality within the OU, with staff development, especially for part-time staff, leading the way. In 1986, the OU formalized its procedures for assuring academic standards in a statement which covered the following conventional aspects of its work (Horlock, 1987):

- External examiner system.
- Academic Advisory Committee.
- Accreditation by external professional bodies.
- Appointment procedures for full-time academic staff.
- External involvement in the preparation of courses.

Very little emphasis in the 1986 report was placed on course presentation and student services or on the role of the regions and regional staff in maintaining academic standards. At that time, neither quality of 'customer services' nor staff development were prominent issues in the University.

The 1980s also saw two major reviews – the *Long Term Review* (Open University, 1984) and the *Strategic Academic Review* (STAR Report) (Open University, 1989). The former was partly in response to government financial cuts, but it also looked at ways of producing materials more effectively through electronic publishing and ways of classifying courses to ensure that students progressed to more independence – the so-called 'independent learner strategy'. In practice, the *Long Term Review* resulted in little change in the course presentation and student support areas.

The STAR Report, although received as a strategic review of the University's academic policies, ranged freely and widely over much of the institution's activities. Conducted in a less punitive financial climate, it led to a renewed burst of energy and thinking within the University and a number of staff were able to use the process to support a number of long-cherished views relating to quality of service to students.

A major issue arising from the strategic review was the agreement of the University Senate to distribute or decentralize the University's admissions process to regional centres, the main aim being more control by the latter over this process and consequently a better service to enquirers, applicants and students. A steering group on enquiries and admissions was set up and the resulting changes are being implemented in the autumns of 1991 and 1992. This is a major change, one which will radically affect regional centres in particular over the next few years and it is likely to be the forerunner of many developments which place more emphasis on and give responsibility to OU regional centres and to the presentation and support aspects of its student services.

The STAR Report also recommended a thorough review of the quality of tuition and, in 1990, a quality tuition working group was established under the chair of Scottish director John Cowan. This group's report, with over one hundred recommendations, is a seminal document in the development of the University. However, despite its welcome restatement of good practice ensuring the quality of services to students, not all of its recommendations will be implemented immediately because of resource implications. Nevertheless, the process itself has led to a significant review by faculties of their practices and policies from the viewpoint of quality teaching. The Report includes references to student charters, student feedback and the vital importance of monitoring the quality of activities. These issues provide a significant challenge to the OU with its high student volume and increasing diversity of provision. Its main concept is that students, irrespective of their ability to attend face-to-face tutorials, should receive equivalent tutoring.

One other move towards improved quality currently under discussion is a review of a University-wide counselling service which is more student-centred than the current approach and which would be available locally to all students within the institution, regardless of their course or programme.

The interface between the educational and bureaucratic procedures, as currently operating at the University, provides a case in point. For example, Patrick Kelly, a senior counsellor, wonders about the effectiveness of past efforts to serve students:

> We have landed ourselves with the worst of all worlds, the system which looks responsive to the individual but is in fact crude and mechanistic and wasteful of staff time. For a change, let's start with the student and work back to the procedures and keep the procedures simple (Kelly, 1991).

In its attempts to put the student first, the OU has a complex bureaucratic system of exceptions which allow, for example, students to be excused from summer school, or to receive fee waivers if they are unable to continue courses because of illness, etc. Within the University, there is a raft of activity dealing with these exceptions and, currently, a full-scale review of how requests for such consideration are handled is in progress.

This review highlights some of the dilemmas of finding an appropriate balance across contrasting views of quality. For example, some current issues at the OU include:

- Should the University advertise widely the availability of financial assistance, knowing that students in receipt of such assistance tend to be less successful in the early period of their study? What is quality here?
- Should the University provide face-to-face teaching at considerable expense when it is used by only a proportion of students?
- Does the University over-assess its students? Is quality defined by the volume of assessment? Would a system which allowed students to take fewer formal assignments in their first year, but provided rapid feedback on examination performance be a better quality system than one which was more traditionally rigorous?
- Is returning assignments to students within ten days – with less monitoring and quality control, but more quality assurance – more important than having excellent quality control?
- Should the institution be prepared to give up some of its quality control when collaborating with other institutions?
- Do we 'over-teach' our students? Who determines the length of a course? Are our expectations for our students too high?

These questions highlight many actual and potential difficulties for addressing issues of quality systematically. What is lacking at the OU, despite much support from students, is a clear system of collecting and *using* student feedback. An effective system would be expensive but, if we really believe that quality is perceived by the student, we need to know urgently what our students think about particular aspects of services provided.

The University has agreed to a target of an increase of 10 per cent of new undergraduate students who are non-traditionally qualified, over the next five years. This is the key to a major debate. This target is directly in line with the University's mission. Can it be seen as increasing the quality of the institution when we know that although many students in this category can do very well, on average the group performs less well than those with traditional University entry qualifications? The answer must be that a continuing search for successful strategies to support non-traditionally qualified students is a critical aspect of the quality of management. This issue underlines the importance of being clear on goals and priorities before attempting to assess quality.

Athabasca University

In 1987, through the initiative of Stephen Murgatroyd, Dean of Administrative Studies and consultant in the area of quality of service management, Athabasca University embarked on a strategy of reforming the quality of its services to students. While the University was initially relatively well resourced, the exercise was conducted throughout a period of fiscal constraint. As government grants were diminishing, the strategy proceeded under the rubric 'doing more with less'; something which bred more opposition than might otherwise have been the case.

The first step was a two-day seminar for deans and senior managers led by external consultants. Among the lessons stressed during this session were the need for the full involvement of all employees in a quality programme, the critical importance of 'front-line staff' (those who most directly relate to students – tutors, counsellors and advisors, admissions and records clerks, regional office staff), celebrating success and emphasizing the quality of service to each other within the institution as a prerequisite to improving the quality of service to students.

The outcomes of this seminar were mixed. There was a lot more awareness of quality concerns and one manager in particular (the registrar) initiated a programme of quality control on all services, notably by establishing maximum 'turn-around time' benchmarks which were subsequently monitored and reported on publicly each month. Several departments made commitments to never let a telephone ring more than three times or to ensure that no student enquiry was referred to another person more than once (to avoid a common tendency for students to be shunted around the institution with seemingly no one willing to accept responsibility for solving a particular problem).

Issues were found to be more complex than first presumed. For example, many believed that the notoriously slow return of papers and examinations from markers was a result of recalcitrant staff. An analysis of the problem showed that a combination of University decisions, each with a legitimate rationale, produced delays even if everyone did their work swiftly. Among the problems were a reduction of daily mail services between offices to twice a week (for financial reasons), an inadequate system of monitoring staff absences (hence papers waited for someone to return from vacation or a conference) and requirements introduced in the supposed interests of security and control which led to papers being handled by an apparently undue number of clerks. With the vagaries of Canada Post at each end of the process, it is not surprising that senior managers might think everything was going well, whereas the return of papers was taking a month or more. Too often, it was found, official University reports about service improvements did not match the actual experiences of students.

A further complication was the cross-functional nature of so many processes. Course development was the responsibility of several departments (faculty, instructional design, media, course materials), each of which could blame the others for problems so that one sometimes wondered if anyone was taking responsibility for a particular course project. As long as deans and managers were primarily concerned with protecting their own domains and blaming others for problems, little progress would be made by the establishment of yet another committee or set of guidelines in isolation.

Some managers also attempted to promote a more positive organizational climate, but cynics dismissed attempts at 'celebrating success' as manipulative or hypocritical. It is fair to conclude that the overall impact of this first venture was far less than anticipated by those who initiated it.

A second attempt, in 1990, however, built on the first and produced some additional initiatives. The same senior management group was exposed to a presentation from a senior vice-president (for quality!) of a major corporation which had turned its performance around over the past decade through a very rigorously pursued programme of quality of service management. Among its features were tremendous emphases on measurable performance indicators and on cross-functional teams. The latter were of particular interest – each team had one specific quality issue to pursue, each had both a team leader who was held completely accountable for the team's performance and a process observer whose role it was to help the team work effectively. Each team was disbanded as soon as its initial goal was reached, usually within a six to nine month period.

The translation of the cross-functional team concept to Athabasca University's attempts to reform the quality of service to its students bore some fruit. A number of central service problems were identified and a team developed for each. Each was given specific deadlines to meet and some were quite productive. One in particular, on the efficiency of the course development process, had considerable success where many previous committees and task forces had failed, primarily because of the emphasis on common ownership of the problems, rather than each manager or dean blaming someone else for the problems. This was greatly facilitated by the identification of a single manager with full responsibility for the team's success and by the designation of a 'process owner' for each team.

An objective review of what has been achieved would suggest that a formal programme of service quality is worthwhile, that it can breed results but that it is much more difficult than is first apparent.

The major corporation cited above has been involved for over ten years in a thorough programme and it is still seeking better ways of implementing it. A few seminars and cross-functional team initiatives may be useful but they will have minimal overall impact on what a student experiences unless they are part of an institution-wide programme that stresses pride in the organization, rewards those who give good service (to each other, not only to students) and has very strong leadership from the top. In the Athabasca projects, for example, the process focused on line managers (deans, registrar, director of media services) and did not significantly involve members of faculty.

Despite its success, then, the Athabasca University reforms only really scratched the surface of quality issues. The service quality initiative was conducted during a period of considerable change at the institution. There was a real questioning of the tutor-role as tutors became more unionized, the costs of tutorial support soared and formal student support services were cut drastically in the face of fiscal pressures. Among the questions openly discussed during these processes were:

- Should students be asked to pay extra for such support services as tutoring, counselling and advising? Do students know whether or not they require such services?
- How can one identify and hence match individual learning styles to educational provision?
- How can one increase the participation rates of traditionally disadvantaged students and how important is this goal for the University?
- Can one expect academic staff to function effectively under a rigorous set of benchmarks and performance indicators or are these incompatible with the values of academia?

What is striking is not so much the conflicting opinions within the institution as to the importance of various services, but the lack of agreed criteria for measuring programme and service quality. Ultimately, both teaching/learning and research are extremely difficult to measure in the short term and we are often forced to use less than adequate indicators (formal examinations, completion and graduation rates, number of refereed publications) to represent them.

Some critical perspectives

The examples from the Open University and Athabasca University both underscore the difficulties and the magnitude of attempts to reform quality of services in the open/distance education environment. In this concluding section, we offer some perspectives from our respective experiences which underscore both the complexity of quality issues and the importance of finding more effective ways to address them.

Professional/bureaucratic conflicts

In both national contexts considered in this chapter, there are frequent instances of university leaders expressing concern that pressures for accountability and measurability of product threaten long-cherished notions of academic freedom and university autonomy.

This dilemma is exacerbated in an open university which is, perhaps more than almost any other organization, characterized by sharp conflicts between bureaucratic systems (necessary to ensure effective course development and presentation and to support individualized timetabling, for example) and professional orientations (such as a strong client orientation and professional autonomy, which are central to the role of a faculty member at any university).

Whatever the quality of service indicators (flexibility in course development and presentation, turn-around time on assignments and examination results, number of times a telephone rings), objectivity requires that they be defined in measurable terms and monitored according to established benchmarks. This very quickly can be seen to challenge long-standing notions of academic freedom and institutional autonomy and can thus be cited as a direct threat to the basic values of a university.

While there is legitimate concern here, it is our position that there need not be contradiction between the search for quality and the traditional roles of a university, between accountability and academic freedom. The issue is more about who conducts the monitoring and how, rather than whether or not it is required. Universities are supposed to be about quality, the concept of academic freedom being advanced fundamentally to ensure that the quest for truth can proceed without political interference.

Within the Open University, for example, a system of external examiners and external assessors to moderate the processes and products of the University has long been in effect. Athabasca is in the process of introducing an external review process for each of its academic programmes.

The Open University has an elaborate system of monitoring student grades to ensure some consistency across the country, one which has subsequently been adopted by a number of other institutions. In this case, student scripts are photocopied and analysed by other members of staff to provide effective cross-checks on the quality of evaluation. This monitoring of assignments, however, has been difficult to sustain with increasing student numbers and declining resources, to the point that the whole system almost collapsed recently as a combination of factors, including the positive one of an increased rate of submission of tutor-monitored assignments, occurred. A similar problem has been encountered with the long-standing practice of monitoring the quality of counselling and face-to-face tuition in the regions. The University is faced with a dilemma as to how to introduce and sustain a fair system of appraisal for over 5,500 staff across the United Kingdom and Europe at a time when resources for full-time staff tutors and senior counsellors are diminishing. New approaches are urgently needed to enable more to be done with fewer resources.

While the focus in this chapter has been on quality management of individual institutions, there is a broader notion of quality which emphasizes the importance of an integrated educational 'system'. Protection of institutional autonomy has been cited as a legitimate reason for universities to resist any attempts to fit them into an educational system, but it is increasingly evident that better quality and more efficient use of scarce resources demand that this be challenged. Rationalization of higher educational systems worldwide in recent years has led to major changes in processes and structures and, even in the relatively decentralized Canadian provincial system, cross-institutional liaison and cooperation are the order of the day.

Joint academic programming and research, credit transfer schemes and reductions in residency requirements are just some examples of cooperation and integration in the name of quality and efficiency which impinge on all national systems of education in the 1990s. Increased public accountability and pressures on limited resources are encouraging institutions to avoid programme duplication with rival institutions and to focus, through strategic planning, on their major areas of strength. This is further encouraged by much greater pressures for public accountability, as represented by the recent controversial publication by a national news magazine of an overall ranking of Canada's 46 major universities. While the rating criteria left much to be desired, it is likely that future indicators will increasingly take account of quality of service measures rather than such traditional measureable outcomes as graduation and course completion rates.

Carrots more than sticks

A thorough and effective programme of service quality can be part of this response to new challenges. If we accept Perry's (1991) distinction between quality assurance (broad guarantees to consumers) and quality control (day-to-day performance checks), our focus will be quite appropriately on the positive rather than the punitive aspects of service quality. Programme review should be welcomed as an opportunity to demonstrate excellence and to identify areas which require improvement. Student complaints should be encouraged, not discouraged. Staff should be rewarded, rather than disparaged for trying out new ideas, identifying problems and admitting mistakes.

The chief executive officer should encourage active identification of problem areas, not in a negative fashion but as opportunities for improvement. An organizational climate that encourages problem identification and solution also fosters institutional pride. It is not only the students who benefit when long-standing service issues are resolved or improved for there is nothing better for the morale of a front-line staff member than a satisfied customer, be it student or colleague.

Ironically, experience has suggested that organizations which make mistakes but do a great deal to rectify them often have a better reputation for quality than competitors which make fewer mistakes. It is what is done when things go wrong which is the real test of an organization's dedication to service quality. Hence, one tends to take for granted a dry cleaning company that never loses an order but to be extremely impressed by the one that tracks down a lost order very quickly and has the manager deliver it personally to the customer's home.

In the long run, the quality in distance education is best measured by its impact on students – their experiences from the outset (information, advising and counselling, quality of learning experiences) and, ultimately, the extent to which they have become independent learners.

While the interest here is very much in the product, much of process *is* the product in education. Therefore, both the student and the university are learners throughout. The ironies abound, the tasks are complex and difficult and the demands on university leaders are endless. Effective staff development cannot be overemphasized as it is, in the long run, much more likely to produce a quality support to students than any amount of monitoring can achieve.

This requires value-driven leadership, leadership which is prepared to plan and build for the long run and about which there is no question of other priorities when it comes to resource allocation and policy decisions. The cardinal test of a value system is not what leaders espouse but where they allocate resources.

Doing more with less – the ultimate challenge?
A fundamental question is whether or not quality can be improved while resources are reduced. Whilst most educational institutions have found ways to do more with less in recent years, there is presumably a point beyond which it is no longer possible to preserve quality with diminishing resources.

This viewpoint suggests that it is not possible to operate a quality education system purely on market forces. It is not possible to improve services to students, to widen access and to develop equal opportunity policies without having the necessary resources. It is not possible to maintain quality distance teaching materials if there are fewer staff available to develop them and to go through the processes of writing, working and learning together which are essential to the production of high quality teaching materials.

The counterpoint is that it is highly unlikely that new resources are going to accrue to universities, at least not through the traditional route of government funds. The escalation, not only of costs, but also of demands upon municipalities, hospitals and schools all compete with those faced by universities. While part of the answer is for universities to be more accountable, with their role and importance better understood by the taxpayer, it surely lies more immediately in the way that they conduct themselves. We must find new ways to teach and learn, to conduct research and to harness the potential of new technologies.

It is tempting to seize upon cheaper and easier solutions in the name of efficiency, but sometimes such savings are illusory. There are economies in bringing in courses from outside the institution, but the best courses are those that are written by committed groups of people who involve teaching and counselling staff in their construction, who take note from previous feedback from students, who are concerned for the maintenance of the course once it is offered to students over a long period of time, who feel part of the course, who generated the course and who feel the course is part of them.

Conclusion: a difficult but essential process
One should have no illusions about the difficulties of implementing and sustaining quality management programmes in institutions as

complex as open universities. Cooperative linkages, joint course development and other pooling of resources are helpful, but they introduce new demands and are sometimes counter-productive.

Ultimately, there is no substitute for quality in distance teaching and quality does not come cheaply nor easily, especially at the most fundamental level of ensuring dedicated and exceptional staff. It is not simply how many times a telephone rings before it is answered or whether letters are answered within three or four days. Performance indicators of this kind are important but the fundamental and absolute importance for management in distance education is to ensure that the quality of teaching and learning is maintained. This involves hiring and retaining highly competent, experienced and energetic staff, and providing sustained support for students as they struggle with what has been called the hardest way yet devised to earn a degree, all the time weaning them from dependence on the very support services that the institution has struggled to develop.

While the foregoing has suggested a number of components central to an effective quality programme in distance education, it should also have left no illusions as to the difficulty of attaining this. Real and significant reform is as much about changes in values as it is in structures and processes and strong, consistent and sustained leadership is fundamental to its realization. This is a large order, especially in an institution like a university which should not only value but celebrate dissent. Nevertheless, it is our firm belief, demonstrated increasingly by practice, that a greater commitment to service for students ultimately enhances the institution's commitment to research, scholarship and learning.

In the end, the quest for quality is not just a new management tool, but the very foundation of what a university is about.

8 Reforming a system of distance education

Gavin Moodie and Daryl Nation

An overture: Gippsland's Weekend Schools

It's a sunny Saturday morning in late February. The College campus has the air of a country show. Attendants in dustcoats direct vehicles towards temporary car parks on the lawns. Families unpack and some complete their journey with a late picnic breakfast. Overnighters – both bright and bleary-eyed – are wandering up from the student residences, bearing bags and baskets filled with books, folders and other tools of scholarly trade.

Temporary signs abound, beckoning unfamiliar and partly familiar students to key areas. Provincial values dictate that staff, experienced students and their families assist newcomers with direction finding. All students are drawn towards the despatch area where they will add another package of teaching materials to the bulky bundle which arrived by mail in early February. The bookshop is bustling with eager customers. Classrooms and the library are spilling over. The Caf is abuzz. Stallholders in the market have already made healthy sales. At Pooh Corner the new kids are already into the dress-ups under the guidance of their experienced peers.

Administrative staff are in the last hours of weeks of overtime. They look jaded but in the face of last minute crises they refuse to panic – just. Smiles and thanks from academic staff and students keep them going as they get on with their various jobs. Today the boss is at the counter and she is gathering much useful data for her MBA case study on total quality management.

Energy-charged academic staff head for classrooms, with the sure knowledge that they will be physically drained and intellectually invigorated by their engagements with students new and old. New students want to check their understandings of the first study guides with their tutors. Experienced students are checking with each other before mounting a campaign against their lecturer.

By late on Sunday the caretakers and cleaners arrive to ready the campus for orientation week and this year's freshers. The rest of the staff will return tomorrow to teaching and administering 'the other half' of the College in the same buildings, but with a different timetable and cultural atmosphere.

Gippsland is proud of its Weekend Schools. For most staff and many students they are the significant context for contact, in all senses of the word, within the College's external studies programme. They have evolved over two decades; the immense growth in courses offered and student enrolments has not caused any significant change in the basic concept fashioned in the mid-1970s.

To the best of our knowledge, Gippsland's Weekend Schools are unique in distance education. They fit within the generic category of tuition which institutions teaching at a distance often provide as a complement or supplement to 'packaged' teaching materials. These are named variously: residential schools, tutorials, day schools, summer schools, teletutorials, computer seminars and weekend schools (see also Chapter 5).

The distinguishing features of Gippsland's Weekend Schools are their location at the College's campus and their attempt to cater for most courses and most students in a series of four two-day events in each teaching semester. The College has a two-semester academic year, with commencement in February and July. The vast majority of new students begin in February. There is a Weekend School at the beginning of each semester. Prospective academic staff are advised when they apply for positions at the College that they are expected to teach at Weekend Schools. For many members of the College community, the February Weekend School is the highpoint of the year.

In terms of potential volume of traffic in people and vehicles, the February Weekend School is approximately equivalent to that of the first teaching week for on-campus full-time students. In 1991 there were about 1500 of these students and 3500 part time off-campus students; just over half of the latter attended the February Weekend School.

The purposes of this chapter
This chapter reviews attempts made between April 1989 and May 1991 to reform the approach to distance education created by the Gippsland Institute of Advanced Education as it became the foundation of the Monash Distance Education Centre, which was created following the Institute's merger with Monash University in July 1990.

The significance of the Weekend Schools and the system of distance education, of which they are an important part, is discussed in the context of the political and social circumstances from 1972 to the mid-1980s. Monash University had been expected to develop external studies in the 1960s, but had resisted political pressure to do so in the late 1960s and early 1970s. By the mid-1980s, a Monash administration with a key sense of educational entrepreneurship was keen to acquire a strength in this field as part of the opportunities that presented themselves during the national government's restructuring of higher education.

The changed circumstances required both reassessment and reform of the system of distance education which had been created at Gippsland. The difficulties in making changes to teaching practices are revealed. Emphasis is given to the important weight of tradition as a restraint upon educational innovation – even when these traditions have been relatively shortlived.

The chapter adopts a narrative style and eschews links to theory and research. It is intended to be read in the context of the theoretical discussions which abound in the book.

Gippsland's approach to external studies

In the mid-1960s the Australian Commonwealth Government decided to expand the nation's higher education by creating Colleges of Advanced Education (CAEs) from technical colleges and teachers' colleges. Thus emerged a 'binary' system of higher education within which universities and CAEs had different functions. The latter were to concentrate on vocational courses and the former would continue their traditional functions of research and the creation of new knowledge, teaching in the general arts and sciences and providing a preparation for the prestigious professions (Meek, 1984, pp. 25–49).

With just over 200 students in its tertiary courses, Yallourn Technical College was next to the smallest of Victoria's new CAEs at its transition to its new status in 1968. The college was located 135 kilometres east of the state capital Melbourne in the Latrobe Valley, the centre of Victoria's electric power generation industry. Its *raison d'être* had been to educate the tradesmen, technicians and some of the professionals for the power industry. Despite decades of constant pressure from the people of Gippsland governments had never been persuaded to establish a teachers' college in the region (Meek, 1984, pp. 50–97).

In the cities of Ballarat, Bendigo and Geelong, which service much of the rest of provincial Victoria, technical colleges and teachers' colleges had been established for many decades, were larger and offered a wider range of courses. Starting from a less than substantial base, the Yallourn Tech faced a severe challenge as it competed with Victoria's other provincial colleges and their bigger counterparts in a rapidly expanding metropolitan Melbourne for funds and attention from governments.

In appointing Max Hopper as principal in mid-1970, the Yallourn College Council had committed itself to developments in external studies. Hopper had been assistant director in the Department of External Studies at the University of New England. From 1966 to 1968, as a UNESCO consultant, he was the foundation director of Correspondence Studies at the University of Zambia. Hopper convinced the College's selection committee that an external studies programme was 'the way of increasing enrolments, raising academic standards and extending the diversity of courses offered' (Wearne, 1989, p. 18). During the next few years he convinced the college and its regional community that the external studies programme was central to the College's capacity to serve its entire region. His views on these matters met with considerable respect in Victoria and nationally (Hopper,1974; 1976; 1979).

Within a year of his appointment, Hopper led the College to cut itself adrift from Yallourn Tech, to form Gippsland Institute of Advanced Education. Its move to a green field site in the new town of Churchill symbolized its renaissance as a CAE serving Gippsland. The principal's position was retitled 'Director'. The Institute sought approval to award degrees and it pursued the creation of new schools for visual arts and education.

The first tangible support for the external studies developments came from a traditional source: school teachers seeking to improve their qualifications. The Education Department, the Teachers' Tribunal and the Victorian Teachers' Union offered vigorous assistance. The Director chose the Diploma in General Studies, a three-year course with majors in economics, mathematics, media studies, politics, psychology and sociology, as his vehicle for this development. The scheme he created established the enduring 'Gippsland approach' to distance education. The planning document put it as follows:

(a) It is accepted that the provision of facilities for part-time students is a normal responsibility of Colleges of Advanced Education. A metropolitan college can fulfil its responsibility by conducting evening classes. In a country college, evening classes can serve only those who live within a radius of no more than fifteen or so miles of the college. The Council of the Gippsland Institute, accordingly, sees the provision of external courses as a necessary function of a regional college. It is readily accepted that a teaching institution must provide lecture rooms, black-boards and chalk and various other aids to facilitate communication between lecturers and their full-time on-campus students. The introduction of external courses must be seen as no more than the provision of the facilities necessary to allow teaching staff to communicate with their part-time students – the majority of whom, in our situation, are unable to attend classes on the campus.

(b) The facilities necessary for external teaching are essentially:

    i. An adequate administrative service based upon carefully devised administrative procedures.

    ii. Facilities for the production of teaching materials. Initially, these might be no more than a typewriter and a duplicating machine. As enrolments grow and the number of courses offered increase and diversify, more sophisticated facilities can be added – for offset printing and the production of tapes and other audio-visual materials.

    iii. An educational service to provide guidance for students and information and guidance for teaching staff, expert advice on production of teaching materials, and in-service training of staff in teaching methods.

    iv. An adequate library service.

Since it is fundamental to this concept that external teaching is a normal activity of a regional institution and a responsibility of all teaching staff, and since all the above facilities are required, in any case, for on-campus teaching, the Council intends that the facilities listed above should be developed within the central administrative and academic services of the Institute and not in a separate department (Hopper, 1971, pp. 1–2)

The programme commenced in 1971 with 94 part-time students enrolled in the following subjects:

Mathematics 1G	14
Media Studies 1	33
Modern Government 1	20
Psychology 1	49
Sociology 1	26

All students were residents of Gippsland and half of them were primary teachers (Meek, 1984, p. 62; Young, 1972, p. 1). At very short notice the academic staff began preparing teaching materials following examples of printed study guides Hopper had brought from New England. These were typed on 'state of the art' electric typewriters and printed on a rapidly acquired offset press by a highly skilled printer who thrived on crisis deadlines. A 'just in time' system of developing, printing and despatching teaching materials had been created.

An educational services unit was established to administer the programme. The unit supervised teaching materials production and despatch and liaised between the external students and the academic staff. Its head, Keith Smith, had a background in curriculum development; one of his duties was the difficult task of introducing academic staff to teaching at a distance. The unit and the teaching staff were never able to devote much time to discussing and debating principles: the demands of contemporary practical realities were always dominant!

The first Weekend School was held in May 1972 and a week-long vacation school, coinciding with the school holidays, was held in August of that year. These were based loosely on their University of New England namesakes, but it was really the pioneering staff and students who created the Gippsland approach – by trial and error. Within a decade there had been remarkable increases in courses available and student enrolments. By 1981 courses existed in applied science, computing, business, education, engineering, humanities, social sciences and welfare, with a total of 195 semester units being offered. Enrolment numbers jumped to 721 in 1975 and by 1981 had reached over 1,500. In 1978 Gippsland began to recruit external students from outside the region. By 1980 about half the external students were from outside Gippsland; 31 per cent resided in Melbourne, 12 per cent lived elsewhere in Victoria and 5 per cent resided in the rest of Australia or overseas (Meek, 1984, p. 63).

By the early 1980s, Gippsland's external studies programme could be described as follows:

Myths abound which relate tales of academic staff who were met at Melbourne airport on Friday, and were teaching at a Weekend School on the following Saturday, and who went home to their tea-chest strewn flat to write a study guide on Sunday which was typed, printed and in the mail by the next Thursday. In the best traditions of the Gippsland 'peasantry', production staff hold their machines together with wire and get 'their mates' to provide the instant machine servicing which is sometimes necessary.

Today 'the system' stands in need of an overhaul, and a dramatic one has just been commenced. Much of the early 'model' has survived the ad hoc developments. Considered in the light of Keegan's (1980) model it could be summed up as follows:

- most external students live within a 150 km radius of the campus, a few are elsewhere in Victoria, interstate and overseas, many live within 20 kms;
- inevitably an 'organised' process of producing course materials has been developed, but academic staff have considerable autonomy, educational development is available 'on request' and production deadlines are governed by the capacity of the technology and its workers;
- print is the major medium for course materials, there is considerable use of audio-tapes and some use of computers and telephones;
- two-way communication is conducted largely on the basis of student assignments;

- monthly, but largely non-compulsory, weekend and vacation schools are held at the central campus, and are very well attended;
- new technology has been purchased as funds permit, it is 'basic' for the most part, but does contain some very sophisticated elements, all facets of the production and distribution process are highly organised, but they need to be reorganised (Nation, 1985; pp. 8–9).

Despite the goodwill of the staff and students and the vigorous support of many influential individuals and groups within the region, the Gippsland Institute struggled for support with governments and their bureaucrats in Melbourne and Canberra. The Victoria Institute of Colleges, which coordinated the state's CAEs, had not planned any developments in external studies. It supported Gippsland's initiatives without enthusiasm and later approved Warrnambool Institute – then a CAE in SW Victoria, now part of Deakin University – moving into the field. The Australian Government-funded places to fuel these developments were provided at an increasing rate, but fell well short of demand from students.

Lindsay Thompson, the Victorian Minister of Education, supported the Gippsland and Warrnambool developments, but he harboured grander plans for external studies. These were targeted at Monash University, the state's second university, which was created in 1958 and commenced teaching in 1961.

Monash resists external studies

Monash University had a statutory obligation as follows:

To provide facilities for University education throughout Victoria by the affiliation of existing educational institutions to the University, by the creation of new educational institutions to be affiliated to the University, by the establishment of tutorial classes, correspondence classes, University extension classes and vacation classes and by such other means as the Council deems appropriate ... (Monash University Act, Victorian Government, 1958, Sect. 5[d])

The University's interim council moved swiftly on these matters with the assistance of a Country Colleges sub-committee, which included representatives from provincial Victoria. By late 1959 the sub-committee had recommended:

Provision should be made for external studies as soon as teaching in the Faculty of Arts begins. We should provide assistance for external students by using part-time tutors and by lecturers visiting country centres where the number of students warrants it. The immediate appointment of a Director of External Studies is recommended (Monash University, 1959).

The sub-committee did not recommend affiliation of the provincial technical colleges, but it made many recommendations relating to University recognition of the courses taught in the colleges. Despite discussion at council level these recommendations were never accepted. Only the Dean of Education, Richard Selby-Smith, demonstrated any enthusiasm for external studies. The vice-chancellor had kept the issue under discussion without positive encouragement until the mid-1960s. In a memorandum of 22 October 1964, the Dean of Arts, W A G Scott, probably reflected the views of his colleagues by stating, 'I hope that we shall not have to cater for external students in the next triennium (if ever)'.

By the late-1960s Monash was subject to intense pressure from Minister Thompson and Australian Government education ministers to establish external studies. Offers of special funds and bureaucratic prodding produced some action within the University. The professors of French and German proposed a carefully constructed plan based on detailed knowledge of the University of New England's approach. In 1970 the Vice-Chancellor, fortified by reports of the success of the Open University in Britain, proposed:

... the formation of an affiliated college to conduct these courses which would be under the academic control of the University and have its own director and a tutorial staff, but would be financially independent. In this way it would be possible to ensure reasonable academic standards while, if its grants were separate from those of the University, it could impose no burdens upon our main work. Students would apply in the normal way and their applications for status would be processed by our faculty committees as usual. Teaching would normally be conducted by post, with written or tape recorded comments on assignments; a loan library would be established; vacation courses organised; the normal internal examinations would be used. Professors would be responsible for the appointment of staff and for keeping a general eye on the teaching but the whole organisation would be run by the Director (Monash University File, 1970, CF/0/ 1.3 folio 18).

As the Vice-Chancellor acknowledged, most of the professors were 'luke-warm about external studies'. It was not surprising, therefore, that the Professorial Board twice resolved to resist the politicians' pleas. The Board endorsed a recommendation of the Vice-Chancellor's committee of enquiry 'that the Victoria Institute of Colleges through its affiliated colleges of advanced education was better suited than a university to offering external courses'. A detailed account of these matters has been provided by Moodie (1991a).

With his patience exhausted, Thompson spurned Monash University, ignored the advice of its professors, and determined to introduce university-level external studies by establishing a new university. He did this through an Act of Parliament in 1974 which created Deakin University at Geelong by amalgamating the Gordon Institute of Technology with the local teachers' college. As a consequence, Gippsland and Warrnambool Institutes had a new and potentially powerful rival in external studies.

Deakin's new dimension

Deakin University has been substantially responsible for introducing the forms of teaching and teaching materials production pioneered by the 'open universities' to Australian higher education. Fundamental to these approaches have been forms of course development, employing 'courses teams', which provide academic staff with sufficient time and resources to produce high quality teaching materials well before they are needed by students. As expressed by the early planners, who included Hopper:

> This integrated approach means ... that all courses and materials are developed by a course development team involving all members of a department in consultation with specialist advisors on curriculum development and educational technology. It will ensure staff commitment to this educational philosophy from the beginning.... The acceptance of this principle means that Deakin will not just be another Australian university but an unique institution in Australia (Dean, 1975, p. 1).

Deakin adopted many aspects of the proven student administration and support, library and teaching materials despatch systems used by institutions such as the University of New England and Gippsland Institute. Taken together with its new form of course development, and backed by resources commitments which other institutions had been unable or unprepared to make, Deakin became, by design, a pace-setter for the field.

While attending closely to the needs of its Geelong region, the new university employed a national perspective in its quest for students. Further, it embarked upon an aggressive campaign to win government support to coordinate external studies in higher education for Victoria. This push was resolved with a government enquiry by the Wishart (1981) committee which rationalized external studies in Victoria using a framework in harmony with the binary system. As the only university in the state involved in distance education, Deakin was given an exclusive franchise in the high-demand market of general arts degrees. Business degrees were the only area of high demand open to Gippsland and Warrnambool, which had neither the resources nor the incentive to pursue goals of 'national excellence'. While Deakin had not succeeded in taking over distance education in Victoria, it had established itself as the leading institution in the state. It had established standards in teaching materials which challenged other institutions to improve theirs. It had provided plausible arguments to question the educational legitimacy of the residential schools at the ideological heart of the New England system (see Dean, 1975).

Rationalizing external studies

From the early 1980s all the Australian universities and CAEs providing distance education faced the threat of an Australian Government determined to bring 'efficiency and effectiveness' to the system. Eventually, a series of studies and policy proposals relating to these themes were swept into the massive reforms initiated by Australian Government Minister John Dawkins from 1987. Dawkins engineered the collapse of the binary system in a restructuring which fostered larger universities and incorporated the CAEs into existing universities and/or transformed them into universities. In this context, in 1988 the Australian Government proposed to create 'about six' Distance Education Centres (DECs) which would be the major providers of distance education at university level. Much has been written about these developments elsewhere (Campion and Guiton, 1991; Johnson, 1991a, 1991b; Kelly, 1987; Livingston, 1990; Scriven, 1990).

Richard Johnson has been a key policy adviser in Australian distance education since he was commissioned to report on external studies in the universities and colleges in 1982. His respect for the 'open university' type of operation is reflected in all his policy advice. Minister Dawkins appointed him as chair of the assessment team which examined the submissions made by the 14 institutions seeking to become DECs. Johnson's account of these matters is comprehensive. He notes that 'apart from the variations caused by amalgamations' the DECs are those institutions identified by him and his fellow policy advisers as the 'principal providers' of distance education in the mid-1980s (1991a, p. 16). The report of his assessment team takes the criteria developed in those earlier reviews as its basis. Accordingly, the DECs were to possess the following: the capacity 'to provide support services for external students on a national basis', a wide range of courses, a capacity to attain at least 3000 enrolments of external students by 1991, investment in capital and staff dedicated to distance education activities, high quality teaching materials and 'open' entrance policies (Johnson, 1989, pp. 2–5). With regard to the vexed issue of residential schools, the team remarked:

There are clear differences of opinion over the educational benefits of residential requirements given the costs involved for institutions and students. The assessment team recognised the importance of interaction for external students and that providing distance education nationally will require some institutions to use alternative support and teaching mechanisms more widely than in the past. Residential schools will continue to have a place, in some areas more than others, but institutions will clearly need to provide students with ready and affordable access if attendance is considered essential (Johnson, 1989, p. 5).

The Minister accepted the report and in April 1989 announced the granting of DEC status to eight institutions. Five of the eight DECs are located in amalgamated institutions and another serves a consortium of three in Western Australia.

The DEC Working Party emerges

Gippsland Institute's application for a DEC had been made jointly with Monash University in the context of the ensuing amalgamation in response to Dawkins's push for larger universities espousing both elements of the binary system. Gippsland had rejected an earlier proposal from the Vice-Chancellor of Deakin University, Malcolm Skilbeck, which attempted to create 'a provincial university' based at Geelong and incorporating the colleges in Ballarat, Bendigo, Churchill and Warrnambool. This would have achieved one mega-DEC in Victoria. For the country colleges this was a familiar re-run of earlier imperial attempts by Deakin. It was handled ineptly and was resisted vigorously by each of the CAEs. Ballarat and Bendigo eventually chose to affiliate with the University of Melbourne and La Trobe University, respectively. Gippsland responded positively to an overture from Monash. Warrnambool, after much vacillation, agreed to merge with Deakin.

Gippsland Institute formally affiliated with Monash University on 28 November 1988, one month after the two partners despatched their application for a DEC to Canberra. A merger agreement was signed on 5 March 1990 and the merger came into effect on 1 July 1990. Under this agreement the Gippsland Institute of Advanced Education became Monash University College Gippsland, a college with partial autonomy within the University. Substantially, the University College retained its internal academic and administrative structure; it relates to the University through its chief executive officer, an academic board which advises the University Academic Board and an Advisory Council which reports to the University council. Regarding the DEC, the agreement states: 'Monash and Gippsland will work together to fully realise the potential of the

Distance Education Centre which will be developed using the established expertise at Gippsland'.

A DEC Working Party was established at the College in April 1989 soon after the granting of DEC status. Its origins are unclear, even to its founding members. It arose in the context of the College's senior management committees which were considering the merger proposals. The initiative came from Len Cairns, Head of the School of Education. On the suggestion of the Head of the School of Social Sciences he approached Nation. He also approached John Evans, the Head of the External Studies section. Following a meeting, John Harris, a senior member of the School of Applied Science was invited to join. Evans and Harris had been responsible for drafting the application for DEC status.

Len Cairns, assumed the role of chair of the Working Party and was able to establish the right to report to the senior management committees. The then Institute Director, Tom Kennedy, approved these arrangements and soon began to use the Working Party as his advisory committee for distance education. The Working Party set itself two short term goals: to develop processes for better informing the College of the consequences of DEC status and to offer advice to the Director and management committees on the organizational structure of the DEC.

Discussion and direction papers
Members of the Working Party were concerned that few members of the college community seemed to understand that in accepting DEC status the College would need to reassess thoroughly its distance education programme. Indeed, there was an air of 'business as usual' and many believed that in granting DEC status the government had legitimated Gippsland's long-standing claim as a significant performer in the field. A close reading of the assessment team's report revealed important reservations about the Monash/Gippsland capacities in key areas. Indeed, it proceeded from assumptions which were problematic for the Gippsland system, especially in its demand for a national approach and its questioning of residential schools.

The Working Party decided on a course of action in which it would draft a series of 'discussion and direction papers'; these were to create, even provoke, discussion and debate (DEC Working Party, 1989a). Written responses were encouraged. It was decided to move beyond discussion and detailed recommendations (aimed towards a 'new direction') were also provided. These papers were put together within a few weeks and were in circulation by May 1989.

Two papers provided background information. One offered a

summary of the assessment team's report and outlined the pertinent aspects of the 'rationalization' policies, which had been little discussed outside administrative circles. Another attempted to codify the Gippsland system; it had been poorly documented within the institution. There were proposals for the trial of innovative approaches and arguments for additional resources.

Administration and course development and delivery were the two key issues. The recommendations proposed substantial changes:

DEC Administration

(i) Monash University and Gippsland Institute agree to establish the Centre for Open and Distance Education (CODE).

The Centre's functions would include:

a) The overall operation of distance and open education including materials preparation, student support and course development.

b) Monitoring and quality control of distance and open education materials and teaching.

c) To advise on and overview the development of continuing education and short courses in a variety of modes and other entrepreneurial activities.

(ii) An interim CODE committee should be set up to make policy for the introduction and co-ordination of all distance education courses....

Course Development and Delivery Style

(i) The Institute should move quickly to accept the **course team** as the basic unit for course development and delivery.

Course teams should involve all academic staff involved in teaching an award course along with appropriate personnel from the CODE.

(ii) All new courses should have adequate developmental time and a cyclical system of revision has to be developed for existing courses.

(iii) Building on the existing courses taught at a distance about six courses should be developed and taught nationally through the CODE over the five year Distance Education Centre contract.

These nationally offered 'flagship' courses could emerge from identified new courses from the present Monash, Gippsland and Chisholm centres as well as from within the existing distance offerings at Gippsland Institute (DEC Working Party, 1989a, pp. 33–4).

A review process was proposed which requested schools and divisions to assess their practices and plans against a set of criteria. The Working Party undertook to engage in a parallel review and to collate reports from the other reviews. Individuals were invited to make responses directly to the Working Party. A decision-making timetable was proposed: a management committee would approve the discussion papers and the process for review in May 1989; schools, divisions and individuals would have two months to undertake reviews and offer responses; the Working Party would 'collate reviews' and 'formulate recommendations', which would be taken to management committees and the Institute's academic board for discussion and decisions in August and September.

Interim decisions by the Institute and the University

In June 1989, in the context of discussions between the Institute's director and the University's Vice-Chancellor, Mal Logan, relating to merger arrangements, the Vice-Chancellor requested the Director to provide him with advice on the nature of the DEC. The Director formally requested a management committee to develop the advice and requested the Working Party to do the detailed drafting. Acting on the basis of its constant deliberations and the discussion and direction papers and following many meetings with the Director, the Working Party hastily drafted a three-page statement with an accompanying organizational chart of the proposed CODE. In the course of these deliberations, it became clear that the Director and the Working Party had considerable confidence in each other. Kennedy had determined to use it as an advisory committee in two related senses: he accepted its own definition of its role in policy formulation and he consulted it as a sounding board in his own decision-making.

Essentially, the advice to the Vice-Chancellor was an 'executive summary' of the discussion and direction papers, which covered the issues mentioned above in a little more detail. It included a brief but ambitious request for more resources for the CODE, based upon 600 new student places annually for five years. This was calculated to increase student numbers from 3000 in 1989 to 5000 in 1994. A development fund was also requested.

In August 1989 the Director was able to announce:

After consultation with Monash, it is now agreed that:

- the major part of the DEC activities, related to course development, production and student liaison, be located at Gippsland;
- a small office of distance education be located at Monash, staffed with an Assistant Registrar:
- an Advisory Committee on Distance Education be established;
- a small number of courses be designated for development as national courses to comply with expectations of a DEC (Kennedy, 1989, p.1).

The Assistant Registrar's role would be 'to assist the development of distance education activities at the Monash University and Chisholm campuses' and its incumbent would be 'seconded to the Distance Education Centre to work with the Centre's Director.' In November 1989, Gavin Moodie was appointed to this position with the title, Distance Education Manager. Kennedy chaired the Advisory

Committee, which reported to the Vice-Chancellor, and Moodie was its executive officer. The members of the Working Party were appointed as 'Gippsland representatives' and seven senior staff 'represented' the Melbourne campuses.

In February 1990 the Vice-Chancellor appointed Kennedy as 'interim' director of the DEC; he still holds this position.

Working towards policies

By June 1989 the timetable for the review process was proving very tight for the schools and divisions, but there had been numerous responses from individuals and groups in the Institute. Many of these responses had been in writing and many had been communicated orally to members of the Working Party. At this time the schools and divisions were given a reminder of an August deadline. All those involved in distance education were able to meet this.

In a short paper to heads of schools and divisions at this time the Working Party asserted confidently: 'none of the submissions showed any major disagreement with any of the recommendations in the Discussion and Direction Papers'. However, the Working Party's own cryptic summaries of the 'significant issues raised' suggested considerable resistance to the directions it had endorsed. Particularly pertinent were the following:

- the importance of maintaining face-to-face contact (student-student and staff-student) via weekend schools and/or other methods;
- argument for flexibility of structuring study materials;
- the importance of avoiding alienation of staff currently involved in distance teaching (DEC Working Party, 1989c, p.1).

Put baldly, many of those who had taken the trouble to communicate with the Working Party were supporting 'business as usual' for Gippsland. Their suggestions could be represented by two common statements: 'leave our weekend schools as they are' and 'don't foist a Deakin-style course development and production system on us'!

The school reviews confirmed the existence of these reactions. There was no general acceptance of the need to establish 'new directions'. There were muffled messages of willingness to discuss possible changes. Most schools, however, were able to propose courses which could be offered nationally.

Adhering to its timetable, the Working Party began to grapple with its promised 'recommendations' paper. The decisions of the Director and the Vice-Chancellor had taken consideration of the organizational structure of the DEC off the agenda. After lengthy debate, it was decided to recommend various courses for national offering, to create a draft 'Policy for Development and Production of Distance Education Courses' and to develop a discussion paper, 'Weekend Schools and National Distance Education Provision', which recommended reducing Weekend Schools from four to one per semester. These began circulation in September 1989.

Eight Gippsland courses were recommended for national offering in 1990; subsequently four Gippsland courses and four courses from other Monash campuses were considered for offering from 1991. The Working Party established the following criteria for national courses:

- The course material and delivery must be of high academic, instructional and presentational standard.
- Each course must demonstrate suitable strategies for providing for any essential face-to face tuition. Additional support must be committed for the development of alternative strategies to face-to-face tuition (eg, tele-tutoring) (DEC Working Party, 1989b, p. 1).

The development and production policy provided the detail for the recommendations relating to course development and delivery style referred to above. It made course teams the basis of course development. It provided for the employment of instructional designers, or course developers as they are known locally. It created a four-year cycle of production for teaching materials. It lengthened considerably Gippsland's comparatively short lead time for materials production to 15 weeks – which is still very short in comparison to other providers of distance education. It introduced a standard pattern for printed teaching materials: a unit guide, which would change annually; unit books, which would be the central teaching texts and which would remain unchanged during the four-year cycle; and resources materials, which would be collections of reprints. Considerable scope for variations were allowed and non-print materials were encouraged.

The drafting of the discussion paper dealing with Weekend Schools created considerable difficulties; responses to the earlier papers had revealed that for many staff Weekend Schools had a treasured, almost sacred, status. The paper repeated the earlier argument that Gippsland's Weekend Schools were more appropriate to a regional than a national approach to distance education. The paper listed arguments in support of Weekend Schools which had been put to the Working Party. Each argument was countered with either contradictory facts or proposed alternative forms of teaching. Recommendations for change were made. These encouraged the development of alternatives to Weekend Schools. A deliberately provocative recommendation advocated either reducing Weekend Schools to one per semester or eliminating them entirely.

The Working Party was not surprised by the outbreak of protest against these recommendations. It was surprised by the energy which many staff and students put into a very political campaign against them. Posters went up, especially at Weekend Sschools. 'Save our Weekend Schools' became the rallying cry. Letters began to flow to the Director, Heads of School and the Working Party. It was clear that 'the numbers' would not exist in the academic decision-making bodies to approve these recommendations. Conceding defeat, in putting the Weekend Schools discussion paper to the academic board the Working Party deleted its recommendations and the paper then closed with the following statement:

Putting Alternatives in Place

Each School proposing to offer a national course should be required to designate the methods it will use to replace part or all Weekend School attendance, and the extent of School resources it will commit to these processes. Some central funds should be made available for which Schools can bid. Monitoring and evaluation of the processes of weekend school replacement should be carried out over the next two years (DEC Working Party, 1989d, p.3).

The Weekend Schools discussion paper and the 'Policy for the Development and Production of Distance Education Courses' were considered by the Academic Board in June 1990, after eight months discussion in the schools. The latter was adopted with little debate and without dissent. Regarding the discussion paper the Academic Board resolved:

To note the responses from the Boards of Studies, and to encourage the continuation of the re-development of weekend school programs and initiatives and alternatives in distance education teaching (Monash University College Gippsland, 1990).

An academic approach to policy-making

The Working Party had prepared itself for the Academic Board decision which, in effect, recognized that any movement away from Weekend Schools towards alternative forms of teaching would be very gradual. It was also surprised by the easy passage of its development and production policy. Upon reflection, the Working Party believed that, despite its acceptance at decision-making tables, many elements of this policy would need considerable assistance with their translation in the practical realities of distance education at Gippsland.

While discussing these matters and taking a long-term view, the

146

Working Party became concerned with the need to involve colleagues from other campuses of the new University both in policy-making and its implementation. Moodie accepted an invitation to join the Working Party as a step towards addressing these issues. His capacity for energetic drafting and re-drafting of papers would both influence and assist the course upon which the Working Party decided to embark. The next move would be both 'academic' and 'cultural'. It would be cultural in the sense that it would seek to both document and celebrate the culture which had developed with and continued to inspire the 'Gippsland approach of distance education'. It would be academic in that it would review the Gippsland system not only in terms of the ideas of the 'rationalizers' from Canberra, but in terms of the 'literature' of distance education. The Working Party spent four months carefully drafting a lengthy discussion paper. Its introduction sets out its objectives:

The paper begins with a discussion of some background relating to policy development within the DEC; it proceeds to outline the Gippsland model of distance education; it then deals with the relationship between teaching materials and complementary forms of tuition in distance education; and concludes by suggesting alternative approaches for consideration.

It proceeded in a spirit of reconciliation:

The Working Party has recognised that its strategy relating to Weekend Schools was a failure. The attempt to 'rationalise' Weekend Schools struck at the heart of the culture of distance education at Gippsland, as was borne out by the rhetoric and administrative strategies adopted by those staff and students who resisted the policy change. Nonetheless, the motion adopted by Academic Board said that alternatives to Weekend Schools should be investigated. This paper puts the case from a more comprehensive strategy which regards Weekend Schools as one important means of tuition which are used as a complement to teaching materials in the Monash-Gippsland Distance Education Centre at present and are likely to continue in this role for the foreseeable future. This approach would endeavour to celebrate the pioneers of the Gippsland model of distance education and their major practical achievement – our system of Weekend Schools. It would do this with full recognition that there are imperatives stemming from both Australian Government and University policy and our current practical realities which require a thorough reform of our approaches to complementary tuition, in general, and Weekend Schools, in particular (DEC Working Party, 1990, p.1)

Fundamental to the argument in the paper was an attempt to clarify the connections which exist between teaching materials and complementary tuition in good quality distance education. The nature and mixture of these depend on circumstances and, of course, the resources available.

From the outset, the Working Party's agenda had provided for a lengthy process of information provision, discussion and debate which would become the foundation for a new policy statement. The discussion paper, 'Towards a new approach to distance education', was released in November 1990 and written and oral comments were solicited. This was followed by a position paper, 'Diverse forms of complementary tuition', which was released in February 1991. This was followed by a series of forums at a Melbourne campus and the Gippsland campus. Invitations for other comment remained extant throughout. All discussions were well attended and many of the staff new to distance education were involved. Key antagonists of the Working Party were invited to make presentations.

Taking the comments from the public discussions and other comments into account, the Working Party developed a draft of a new 'Policy for course presentation in distance education'. It also revised the 'Policy for development and production of distance education courses'. This was necessary for two reasons: it needed to be linked thoroughly with the course presentation policy and it was necessary to make some changes in style for it to make sense as a University-wide policy. At the time of writing, both policies had been approved by the University's Distance Education Advisory Committee and approval by the University Academic Board was anticipated.

The essential aspects of the course presentation policy are expressed in the paper as follows:

Course development includes developing study materials and complementary forms of tuition which together constitute course presentation.... Course presentation for a distance education course would normally be a combination of some of the following:

- assignments, exercises and projects
- computer mediated communication
- correspondence tuition
- individual telephone tuition
- informal study groups
- local area tuition
- short answer tests
- teletutorials
- video conferences
- weekend schools...

Major reviews of course presentation will normally occur every four years as part of the revision of Study Material ... (Monash Distance Education Centre, 1992, p. 2).

Having assisted in the development of these policies, the Working Party believes it has made a useful contribution to the reform of the Gippsland system as it becomes the Monash system. Members of the

Working Party understand that the more important challenges lie ahead in the tasks associated with convincing their colleagues to practise the principles entailed in the policies. Most staff can be expected to make commitments based upon their own involvement in the debates surrounding the creation of the policies. The staff who work in the administrative and production infrastructure of the DEC are committed to the policies. The policies give major responsibility for compliance to Heads of the Schools and Faculties. Significant innovation can be expected from those academic staff from various campuses with incentives to teach differently, such as those who need to serve students who are necessarily remote from a campus and who study part-time.

It is significant that a university which once resisted distance education has seen fit to welcome it to the fold. This chapter offers no complete reasons for these changes. It does demonstrate how competing ideas clash together in the creation of new forms of teaching. It provides evidence that innovations in distance education are partially guided by grand plans and are usually the result of compromises born from devotion to the solution of practical problems.

Endnote
We would like to thank our colleagues on the DEC Working Party for their critical review of the group's work. We also would like to thank John Evans for his editorial assistance.

9 Critical Reflections on Developing an Equal Opportunities Action Plan for Black and Ethnic Minorities

Alan Woodley, Lee Taylor and Bernadette Butcher

Introduction

Open and distance education have often been seen as vehicles for the promotion of equal educational opportunity for people who are disadvantaged. Issues of openness and equal opportunities in distance education are frequently open to public scrutiny because of the public nature of teaching materials and the expectations politicians and others have of such institutions. The problems and innovative solutions which have emerged in these forms of education – although the key issues of teaching and learning remain the same – can illuminate the whole area of education in its approaches to 'equal opportunities'.

Equal opportunities is a relatively new phenomenon in Britain. It was only during the 1980s that a number of institutions, led largely by the local government sector, declared themselves as having an equal opportunities policy. According to Cockburn 'they were prompted by the Sex Discrimination Act 1975, and the Race Relations Act 1976, themselves products of pressure from the women's movement and the anti-racist movement of the preceding decade' (Cockburn, 1989, p. 213).

While few publicly dissent from the view that equal opportunities is 'a good thing', either from the viewpoints of human rights or of the efficient use of human resources, there has been a lack of clarity concerning what equal opportunities means and how it might be achieved. Allen (1991), when talking about equal opportunities and access to higher education, noted that the imprecise conceptualization of equal opportunities had led to 'a plethora of different understandings, assumptions and policy implementation'. A study of the equal opportunities literature did not help in establishing a theoretical framework because it tended to be 'prescriptive rather than analytical' (Cockburn, 1989, p. 214). However, studies are now beginning to appear that attempt to theorize institutional policies and practices in relation to equal opportunities.

Jewson and Mason (1986) identified 'liberal' and 'radical' models of equal opportunities and, whilst their concepts have emerged from studies carried out in the general employment area, they can be applied to the development of equal opportunities in institutions of higher and distance education. For them, the liberal approach,

argues that, in principle, equality of opportunity exists when all individuals are enabled freely and equally to compete for social rewards .... Policy makers are required to ensure that the rules of competition are not discriminatory and that they are fairly enforced on all (Jewson and Mason, 1986, p. 313).

The liberal model can be said to be limited because it focuses upon the concept of 'fair procedures', which supposedly guarantees that each individual, regardless of race, class, gender and disabilities, will be able to compete on an equal basis for social (educational) rewards based on the individual's qualities and performance. According to Allen, the liberal model's main equal opportunities purpose involves the removal of barriers for people and fairness equates with the absence of racial discrimination (Allen, 1991).

Young (1989) identified the policies which flowed from the liberal model. These have been described as 'distributive' and 'procedural', as they proscribe certain forms of discriminatory behaviour and insist on conformity to universal codes of conduct. A second characteristic 'enshrined in such policies is the tendency to equate "equality" with "efficiency" in terms of "good management practice"' (Allen, 1991). It is this approach which is central to the 'market orientated access model', and which many see as the main driving force behind recent initiatives in the access to higher education area.

The radical approach is very different. It 'is concerned primarily with the outcome of the contest rather than the rules of the game, with the fairness of distribution of the rewards rather than the procedures' (Jewson and Mason, 1986, p. 315). The radical approach is also explicit in targeting specific groups, which has been described as 'positive action' by others (Young, 1989). With some radical models there has been a deliberate manipulation of selection processes in the pursuit of proportionality, this mechanism being seen as necessary for an initial breakthrough for the interest group. Some researchers see the radical model as being restrictive because it is 'regressive in further dividing the already fragmented powerless groups' (Cockburn, 1989, p. 217). Also, the model lacks an organizational dimension. It seeks to give disadvantaged groups a boost up into the institution whilst leaving the structure of the organization, and the institutional barriers it entails, unchanged. Cockburn has suggested that the radical model,

> fails to address the processes in the life of the organisation that, if the on-going chances of all groups are to be equalised and sustained, must be democratised and opened. It does not question the purpose and role of the organisation. It does not change its attitudes and its cultures (Cockburn, 1989, p. 217).

The Open University context

The Labour Party declared that the new university which it proposed to establish in Britain (eventually called the Open University) would mean the first chance of equality of educational opportunity for millions of people (Labour Party, 1966). The fact that no entry qualifications would be required and that study could be combined with full-time employment, suggested that the opportunity to participate was available to everyone. However, for many critics, 'genuine' equality of opportunity would only be demonstrated by a greatly increased participation rate (over traditional universities) among groups traditionally under-represented in higher education. When details of the characteristics of the first intake of students became public knowledge, articles were published by outside observers suggesting that the University had failed in its attempt to attract the educationally disadvantaged (for example, Pratt, 1971).

Defenders of the Open University (OU) responded in two ways. Jennie Lee, the politician chiefly responsible for implementing Prime Minister Harold Wilson's plan, denied that it was ever their intention to create a university for the working classes. She claimed, 'It is *not* a working class university. It was never *intended* to be a working class university. It was planned as a *university*. It is an Open University' (Lee, 1971).

A second defence drew on research which showed that, although the OU had attracted relatively few 'disadvantaged' students, many could be described as 'initially disadvantaged' (Woodley, 1981). For example, one in five new undergraduates in 1975 had taken no examinations at school and the fathers of one half were manual workers. The University was attracting people who had experienced a great deal of upward social and educational mobility since leaving school.

As the OU became more secure, some of these defences were lowered. Perry, the University's first Vice-Chancellor, talked of the groups for whom the OU was initially planned: those with low socio-economic status who were also generally the most educationally deprived (Perry, 1974). Jennie Lee said that she did indeed want to attract working-class people but that 'the problem was, how could you devise a scheme that would get through to them without excluding other people? The last thing we wanted was a proletarian ghetto!' (Lee, 1979, p.4).

Of course, equal opportunities analyses not only include socio-economic class background, but also focus on a range of potential disadvantages to achieving success in higher education, including gender, ethnic minority background, disability, religion, political beliefs, age and sexual orientation.

During the 1980s a number of equal opportunities groups in faculties and regions considered various aspects of equal opportunities in relation to their own unit's work and provided the impetus for wider-ranging debate within the University. In parallel, the OU unions drew attention to certain equal opportunities issues in staffing. In 1987 the Senate debated the issue and called for the following action:

i) an agreement with joint negotiating committees on an equal opportunity employment policy and its implementation as soon as possible;
ii) the development of policies to 'increase the recruitment of and provision of services for students from racially, socially and economically disadvantaged groups';
iii) the routine collection and maintenance of data on 'major relevant parameters including ethnic origin (as defined by the student)' (OU Senate S/87/min 21.6).

This led to several initiatives, including the agreement in late 1988 to review the University's policies and practices against equal opportunity goals and recommend a five-year action plan in the area. The University agreed to an action plan in 1990 – which it is now implementing – and to developing further policy. The present authors have been involved in these activities, as follows.

Equal opportunities team

The team's brief was to review current practice and to devise a strategic five-year plan for the University. Lee was the planning director, leading the team, and has since been appointed as the University's first Director, Equal Opportunities. Alan was also a member of the team.

Ethnic monitoring for students

Alan worked as a member of the Student Progress Committee on the design and implementation of this policy.

Research project in the West Midlands

Bernadette was employed on a two-year contract to lead an access project which was aimed at black and ethnic minority students. The project was funded by the Training Agency and arose from an initiative by members of staff in the Open University's West Midlands Regional Centre. Alan worked with her on a number of postal surveys that were carried out as part of the project.

In this chapter we want to focus on a key issue within the overall equal opportunities remit, namely ethnic background, and look at how such an issue emerges and is handled in an open and distance educational institution. In a more general sense we want to use this example to examine the model of equal opportunities that is being pursued at the OU and to consider how institutional change can be achieved. We have attempted to cast light on the process by critically reflecting on our own roles as participants in the process itself. While we share a commitment to improving equal opportunities and a belief that the OU has a unique role to play in this respect in British higher education, we have different perspectives on how this might best be achieved. We have different ethnic backgrounds, different professional backgrounds, and different professional roles with the equal opportunities process. These differences are depicted in our three 'tales'.

The Equal Opportunities Director's tale

The establishment of a major institutional review process on equal opportunities was a challenging and exciting development. Although some other institutional reviews had been published (for example, Eyland et al., 1983), it was the first time that a UK university had devoted resources to such a comprehensive review. Within higher education in the UK, a survey by the Commission for Racial Equality in the late 1980s presented a bleak picture of equal opportunities. The authors concluded that there was a 'lack of understanding and progress to date. A tone of moral complacency plus ignorance of the issues and available evidence was pervasive . . . discrimination or bias (was seen as) unacceptable but most unlikely to occur'(Williams *et al.*, 1989, p.24). The situation by early 1992 was radically different. Prompted by guidance from the Committee of Vice-Chancellors and Principals, a majority of universities had equal opportunities policies and most were working in some respect (usually in employment) to improve organizational awareness of the issues and to develop action plans. The polytechnics and colleges, partly because of their earlier statutory links with local authorities, had also made considerable progress. Some institutions could point to significant moves towards agreed targets to redress previous imbalances in the student and staff populations.

In 1989 the OU advertised (internally) for a Planning Director at senior lecturer level, and appointed a team to undertake the review of equal opportunities at the University. It had been expected that an academic ('with institutional clout') would be appointed. However, interest was limited, possibly because it was a short appointment (ten months), and the task was seen as difficult due to the amount of work to be undertaken in a short time, the range of views within the University on the usefulness of such a review, and the acceptability of likely recommendations. My background was in administration, but I had demonstrated interest and activity in equal opportunities, particularly in gender issues.

The appointment of the team members was made by the Pro-Vice-Chancellor (students) which, predictably, caused some controversy. This was was focused on the desire to ensure 'representation' of all groups; and on the method of appointment. Many equal opportunities groups in the OU felt that some, if not all, the members should have been elected. An effort was made to balance male and female members and categories of staff, and to include a student member. A member of black staff was appointed, who was then a secretary. One member of the team was registered as having disabilities. One of the team was appointed largely because of a background which did not include equal opportunities work. Although the Students' Association nominated their Deputy President, the team was not composed of senior members of the University staff. However, I would argue that members individually were known and respected for their work within the institution, so that formal status was less crucial. This sense of credibility within the organization proved important when the action plan came to be debated.

Prior to the review, there was a paucity of information on black students and staff in anything but an anecdotal fashion, so the monitoring process was crucial. However, while the team totally supported the idea of monitoring, the details of how it was to be carried out were outside its control. Alan analyses the issues surrounding the actual process of monitoring in his section later.

As an almost exclusively white group, the team felt tentative about making recommendations about black and ethnic minority issues, and hence supported the setting up of a black staff group. The University community was mixed in its response to this group: some (including many senior members of staff) felt that a separate group was antithetical to the development of equal opportunities. Some staff were less than happy about being identified as black or ethnic minority and did not wish to align themselves with the group. However, the team fully supported the small black staff group and the group has been influential in raising issues and has been recognized as a legitimate source of comment on policy. In order to raise the profile of the issue, a seminar was held entitled 'Race and the OU: What are the Issues' which featured speakers from the Commission for Racial Equality and from the Race Equality Unit at Lancashire Polytechnic. The seminar was introduced by the most senior black academic in the University, the highly respected Professor Stuart Hall, who made a telling set of comments about the insidious nature of indirect discrimination within so-called liberal institutions, such as universities.

The equal opportunities team published its report in April 1990, together with a statistical digest analysing student and staff figures against various equal opportunities measures. There were over 120 recommendations for action, which were condensed into 25 key recommendations in the executive summary. Many of the findings related directly or indirectly to black and ethnic minority students.

The University only began to collect information on ethnic origin in 1989 in a pilot survey. Recent data from 1990 and 1991 on applicants for the undergraduate programme indicate that the University attracts new black and ethnic minority students into the undergraduate population in proportion to the population (around 5.5 per cent). There are, however, significant differences between the initial foundation course choices of different ethnic minority groups. Of course, admission to the system is only the start; it is also crucial to ensure support for progress through the system. Here, the indications are that there are also differences between different ethnic minority groups. Incomplete data from staff returns indicate that there are significantly fewer staff from black or ethnic minority backgrounds than would be expected either for nationally or locally recruited staff.

The University agreed to the 25 key recommendations across the spectrum. It heralded a new statement of principles to employment, student access and progress, curriculum, codes of practice and the organizational structure to implement its plans.

There were few specific recommendations in relation to black and ethnic minority students and staff – partly because the team did not feel it had sufficient data on which to base detailed recommendations. The most important one related to student access. The University accepted the recommendation of the equal opportunities team that on the basis of the monitoring information and other limited qualitative information, no specific targets be set for black and ethnic minority groups, but rather a general umbrella target aimed at increasing by 10 per cent the intake of students with low previous educational qualifications (defined as less than sixth form [year 12] qualifications).

The team felt strongly that acceptance of this broad-brush target would move the University towards more detailed action planning to increase the numbers of students from all disadvantaged groups because, broadly speaking, women, older people, people with disabilities and people from ethnic minority backgrounds tend to have lower education qualifications. However, the target was criticized from a number of perspectives. First of all, there were those who wished to have detailed specific targets for different groups, in the way that some US institutions have. There was a strong view that taking the broad approach perpetuated stereotypes, for example, suggesting that all of ethnic minority origin were less qualified. Others were concerned about the notion of a target, and whether there was a difference between a target and a quota. Few wished to alter the University's fundamental 'first come, first served' principle at the point of admission, and there was substantial debate about the role of targeted advertising, admissions counselling, access courses and guaranteed admissions schemes. Some felt that these compromised the University's openness, whilst others (led by the team) believed that positive action in these areas began to improve access for all groups.

The equal opportunities team believed that monitoring is the cornerstone of an active equal opportunities policy. Unless there is a factual analysis of the current position, it is difficult to make strategic decisions about future action. Alan's later contribution points out that there are issues around monitoring that may make it less of a firm foundation. However, it is clear that some of the statistics published by the team were particularly influential in determining future policy. I would pick out two relating to black and ethnic minority issues:

1. The grouping of new students entering the undergraduate programme into three almost equal cohorts according to previous educational qualifications: those without the entry requirements for higher education, those with such qualifications, and those with some higher education qualification.
2. The statistics on black and ethnic minority students, including their choice of foundation course, the variations between different ethnic groups, and disappointing progress rates within the system.

It is interesting that the information on the first has been available for some time, but not widely published. It was, however, timely for the OU to engage in monitoring ethnic origin: both the Polytechnics Central Admissions System (PCAS) and the Universities Central Council on Admissions (UCCA) began their monitoring in 1990 and, as systems take some time to establish, it is only now that the OU can claim to have statistics on applicants and limited information on their progress. It is also interesting that the figures related to disability and gender have initiated far less debate, despite more active groups concerned with women and people with disabilities. An audit should provide the basis for developing a comprehensive plan to make changes according to institutional decisions. In the case of the OU, statistics (however incomplete) have provided the impetus for developing significant new strategies (once again, however incomplete) for students from black and ethnic minority backgrounds.

The University has acknowledged that it has started a new phase of increasing the diversity of its already considerably diverse student population. Many issues will need to be considered, including course design, institutional barriers and the existence of racial harassment before participation can be considered equal. The next step for the University is to request all its regions to refine their overall access targets to conform to what is appropriate and realistic for their contexts. As a result of this, and some short-term finance available for access projects, there has been heightened activity on issues concerning black and ethnic minority students, as well as other groups.

Much has been written about successful strategies for increasing diversity on campus, particularly in the North American context.

The American Council on Education has recently suggested in a *Handbook for Enhancing Diversity* that it is necessary to have a comprehensive programme, encompassing a range of tactical and strategic issues, in order to achieve success in this area (Green, 1989). This is borne out by our experience at the OU. Monitoring – the institutional audit – is only the first practical step. It is simply not possible to address a value-laden area such as equal opportunities without broad institutional involvement (not necessarily support), leadership from the top, assigned responsibility to a 'champion' in this area, resources and manageable goals, together with the involvement of minority people and the support of minority networks.

Using these criteria, the OU has taken some of the necessary steps; and the research that is being carried out by Bernadette and others is likely to provide the stimulus for a further round of consideration and activity. The OU has made a start. As Director of Equal Opportunities, my perspective is grounded in the belief that the University needs to make recognizable and speedy progress in this area. My wish for an overall strategic plan, firmly linked into organizational objectives, is tempered by a pragmatic and sometimes opportunistic attitude to fostering change. There is the difficulty of balancing being part of the management and the 'champion' of those challenging the status quo.

The field worker's tale

While the OU has decided to target non-traditional groups as part of the implementation of its equal opportunities policy, it has been recognized that much more information is needed if the policy is to be truly effective. If the University is to be responsive to the needs and circumstances of these groups it must take steps to find out their educational requirements and any barriers to access. For those who become students, the University needs to follow their progress, to record their reactions to the courses and to the institution, and to document study outcomes in terms of subsequent employment, other courses, personal development, etc.

In order to address these issues the University has sponsored, or has obtained external funding for, a number of access projects, some of which were targeted particularly at black and ethnic minority groups. I was employed as the field worker on one such scheme, namely the 'West Midlands Access Project' which began in January 1990. The primary aim of the project was to produce an increase in the access of black and ethnic minority groups to the OU. This was to be achieved by:

a) identifying good equal opportunities practice in respect of the OU's marketing and promotional strategies, and support services; and

b) exploring aspects of curriculum development in relation to the educational needs of black and ethnic minority people.

Policy-makers and practitioners usually adopt a 'top-down' approach when determining issues such as the nature of higher education and access to it. Tight suggests that 'Those who work in higher education, particularly at a senior level, largely determine the nature of what it is that they offer to the rest of society ... [Furthermore] there is an underlying uniformity in their assumptions and practices which, despite the apparent diversity within the system, sustains a dominant model of teaching and learning (1989, p. 90). In the case of the Open University, characteristics of the dominant model include length of courses, study centre locations, summer schools, curriculum developments via course teams, recruitment and selection of tutor counsellors, costs of study and the recruitment and selection of students.

In our project we consciously chose a 'bottom-up' approach which enabled black and ethnic minority students to articulate their educational experiences and needs in relation to the dominant characteristics of the OU listed above. Much of the early research took the form of 'outreach work' and involved semi-structured interviews with community groups and different black and ethnic minority student groups within the University. Building upon this, three large-scale postal surveys were carried out on: a) people who had declined the offer of a place; b) students who had dropped out; and c) continuing students. In each survey the sample comprised all those who had categorized themselves as 'Black' or 'Asian' plus a control group of 'White' applicants/students (see Figure 9.1). As far as possible, the design and interpretation of the research has been guided by emerging theoretical frameworks in the area of equal opportunities. Furthermore, the research results have been integrated into the overall OU statistics concerning the characteristics, the course choice and the academic progress of black and ethnic minority students.

The project did not run smoothly. Looking back, it seems to me that at least some of the difficulties arose because, as with most equal opportunity developmental work, the day-to-day running of the project was very much left to the field worker. The methods which

A. The Open University Application Form

ETHNIC ORIGIN

This information is to enable the University to monitor its Equal Opportunity Policy (see the Guide page 25)

E1 Please read the list below, choose ONE term that you feel most nearly describes your ethnic origin and enter its code in the box opposite.

ASIAN: Asian–British = E
            Bangladeshi = C
            Chinese = D
            Indian = A
            Pakistani = B
            Asian–Other = F

BLACK: Black–British = J
            Black–African = H
            Black–Caribbean = G
            Black–Other = K

WHITE: White–British = L
            White–Other European = N
            White–Other = P

ANY OTHER ETHNIC GROUP = R

B. The 1991 Census Form

Ethnic group

Please tick the appropriate box.

White	0
Black–Caribbean	1
Black–African	2
Black–Other	
please describe	

Indian	3
Pakistani	4
Bangladeshi	5
Chinese	6
Any other ethnic group	
please describe	

If the person is descended from more than one ethnic or racial group, please tick the group to which the person considers he/she belongs, or tick the 'Any other group' box and describe the person's ancestry in the space provided.

Figure 9.1 *The Open University and the 1991 Census questions on ethnic origin*

were adopted were thus influenced by the published materials of others and by her personal experiences of work in the field. However, while field workers have to evolve their personal research strategies, this often has to be negotiated with some form of steering committee. In my case the steering group was composed of OU staff from the region in which the project was based, representatives from the Training Agency who funded the project, and two representatives from the black and Asian community, both of whom were working in the field of adult education for ethnic minorities. While my background and experience led me towards a 'qualitative' strategy based on interviews and group discussions, the steering committee favoured a more 'quantitative' approach. The compromise solution was to use a mixture of methods.

As a lone field worker carrying out research on an extremely sensitive issue, using qualitative methods and not working from a central university base, I frequently felt vulnerable and isolated. A great deal of support was given by members of the steering committee and by regional staff but, at times, more support was needed and sought from other members of the University who themselves had been working in the area of equal opportunities and who were aware of the nature and sensitivity of the project. They understood the difficulties of developing an equal opportunities research framework that documented the actual needs of a specific group – in this case black and ethnic minorities – yet which was 'academically respectable' and which fulfilled the needs of the institution itself, even though the findings might not show it in a positive light. The project highlighted for me the necessity of 'networking' and other support mechanisms which are available within an institution. It was vital to be able to discuss confidentially and in detail, sensitive and controversial issues which emerged during the project.

As an outsider reading the OU's equal opportunities report, it was apparent to me that there was a lack of referencing to previous equal opportunities developmental work, at the practical, policy and conceptual level, which derived specifically from the past experiences and needs of black and ethnic minority groups. In the West Midlands study I tried to draw on the work in this area, in the field of employment and other areas of education, in order to guide the research design and the interpretation of the results.

Much of the current thinking on race at the OU has focused on the more overt, 'traditional' aspects. These include discrimination and harassment, inappropriate curricula and an institutional climate which might be perceived as hostile. While these aspects are undoubtedly important, our research findings suggest that the experiences of black and ethnic minority students at the OU are actually the result of a complex interplay of matters concerning race, gender, class and previous education. Any equal opportunities strategy aimed at increasing access for black and ethnic minority students must take into account the great diversity in people's backgrounds and circumstances. To take a concrete example, a strategy designed to help well-educated black single-parent women who are working is unlikely to be appropriate for an unemployed poorly-qualified black man.

If the results of such a study are acknowledged by an institution as being a valuable contribution towards institutional change within the context of equal opportunities, it can only enhance the development of education provision for all existing students. It will also serve to remove barriers to access for a wide range of people from disadvantaged groups, regardless of their ethnic origin.

The institutional researcher's tale

Phrases such as 'the routine collection and maintenance of data' and 'ethnic monitoring' imply a bureaucratic, non-problematic function that institutional researchers can be entrusted with. Having spent a significant portion of my recent working life negotiating the wording of the 'ethnic origin' survey question, the analysis of the data and the dissemination of the results, I am even more aware of the social factors that affect the construction of 'knowledge.'

As an undergraduate I was impressed by Gouldner's writings on values and sociology. In 1961 he attacked what he took to be the dominant professional ideology of sociologists: that favouring the value-free doctrine of social science. In 1968 he returned to the fray because he feared 'that the myth of a value-free social science is about to be supplanted by still another myth, and that the once glib acceptance of the value-free doctrine is about to be superseded by a new but no less glib rejection of it' (Gouldner, 1968, p.103). He took to task Becker and others in the Chicago School (see, for example, Becker, 1963) who sided with the 'underdogs' in their studies of deviant behaviour. They did so on the grounds that it is impossible for a social scientist to do research uncontaminated by personal and political sympathies. Work must be written either from the stand-point of subordinates or superiors because one cannot do equal justice to both. Gouldner, on the other hand, while recognizing the inevitability of bias and partisanship, notes 'the fact remains that two researchers may have the same bias but, nonetheless, may *not* be equally objective' (1968, p.111). He outlines three possible conceptions of sociological objectivity. 'Normative objectification' is the objectivity of the court judge which 'requires his explication of the moral value in terms of which his judgement has been rendered' (p. 113). 'Personal authenticity' is a form of objectivity that involves 'the capacity to acknowledge "hostile information" – information that is discrepant with our purposes, hopes, wishes or values' (p. 114). A third component of objectivity is 'transpersonal replicability' which means that sociologists have described their procedures with such explicitness that others employing them on the same problem would come to the same conclusion.

Gouldner, then, did not see partisanship as incompatible with objectivity. 'The physician, after all, is not necessarily less objective because he has made a partisan commitment to his patient and against the germ' (1968, p.113). However, Gouldner did not address the question of the researcher's position in relation to the different factions. For example, how would it have affected Becker's research if he had been doing the research for the police force, or even if he was part of that police force? As an institutional researcher for the OU, and as an academic member of that university, there are three sets of constraints acting on me: the need to be a professional, objective researcher; the need to act in accordance with my own values – in this case adopting a partisan role towards equal opportunity issues; the need to act responsibly toward, and to seek improvements in, the institution of which I am a member. In what follows, I have attempted to outline how these constraints have worked out in practice in the case of 'ethnic monitoring'.

Initially, the request for ethnic monitoring appeared straightforward. After many years of debate and controversy an agreed and tested question was included on the 1991 Census form. Hence, if this question were used it would be relatively uncontroversial and would eventually have comparable national statistics. In the event we (the Student Progress Committee) devised a very different question (see Figure 9.1). The Census question had only one 'White' category which it placed first. We felt that this implied that 'White' was the most important and normal category which required no sub-divisions as it formed an homogeneous group that was not seen as being in any sense problematic. We placed 'Asian', 'Black' and 'White' in alphabetical order and split the 'White' category into three. In one draft version a 'White-Irish' category was proposed but this was rejected because some felt it would be confusing in the case of Ulster. A counter suggestion to use 'British/Irish' was rejected on the grounds that people from the Republic of Ireland see this lumping together as the remnants of colonialism.

Once it had been established that 'White-British' would be a category, we felt that equity demanded that there should be the parallel categories of 'Asian-British' and 'Black-British'. The Council for Racial Equality, who had approved the Census version of the question, told us that tests had shown that this caused problems as some people did not know whether to say, for example, 'Black-British' or 'Black-Caribbean'. We decided that, on balance, it would cause more problems by not including these options and in reality many OU applicants have used them. The category 'Asian-Other' was also included on the grounds of equity and symmetry.

When we consider the actual questions shown in Figure 9.1 we see that the Census version merely says 'Ethnic group' whereas the Open University explains why the question is being asked and how to answer it. The aim of the University question was to get a purely subjective assessment of 'ethnicity' rather than 'race' or 'nationality'. With hindsight, the question should perhaps have been 'To which ethnic group do you feel you belong?', or words to that effect, because the term 'origin' is problematic. (In one version of the question, black people were instructed to trace their 'origin' back to the Caribbean if necessary, but not back further to Africa!) In the case of the Census, respondents are again asked for a subjective assessment of 'ethnicity' but they would be answering the question for the rest of their household as well as themselves. The only clues as to how to answer the question are in the notes at the bottom and they clearly indicate that it is 'descent' and 'ancestry' that determine a person's group, rather than feelings of belonging.

Despite the injunction from Senate to collect the information, there was continuing debate in the committee as to when the question should be asked (for example, at application or after registration), whether the question should have an option saying, 'I prefer not to answer this question', and indeed whether the question should be asked at all. It was eventually decided that the question should go on the application form on the grounds that it would allow us to examine any differential effects during the admissions process. The question was put in the 'voluntary' section of the form, but it was felt that to give people the 'no' answer option within the question would invalidate the whole exercise.

One debate revolved around why we wanted to collect this data. Some members felt that they might be used as a proxy measure for educational disadvantage and that this should be avoided. Therefore a further, entirely separate, question was devised which asked applicants how much help they felt they might need with language skills, such as reading and essay writing. This potentially useful question was eventually dropped on the grounds that it might raise expectations of help in these areas which regional staff could not provide due to lack of resources.

In parallel to the student progress committee debate, managers in staff services were discussing how to collect data on ethnicity from University employees. They preferred to use the Census question for reasons of comparability and so the University now uses one version for staff and another one for students. Members of the full-time staff were sent a form to complete, accompanied by a letter explaining why the information was being requested and noting the support of the University's senior management, the joint trade union committee and the Equal Opportunities Planning Director.

We now have some early data from these exercises. Roughly speaking, nine out of ten new undergraduate applicants answer the question and about 5 per cent select one of the 'non-white' categories. The available national data suggest that black and ethnic minorities constitute a similar proportion of the adult population and so the Open University has taken some pride in these results. However, there are three reasons for caution. First, while the non-response rate is low, we have to acknowledge that 5 per cent is an estimate and we cannot put confidence limits on this estimate because with such a sensitive question one cannot assume that the respondents formed a random sample. Plainly, if all the non-respondents were white, the population figure for the non-white group would fall to 4.5 per cent, whereas if all the non-respondents were non-white, the true population figure for black and ethnic minority students would be 14.5 per cent. Second, there are some doubts concerning the reliability of the comparative data. This should improve as the Census data emerge but even here it appears that there will be a problem of non-response. Third, a case can be made that, in an institution such as the OU, the proportion of black and ethnic minority people should exceed the proportion in the population in order to compensate for earlier educational disadvantage within these groups. Again we are hampered by a lack of good comparative data but, as British universities and polytechnics are just beginning to collect these data, such comparisons may be made in the future.

As regards the staff data, the results are even more problematic. One third of the staff chose not to respond to staff services' request for information and, therefore, the figures that are available must be treated extremely cautiously. For what they are worth, it appears that the OU recruits very few black and Asian people to its staff.

Relatively high numbers chose to place themselves in the 'other ethnic group' category but it is not clear whether this was because they felt they were 'of mixed descent' or because this choice represented a rejection of the other categories on offer.

Early results on the progress made by black and ethnic minority students are not encouraging. As an 'objective' researcher I have attempted to control for the effects of factors such as previous educational qualifications, course choice and age, but it still seems to be the case that these students are less likely to gain a course credit at the end of their first year. From my own value position, I want to alert the University to the situation and to produce improvements within the system and, as an academic, I expect, and I am expected, to publish useful findings. However, as an employee of the University I have to consider how, in what form, and to whom this information should be released. The University is anxious not to receive bad publicity over what is a very sensitive issue; however, demand for the information is great from outside the university and from within, both by regional staff and by academics developing the 'Race and Education' course. Therefore, the process whereby the research data become public knowledge is one of negotiation and even contestation.

Conclusion

For the first 20 years of its existence the OU has operated firmly within the 'liberal' model of access and equal opportunities. Although its decisions to abandon entry requirements and to admit people on a first come, first served basis were revolutionary moves in British higher education, equality was to be achieved by ensuring that the procedures were applied fairly. With the acceptance of access targets for people with low qualifications, the University has now adopted characteristics of the 'radical' model. It is committed to redistributing educational opportunities so that certain groups benefit more than others. The lack of information on black and ethnic minority students at the action planning stage led to a broad targeting approach, which it has been acknowledged will need refining as a result of more information from monitoring and the outcome of pilot access projects.

It is one thing to set targets and another to meet them. Problems are already being experienced in three areas:

1. *People with low educational qualifications are more likely to drop out.*
    At a time when universities are being judged by crude

167

performance indicators such as cost-per-graduate, it is seen by some as a dangerous move to deliberately recruit more from high-risk groups. One early attempt was made to change the target to raw numbers rather than a percentage, thus in effect lowering the targets during a period when the University was planning rapidly to expand the total number of students.

On a more positive note, steps are being taken to develop courses and packs that are designed to improve the study skills of potential students.

2. *Attracting people from traditionally under-represented groups involves more than placing adverts in specialist newspapers read by the target group.* If the University wants to attract people from such groups it may well have to change the product that it is offering and the way it offers it. The West Midlands project showed that this does not necessarily mean putting on courses in 'Black Studies'. In fact black students said that they would prefer the University to put on courses in law and accounting. Attracting more black and ethnic minority students involves the institution in challenging its current organizational climate; for example, in dealing with harassment at residential schools

3. Race in particular is a 'hot' issue. The University is well aware of its lack of black staff and the dangers of white staff pontificating on black issues. Furthermore, while it is pleased to announce that the numbers of black and ethnic minority students look positive, it is very reluctant to publicize the fact that they fare less well with their studies.

The University has moved on significantly in looking at black and ethnic minority student issues over the past few years. However, the monitoring and initial studies indicate that much more institutional research is necessary to identify the complexity of the variables involved and their interrelationships. At a basic level, we need to collate all the studies and projects undertaken in the institution in this area and relate these to projects and research undertaken outside the institution before moving on to develop new policy objectives.

10 Reflections on Curriculum as Process

Daniel Granger

The British Open University posited an ideal curriculum for all students then planned how to deliver it. Empire State College began with the individual student's curriculum, then considered how to create the common resources and courses which might serve these diverse needs (Hall, 1991, p. 140).

The UK Open University (OU) and Empire State College of the State University of New York emerged during the same historical period and had similar goals of providing education to under-served learners. They both commenced courses in 1971 and since that time academic staff and administrators from both institutions have maintained frequent communication. In 1991, the OU and Empire State College jointly sponsored a conference in Cambridge, UK, on 'The Student, Community, and Curriculum'. Many of the relationships over the two decades since 1971 have been fostered at the individual rather than institutional levels and have arisen from people's particular interests or activities. This form of collaboration has produced a more dispersed understanding throughout the institutions of each other's practices and people, which enables comparisons to be made. This chapter offers a reflection gleaned from some of those exchanges from the perspective of Empire State College, with particular attention to questions of curriculum

James Hall, founding President of Empire State College, in his book *Access Through Innovation* (1991) devotes most of a chapter on institutionalizing innovation to illustrating the institutional choices to be made from the cases of the OU and Empire State College. For him this comparison made sense because 'Both (institutions) focused on the student in new ways, recognizing that in much of higher education the student had become invisible. Both were innovations in the process of learning as well...' (p. 128). As the epigraph here indicates, however, common purposes did not lead to common programmes or approaches. The OU's task was a national one: a strong, high-quality programme which could be offered throughout the UK to many thousands of students. Economies of scale and programme uniformity and consistency were major objectives (Harris, 1987). Empire State College, on the other hand, was one college among 64 campuses comprising the largest university system in the country. Its mandate covered New York State through regional centres and smaller units. It was to focus on those students who were not well served by the existing educational system and, by the College's projections, it expected to grow to 15–20,000 students; however, limited by state resources, it has never exceeded 8,000.

Given the different contexts of student need and available resources, the academic planning of the two institutions inevitably took different turns. The focus of the OU was on the creation of an effective and consistent curriculum of high quality for widespread delivery; the focus of Empire State was on the development of a curriculum for the individual student who, for reasons of age, circumstance, or intellectual inclination, was not well served by the conventional educational system. Hall notes the dual mission for the College: 'not only to increase accessibility to students of all ages but also to extend and improve American higher education through focus on the individual student' (1991, p. 129). Hall goes on to note:

As the result of their differing approaches to curriculum, (the Open University) and (Empire State College) also diverged significantly in early choices about where to allocate capital investment funds. But each made a choice which proved responsive and appropriate for its particular cultural milieu. For (Empire State College) the choice was to invest resources neither in hardware nor in curriculum development, but in people. For (the Open University), the choice was to invest resources in academically sophisticated, pedagogically engaging, and aesthetically attractive course materials ... (p.137).

In 1986, reflecting on the the general acceptance the OU had then experienced, the founding Vice-Chancellor Walter Perry wrote:

Academics all over Britain accept that the Open University has succeeded, that distance learning works, and that the Open University graduates are as good as any others. They (these graduates) have been accepted by every other British university in postgraduate courses without question. The quality of the courses is seen and is commended by the academics in other universities. But emotionally, many of them don't accept it at all. Emotionally there still is a strong feeling that on-campus teaching in the face-to-face situation is the one way of actually teaching and that this is the vital thing in order to train scholars for the future. It may take decades rather than years to overcome this emotional reaction (Perry, 1986, p. 15).

Speaking to the Open University Council in 1990, the new Vice-Chancellor, John Daniel, noted, 'Perhaps the greatest gift of European civilisation to mankind is the academic mode of thinking and teaching, which stands in contrast to the ideological mode' (1991, p. 5).

Both of these remarks are about communities which, by definition, exclude as well as include. Perry's remark explicitly refers to the emotional impulse to exclude, not to accept that which does not have the customary presenting image. Daniel's remark makes a similar, but more far-reaching, exclusionary distinction: that there is an absolute difference between the academic mode of thinking – reflective, carefully scrutinizing to assure objectivity, and the ideological mode – explicitly value-laden, tendentious and subjective. In Perry's example, traditional academics will often accept OU graduates as educated 'others', but not admit them fully into the inner circle of the community. In Daniel's example, the ideological community is simply shut off from the more open and openly critical academic community.

I would like to use Perry's comment as a gloss on Daniel's to suggest that, even in the best academic world with the purest academic mode of thought, entry is not entirely equal for aspirants to membership in the academic community – a community not always entirely resistant to the ideological mode. There is perhaps a continuum connecting those two modes, a continuum of contingencies and assumptions, of variables and givens. A difference may be that the academic mode is seemingly more disposed to examine its assumptions. But even as the academic world seeks to deal with its subject areas with greater precision to assure objectivity, it finds that objectivity an increasingly elusive spectre. As Scott (1990) put it, speaking of modern science, 'The more precise the means of analysis and the more powerful the means of calculation the less sure the answers seem to become'. But the awareness of that indeterminacy and related contingencies, and the need to take them into account, provide a strong base for pursuing education. A recent American study, *The Challenge of Connected Learning*, noted:

Awareness of contingency takes many forms. It is important for students to know that ideas and methods have origins and histories, that they take place in quite particular times and places, that ideas represent interests; that ideas are framed by gender, ethnic, social, political, economic, and other cultural and ideological perspectives (American Association of Colleges, 1991, p.13).

Considered this way, it is clear that virtually every area of knowledge is in some ways indeterminate and that, similarly, each student's pursuit of a particular field is subject to various contingencies. 'Academic' or 'objective' knowledge refers to the current commonly held understandings and assumptions within any particular field. They are 'objective' because they have been subjected to intense scrutiny from a range of perspectives, usually from different intellectual, social and cultural vantages. 'Objective' knowledge has been 'freed' of local particularisms, biases, or perspectives and so should be generally accessible. Mathematics and science represent the most widespread 'objective' knowledge in that their language and discourses are widely approachable, the correlations to the physical environment are observable and replicable and the predictive powers are strong.[1]

Academic disciplines are generally the largest, most established public discourses or conversations about their respective fields. (I prefer 'conversation' for conveying a greater sense of contingency than the more formal 'discourse'.) They often have their own special languages and usages, in order both to be precise and to share a common frame of reference to facilitate communication. For adult students approaching a particular field or discipline, a common difficulty is not lack of understanding (or the capacity to understand) an area, but rather ignorance of the language and usages adopted or accreted over years within the disciplinary community. The power of highly structured or disciplinary study to extend a student's context for understanding beyond the personal and immediate, providing ways of negotiating the wider world, is a fundamental assumption of our educational system. But at the same time those disciplines themselves are often part of that wider world, and access to them must be negotiated by each individual.[2] This is more pronounced for adult students since the continuity and progression of their developing mastery in academic fields has often been broken. Consequently, the process of that negotiation must be carefully attended to in order to bridge whatever gap exists and at the same time to take advantage of whatever additional (though discontinuous) subject mastery has been acquired, even if often expressed in other language and usage.

Curriculum, the course of study undertaken by students in an educational programme, is the mediating vehicle of access for students to the conversations of the communities they wish to join. Curricula are usually progressive and always dynamic. That is, they ordinarily lead students by steps or degrees of understanding and difficulty into a progressively more detailed and complex engagement with a discipline or area. At the same time, the generally agreed or accepted understanding of that discipline or area is itself in a continual state of flux as members of its expert community make new discoveries, achieve new insights and modify existing notions. With the addition of each new member and new perspective to a 'knowledge-community,' the shared understanding of that knowledge is altered, however imperceptibly. Significantly different perspectives – for example, of culture, social background, gender, or economic class – will introduce substantially different perspectives and understandings, but even subtler shadings of experience, knowledge base and biology will colour one's construction of knowledge.

Curricula, as presentations of, and avenues toward, knowledge-communities are by definition dynamic, yet they are frequently perceived and treated by students and even by staff as static, fixed and for the most part unyielding. Their ability to change in response to changes in those communities is bounded by many practical concerns, from lack of general agreement among the expert members on the significance or implications of changes to something as seemingly minor as current textbook availability. The further ability of curricula to change in response to the aspiring learner's needs – from the individual's particular style of knowing and learning to their deficiencies with particular learning skills or an incomplete referential frame – is even more unlikely in programmes designed for a target student profile. Some general assumptions must always be made about students' level of preparation and experience of the subject matter as well as responsiveness to a particular (or the chosen) pedagogical approach.

The mediating role of the curriculum, and thus its effectiveness with diverse students, can itself be enhanced by rendering it more explicitly dynamic; that is, by recognizing and beginning with the contingencies of the individual student as well as the ultimate indeterminacy of the field of study. By conceptualizing curriculum as process, rather than as a pre-determined course of study, one can successfully acknowledge the contingencies and idiosyncrasies of the student, the field of study and their intersections.

As soon as we pose the educative process in that way – the individual, with goals and needs, seeking membership in an established community of knowers – we set up several tensions, especially when dealing with adult students: the individual's own experience of a field versus the academic and theoretical understandings of that field; the perceived constraints of membership in a community of understanding versus following one's own way on one's own terms. Individual students often do not perceive this, assuming a greater fixity in their environment. They speak of their need to be able to do certain things, or to gain a certain credential for advancement, or the satisfaction of learning or knowing certain things. The individual perspective is frequently limited to just that – individual, and thus insignificant in the face of the forces surrounding them. Education, then, is as much the development of a critical awareness of contingency, as it is the mastery of specific skills or gaining entry into specific knowledge communities.

The academic programme at Empire State College is designed to make education responsive simultaneously to the goals and needs of the individual student and to the standards and expectations of the higher education community. In brief, Empire State College's academic programme requires that students gain the skills and knowledge appropriate to the knowledge communities to which they aspire. Specifically, students are required to engage in a comprehensive and detailed degree programme planning process. In this process, students examine their past learning, knowledge and skills – whether acquired through formal instruction or experientially – in the context of their aspirations and expectations for their undergraduate education. From this process emerge the learning needs – knowledge and skills – the student must satisfy to progress toward those aspirations. Invariably, the student must explore the expectations of several 'communities of knowers', whether they be a specific disciplinary community, occupational community, or an intersection of several communities. The student, with the guidance and support of a staff mentor, undertakes this process in a spirit of inquiry. Students' work in an individualized programme is explicitly dialogic. Students' questions about direction are frequently answered with questions:

'What do I have to do?' – What do you want out of this?

'I simply am no good at advanced mathematics, do I have to take it?' – What will it exclude you from?

The College actually has an elaborate process of individual degree programme design which is essentially a negotiation among the several communities the student inhabits and hopes to inhabit. The process begins with a situational self-assessment, in which the student carefully identifies themself in relation to existing knowledge, skills, and reasons for and goals of education. Quite frequently the reasons and goals initially are quite instrumental – for advancement, career change, a credential – and the self-assessment process foregrounds that in a way that the student and staff mentor can directly address: 'So you want to be a CEO. Well, that will take a lot more than a good golf handicap!'

The student aspires to membership in a particular community which has its own admission standards, thus providing the student's incentive (or disincentive) for the necessary learning. All of the academic programme expectations are the expectations of the relevant communities, whether disciplinary, professional or cultural, and the one required process is intended to help the student devise the plan to enable her or him to achieve that, beginning from the individual student's point of departure. These expectations are underscored by the general knowledge and skills expectations which provide the

> ... abilities to live and work in the world successfully. Students come to Empire State for different purposes, with widely divergent backgrounds and experiences. Degree program planning provides time in the student's first months at the College for reflection and exploration of possible alternatives before making a commitment to a particular program of study.
>
> Degree program planning may involve inquiry in specific disciplines or fields of study. It may involve an autobiographical study. It may involve research into career planning and possibilities, or a combination of any of these (Empire State College, 1991, pp. 12–13).

An 'individualized' programme, such as the one described, does not stress the primacy of the individual in isolation, but rather the importance of the individual student's achieving an effective engagement with the appropriate knowledge-communities.

Because many students come to the College with years of practical experience in working life, it is often a significant and difficult task for them to 'translate' what they know personally and experientially into the terms and usage of the relevant academic discourse. Unfamiliar with the statistics or insights of the social sciences, New York City police officers are 'sure' at an intuitive level of their knowledge of ethnic and cultural differences and the social problems arising from them. Students pursuing degrees in business studies have often learned what they know from observing business practices and organizational structures at first hand. Theoretical models of organizational management may well seem both alien and irrelevant to what they know. An industrial employee may have experience of a management practice which contradicts the 'workforce impact' which management texts claim for that practice. Their knowledge of the same phenomena is in fact different knowledge, but it may well be important as part of a 'recognition of prior learning' process.

The process of translation and negotiation often begins early in students' careers at Empire State College and continues throughout their studies. It is in this process, the continual sawing back and forth between personal context and values and broader standards and expectations, that the central strengths of a dynamic curriculum emerge. By taking seriously each student's 'point of departure', the curricular process insistently engages critical skills of analysis, reflection and judgement. Students are encouraged to articulate their own perspectives and engage alternative ones by critical reflection; to use skills and knowledge in contextual problem-solving; to come to terms with their fields of study in ways that satisfy needs that they themselves have identified. It is most important for their learning success that students engage with the various studies of their curriculum for reasons and motivations intimately related to their own sense of themselves.

At the same time, this curricular process is subject to a number of practical difficulties which can jeopardize the outcome. I will simply indicate what some of these are as they confront the two agents of this negotiating process, the student and the staff mentor. For the student, the challenge of explicitly determining their knowledge needs in terms of expressed goals or aspirations as the basis for an individual curriculum is intimidating in several ways. Many students are unaccustomed to asserting themselves, expecting to be given a recipe of requirements in response to a vaguely expressed inclination. 'Oh, you want a degree in business management? Take these courses and then choose something from these columns for your general learning'. The notion that, *as students,* they must articulate their goals specifically enough to evoke particular expectations can produce an almost paralysing anxiety. 'But I'm not sure I want to stay in public management. What if this isn't right? Why don't they just tell me what I have to do?'

Students can get lost in a labyrinth of possibilities, especially if they are pursuing a programme which is not already reasonably well defined in society. The apparently indeterminate nature of the curricular process exacerbates the contingencies inherent in the fields themselves. Further, students' own weaknesses and phobias can influence their stated intentions in unfortunate ways. For instance, students ascertain that the particular approach they would like to take to business studies requires calculus; they may opt for some less demanding approach, thereby limiting their possible progress. Students with a narrowly instrumental approach to their education will often choose the path of least resistance, and the mentor has few policy requirements to use as levers. Empire State College has articulated standard expectations in a number of commonly pursued fields, but these guidelines are only that, and

REFLECTIONS ON CURRICULUM AS PROCESS

students can weave their way around studies they find particularly difficult.

Even when an individual student successfully accepts the challenge of developing a distinctive degree programme which crosses the borders of several established communities of knowers, the student can be beset by an uncertainty about the reality of their membership of any community, particularly when those communities have competing values. If Perry is right about the emotional rejection of OU graduates, the rejection potential for students with unusual degree concentrations may be even higher.

Finally, in any programme which recognizes indeterminacy and strives to achieve a balance between the specific, personal needs of the individual student and the expectations of a well established community of knowers, there is the danger of that balance being tilted by the anxieties or misperceptions of the student, as well as by the current emphases or concerns of the community of knowers. For instance, students in business studies may feel the necessity to understand sophisticated finance and stock manipulation strategies, or international business practices, when the declared goals call for extensive studies in management and inventory control. Here, of course, the staff mentor becomes the agent of facilitation and arbitration. The mentor role is critical in assisting students to negotiate the alignment of their backgrounds, interests and goals within the community or communities to which they aspire. Without an effective and knowledgeable mentor, the students' programmes can become indeterminate, with only weak or partially developed linkages to knowledge communities. It is only when mentoring is done properly that students are able to take their places in their chosen communities as fully engaged and active members, ready to contribute to their conversations.

Aware of both the OU development plans in the early 1970s, and the experience of the State University of New York's then recently demised University of the Air, Empire State College's planners recognized that while each student's degree programme would be individually designed, the actual instruction could well combine structured components with the individually tailored learning contracts. These structured components could provide students with supportive frameworks to guide their study through a particular course and would enable staff to design courses in areas of frequent demand which need little significant individual modification. A structured series of studies can take students logically and incrementally from an introduction to a field, through to a complexly detailed mastery of advanced areas and applications within that field. Structured studies could include introductory courses in many areas from accounting to philosophy, as well as upper-level courses in popular areas such as business and human services.

Empire State College took a number of approaches to this goal before finding one that aligned with the institution's philosophy and served students effectively. At first, as Hall (1991) notes:

> ESC did actually experiment briefly with a BOU-model development faculty but soon discovered that, given the educational culture of New York State and the students' expectations, a fixed curriculum, developed centrally but offered wholly from afar by correspondence, was not likely to work very well (p. 134).

One of the main concerns expressed by staff in regional centres was that the development staff simply were not in touch with the students and their academic needs. The studies produced by the development staff reflected current issues among specialist academics rather than subjects commonly pursued by undergraduates.

In the mid-1970s Empire State College undertook to cooperate with the OU in adapting its courses for use by American students. Empire State College staff worked with a number of OU foundation and lower-level courses: A100 *Arts Foundation*, A201 *Renaissance and Reformation*, D101 *Making Sense of Society*, T100 *The Man-Made World* (technology foundation), E261 *Reading Development* (Lehmann and Thorsland, 1977) and conducted an extensive adaptation and pilot test of D101 *Making Sense of Society: Social Relationships* (Lehmann, 1978). While Empire State College staff found a majority of the course units appropriate and usable, and students participating in the pilot found the courses to be valuable learning resources, all four recommendations following the pilot suggested changes to 'provide an American context' and to 'substitute American articles' or 'more suitable materials' (Lehmann, 1978, p. 5). The report commented further that

> the course assumed that adult students taking the course could read and write at the college level and could handle the level of the course without great difficulty. As such, the course was not designed for students with unique or different background characteristics (p. 5).

Upon conclusion of the pilot in 1978, Empire State College continued to work with OU course materials, but the adaptation work was necessarily labour-intensive and proceeded slowly. Within a short time the National University Consortium (now International University Consortium) was established with the explicit intention of undertaking this American adaptation for member schools. Empire State College joined the consortium and its staff have participated in several adaptation teams. While these adaptations are used regularly by some Empire State College students, they have not become an educational staple for most students. At least one more turn of the wheel was needed.

In 1979 Empire State College established its own Center for Distance Learning (CDL) with the express mission of developing structured learning materials to be used by ESC students. Unlike the former development staff, CDL was not a resource centre apart, but one explicitly connected to the regional centre staff and students. A core coordinating staff and administration for the new centre were taken from the regional centres; courses were to be developed to meet the needs of the College's students and regional centre staff were to be engaged in that development.

The culture of the College and its staff had by this time embraced wholeheartedly the values of student-centred or 'individualized' studies. By assigning the development of the structured courses to staff steeped in these values, Empire State College assured the development of a third approach, characterized neither by the lock-step instructional design (the 'instructional industrialism' of Evans and Nation, 1989c) of conventional distance learning courses, nor by the unstructured flexibility of learning contracts.

What emerged were courses to be offered within a fixed term schedule, with specific content and performance expectations for a defined credit award. Courses included set texts and other materials such as audio/video tapes and computer programs, knitted together by a course guide developed and written by the course team. Fundamental to the course design, however, are the course tutors, who in most cases did not participate in the original development. Given the course 'package' of materials, tutors are expected to work with their distant students (through 'phone and mail contact) in ways they find most appropriate to their various students. With full academic qualifications, tutors are, in effect, the expert guides to the course terrain and can map different routes through that terrain through changes in the assignments as well as the specific work produced by the student. Tutors can add or substitute readings and design assigned projects that build from and with individual students' experiences and contexts. Much as Empire State College's individual degree programme is intended to provide motivation rooted in the student's personal goals, the tutors' capacity to modify courses is intended to link the specific learning to the student's contexts and concerns. Tutors are encouraged to explore with their students possible areas of interest or experience related to the course content. In the words of the Center's *Handbook for Tutors*:

> Your response to their work, and the notion of 'dialogue', embody a view of knowledge and of learning which does not attempt to separate knowledge, as some kind of commodity which can be distributed or transferred, from the act of knowing. While books may appear to many students to 'contain' knowledge, learning implies the reconstitution of such knowledge into their own frames of reference. Thus the firefighter student might typically be expected to integrate new theoretical insights into how people act in time of disaster with his own experience of such behaviors; the history student is enabled to reinterpret her hitherto taken-for-granted view of early America or later Europe (Empire State College, 1988, p. 7).

This paragraph and a revision of the *Handbook for Tutors* in which it appears were drafted by an OU staff tutor, Vincent Worth, on secondment to Empire State College. Worth had been one of the original course team members on D101 and assisted with the ESC adaptation in 1977. He returned in the mid-1980s to work with the Center for Distance Learning and revised the *Handbook*. The notion of the social nature of knowledge and its implications for education has become increasingly recognized and the works of Perry (1968), Brookfield (1986) and Gardner (1985; 1991) are taking their place alongside the classics of Dewey and Piaget. Yet few educational institutions were (or are) designed or organized to implement these notions in any fundamental way. Both the OU and Empire State College, as well as a number of other institutions, continue to grapple with these issues. Developments at the OU have moved much beyond the notion of 'tutor-proofed' courses of the early 1970s, and Empire State College staff continue to seek the balance in each student's curriculum among the needs of the student, the expectations of the communities for their educated members, and the rapidly evolving knowledge of academic specialists.

The joint Empire State College- and OU-sponsored 'The Student, Community and Curriculum' conference in 1991 (see Chapter 1) represented a meeting of the two institutions with colleagues from around the world, including several of the contributors to this book, to grapple with many of these issues. In his introduction to the conference proceedings, Alan Tait of the OU articulated the continuing challenge:

> What we hope this conference will make irrevocable is that the learner has intruded into the curriculum, and that in distance education and open learning it will be accepted that the tutor and counsellor have an educationally critical role acting as facilitator to the new knowledge that will be created as the student, in

his or her community(ies), relates to the educational institution (Tait, 1991, p. 2).

The commitment to that on the part of both the OU and Empire State College and their respective faculties continues, as does the determination to develop institutionally and programmatically not in similar ways but in ways most appropriate to different student needs and contexts. The parallels and counterpoints articulated through the various exchanges over the years have continued to provide grist for reflection, engendering insights, perspectives and valuable support within the small but growing community of educators committed to reforming their practices and institutions to serve their students.

Notes

1. Yet while the predictive power of the theory of quantum mechanics has led to important scientific breakthroughs, its correlation with or representation of 'reality' is admittedly open to question (cf Penrose, 1991).
2. See, for instance, the work of Tobias (1990) on the problems and varieties of approach to mathematics and sciences.

11 Deconstructing Contiguity

Garry Gillard

I work as an instructional designer in a school of humanities; I also teach in the school in both the internal and external modes. So it is logical – if not inevitable – that I should be trying to relate the two parts of my daily work, as I do in this chapter.

Important work is being done in the humanities with the concepts of production and reproduction. It is said by some feminists, for example, that under patriarchy woman is produced as a sign or as exchange value and reproduced as use value (see Rubin, 1975) so that in a traditional Christian marriage ceremony a man 'gives' the woman to be married to another man. Women are exchanged by men as part of the network of the transactions that maintain patriarchy and the control of women by men. Women are not allowed to see themselves as actors and producers, but only as acted upon and produced.

An analogy can be drawn between this scenario and that concerning students under contiguous education – being taught face-to-face.[1] They are also produced as listeners and learners, partly in order to maintain the status quo of the educational institution and of its main beneficiaries, lecturers; students are also reproduced as citizens through the agency of this most powerful but most latent of ideological state apparatuses: the educational system (Althusser, 1971).

In the distance education situation, on the other hand, institutional control over the construction of the learner is considerably weaker and learners are given the opportunity to produce themselves as such in a dialectical movement between ideological reproduction and individual production. With that freedom, of course, goes greater responsibility – which is one reason for the higher dropout rate in distance education as compared with contiguous education. Taking responsibility for self-production is considerably harder than allowing oneself to be subjected to processes of reproduction. But there it is: 'In its essence, distant study is *individual* study' (Bååth, 1982, p.7).

In texts produced by face-to-face teachers the voice is one that speaks of authorship – and the texts are produced to some extent for the pleasure of the teachers. On the other hand, and paradoxically perhaps, the text produced in writing by distance teachers is one that produces readership, that interests itself in the implied reader (Gillard, 1981). Because of the opportunity for reflection that the writing situation presents, it is more difficult for producers of distance education texts to speak with authority than for lecturers who, in the stressful demands of the moment, must rely on what they can draw from their individual selves. Distance education writers have the leisure to be empathetic towards their invisible readers.

The relationship between writers and readers is one in which more consideration is given for the situation of the Other. Consideration of theories of post-colonialism, and of the kinds of Other to which teachers relate, suggests that distant students are in a much more intimate and sympathetic relationship with their teachers, who typically write to them on a one-to-one basis as to a younger friend or offspring. Students confronted *en masse* in the lecture theatre by contrast represent a palpable Other with different presuppositions and expectations, often of a different generation, and who are there for different reasons; they are a potential threat: rebellious peasants, uncontrollable children, irresponsible and perennial youth. They must be treated as inferior, kept in their place, controlled by the language of authority. Writers of distance education texts, on the other hand, have, as their historical models, the caring epistles of the apostle Paul, the wise dialogues of the philosopher Plato, the society of the novels of Jane Austen and George Eliot.

This is a reflection on the meaning of 'distance' and on aspects of distance in education, some of which are beneficial, some dysfunctional – attempting to do in a philosophical context what Evans has already done in a sociological one (1989b).

When distance educators set out to define 'distance education' they usually proceed by contrast, in the negative, by working from what it is not (Bååth, 1981; Keegan, 1980). What I set out to do here is to deconstruct the ideology which privileges face-to-face or contiguous education over distance education, and also to show in which specific ways distance education is *prior to* contiguous education. I use an opposition between contiguous and distance education, albeit a rather artificial one, to make some contrastive points about both. I try to show that distance education is not an inferior and regrettable alternative to education on campus, but is in many ways prior to it, more original, better. This is of course something that all distance educators already know, but I think it is still worth considering the philosophical underpinnings of the craft and the historical basis of the development of one or two of the assumptions which underlie the understanding of the place of distance education in the broader context.

I also attempt to suggest, in practical terms, what conventional educators can learn from the designers of modes of education designed for individual use. The main argument of the chapter is in support of the usefulness – for reforming conventional education, whether 'open' or 'closed' – of distance-educational techniques and ways of thinking.

In the same way that anthropologists have defined 'the primitive' as being the absence of writing (Lévi-Strauss, 1972, p.101), in this discussion I am using as the *mark* of distance education *the absence of the teaching voice as the primary medium of teaching.* I take it that, whether consciously or not, speaking is perceived as the most essential means of carrying out conventional higher education. I wish to show that it is only one among a great many media and technologies. Contiguous education privileges the voice and so conceals the availability and effectiveness of these other media in the service of an ideology of control. Distance education offers the use of a greater range of means of communication and modes of teaching in the service of an ideology of empowerment.

The alleged precedence of contiguous education over distance education is a kind of confidence trick, an ideological assumption at best. Contiguous education in its most typical form – as conducted in the lecture theatre – is negative (with regard to the position taken in this chapter) in some of its essential elements. This may be seen, for example, in spatial arrangements which display iconically the unequal power relationships existing between lecturers and students through the binaries centre/periphery, one/many, high/low; and in any other of the elements of power which issue from a politics of education which keeps students in their place, rather than setting out to empower them. The typical structure of the lecture theatre from the centre of which the lecturer's gaze can engage with that of any student is similar in design and intention to the Benthamite Panopticon discussed by Foucault in *Discipline and Punish* (1979), a prison designed in such a way that the warders at the centre of a wheel-like structure can look down any of the spokes to see what any prisoner is doing at any time. All the prisoners are visible to their guards all of the time. The structure of this environment produces not only unequal power relationships but a magisterial style of teaching as well. And it has these results: alienated and anomic students.

The great Saussurean discovery was the arbitrariness of the sign,[2] the total dependence of meaning on itself, in the sense that at the linguistic level any sign achieves its meaning only in relation to all other signs and particularly those which are most nearly its opposite; hence its key oppositions: langue/parole, syntagm/paradigm, synchrony/diachrony (de Saussure, 1959). However, the Saussurean moment is only one in a series of binarisms, preceded by others: a/not a (Plato), mind/body (Descartes), nature/culture (Rousseau). And, of course, followed also: the writerly/the readerly, exogamy/endogamy, Self/Other, patriarchy/feminism, centre/periphery ... distance/contiguity.

Such oppositions may have ideological effects and socio-political outcomes, because such oppositions readily become, already are, political. As Godzich (1986) writes, the concepts in such oppositions as centre/periphery are not innocent concepts:

> There is nothing 'natural' or 'inevitable' or to be taken for granted in the setting up of center and periphery. It is always the result of specific and discernible operations: rhetorical ones in texts, power ones in the broader social area; though there may well be a gain in describing the latter in terms of the subtle analytics of textual operations (p.11).

Derrida (1981) deals with this at a greater degree of abstraction, a higher epistemological level:

> In a traditional philosophical opposition we have not a peaceful coexistence of facing terms but a violent hierarchy. One of the terms dominates the other (axiologically, logically, etc.), occupies the commanding position (p.41).

One might ask: is this the case only in philosophical oppositions? There is an assumption, not necessarily shared by distance educators themselves, but prevalent among those who work in or who are affected in some way by the education system, that distance education is an inferior form of teaching and learning. In this view it is obviously merely a substitute process maintained for the benefit of those unfortunates who cannot participate in the Real Thing, people such as prisoners, the handicapped, those living in places remote from population centres and women pregnant or with young dependants. It is a substitute for a learning situation where there a is teacher present who speaks, responds to learners and interacts with them in contiguous space and time. It is inferior because although teaching is also privileged over learning, it is assumed that they share a simultaneity of communication, the instantaneous experience of the meeting of minds.

I deploy a deconstructive approach to the epistemology of distance education, because 'to deconstruct the opposition is above all, at a particular moment, to reverse the hierarchy' (Derrida, 1981, p.41). The hierarchy in question is that which at this moment still privileges contiguous teaching over teaching-at-a-distance, internal over external, on-campus over off-campus, intramural over extramural, the lecture over correspondence, the school over the home, listening over reading, speech over writing. And the intention is to deconstruct the discourses which this privileging inhabits, from which it derives its being, for the reason given and by the process suggested by Culler (1983):

> To deconstruct a discourse is to show how it undermines the philosophy it asserts, or the hierarchical oppositions on which it relies, by identifying in the text the rhetorical operations that produce the supposed ground of argument, the key concept or premise (p.86).

Such a key concept is, paradoxically, the model that namers and definers have in mind: that of the *lecture* (which etymologically = reading). Whereas in its origin a text was read and exegeted, the lecture nowadays is a spoken text, spoken around the conception of the lecturer (although the whole thing may in some cases be a reading of a fully written-out text). The speaker, it is thought, has something to get across and will preferably talk *to* the idea in a conversational way suited to the audience. Thus: 'The explanation of DNA you would give to 14-year-olds may be very different from the explanation you would give to second-year undergraduate biochemists' (Brown and Atkins, 1988, p.21). 'DNA' is thought somehow to remain the same, although the discourse is to vary with the needs of speaker and listeners.

I begin where Derrida does, with the undermining of the phenomenological theory of language, in which language is essentially human (and non-natural). A key idea for Husserl is 'expression', which 'is meant, conscious through and through, and intentional' (Derrida, 1973, p.33). That is, meaning is found not just in the meaning of the words used by the speaker, but in what she or he *intends* them to mean. The concentration on expression leads on to the consequent importance of voice. With clear implications for the situation of a university lecturer, the assumption can be characterized in this way:

In person-to-person speech, the speaker is standing directly in front of the hearer, who can more readily imagine and locate the required act of animating consciousness. In such a situation, the meaning may well seem to be controlled behind the words, especially if the speaker imposes an authoritative interpretation: 'No, what I meant was ...', 'No, what I was trying to say was ...'. It is as though the very airiness of words on the breath, the very transparency of the medium in which spoken signifiers so briefly live, actually allowed the hearer to look straight through into the speaker's mind (Harland, 1987, p.126).

It is often thought that the availability of feedback is an essential characteristic of contiguous teaching so that, for example, 'non-verbal signals of puzzlement, bewilderment, and so on can be monitored by a lecturer' (Brown and Atkins, 1988, p.21). And the use of locutions such as those in the quotation may be seen as a putative response to the recognition of possible difficulties for an audience. They give something else away, however. What the Husserlian model of language implies is that the speaker already knows what he or she intends to say and through the transparent medium of the voice will transfer the information to the listeners, filling the little pitchers with the pure fluidity of knowledge. What the redirecting words ('what I was trying to say was') indicate, however, is that the first form of words used might not have conveyed what was desired at all and another, *supplementary*, form must be tried. The example – of the speaker casting around for the right words with which to construct her text – shows, not that there is an essence underlying the expression which will be conveyed if the appropriate form is found, but that it *is* the form of words which conveys the meaning. There is more than one 'DNA' – in fact an infinitude of them.

Brown and Atkins has been chosen as a text representative of a conventional pedagogy which discusses the importance of effective teaching. The emphasis in their writing in the experience of the lecture theatre is on the originary and on the experience of lecturers (rather than that of students). Brown and Atkins write that lecturers monitor signals from the audience, and modify what they say accordingly. There are several assumptions on which assertions of this kind rely. Learning is assumed to be a transfer of information from the mind of speakers to those of listeners through the pure medium of speech, as if the text of the lecture could be transferred whole, sentence by sentence. If a sentence or paragraph is perceived to have been ineffective with regard to this objective – as observed through audience reaction – another sentence or paragraph will be offered to replace it, until good communication has been achieved. Good communication here comprises a message from a sender to a recipient via a relatively noiseless medium. Knowledge is structured, not merely *like* a language, but *in* specific texts, uttered by speakers and received intact by listeners. If the message is correctly structured at source, it will very likely be rebuilt in the knowledge structures of listeners.

There is another assumption which is more concealed and more insidious, more ideological – being more unconscious – and that is that the experience of teachers, the pleasure in the production of the teaching text, is important. Pedagogy is written by teachers for teachers, to some extent for their pleasure and re-empowerment, so the emphasis there is on the body of teaching rather than on the student body. The interests in question are those of the teachers rather than those of the learners – and yet it is always piously assumed to be the case that the enterprise only exists for the sake of learning.

When they turn to the 'Component Skills of Lecturing' Brown and Atkins do not commence, as they might perhaps have, given the assumptions sketched above, with some notes on voice production or reading aloud; they immediately begin with supplements to the lecturer's voice: 'Using Audio-Visual Aids'. The implication seems to be that essential skills in lecturing include the employment of things which are additional to 'lecturing'. Perhaps because there is an assumption that lecturing is a 'natural' activity in which lecturers all engage more or less effectively, according to their inherent talents, the attention turns immediately to those extras which are more manageable by the pedagogue and which can be wheeled in to improve the given situation. Perhaps there is a simple assumption that all lectures can only be improved by such supplementation.

The *supplement* is a key idea for Derrida. One of his own examples refers to education. He points out that although Rousseau argues (in *Émile*) that a child is born in a state close to perfection, yet it is found to be necessary to subject the child to a process of education, to add something to the fine natural condition in which it arrives in the world, so that it seems that, in this case, although nature precedes culture, and is complete in itself, a plenitude to which education is an external addition, it is nevertheless *necessary* to supplement nature with education. There is, therefore, an *inherent* lack or absence within nature (Derrida, 1976, p.145–7). Similarly, it is necessary to supplement the oral lecture. The various processes of supplementation will usually begin well before the lecture hour with the lecturer writing notes, or perhaps the whole lecture. Some of these notes may be given to students as lecture outline 'handouts', some may be reproduced as overhead projections. There may be pre-tests and post-tests. The time of the lecture is a time which necessarily implies a past of pre-learning and preparation and a future containing review and recall.

Thus, for Brown and Atkins, the audio-visual 'aids' *are* the lecturing skills, and students learn by looking at – reading – the visual aids and by listening to the audio aids. The spatiality of the visual crosses the linearity of the lecture, with its assumption of additive learning. Time is persuaded to stand still for a moment and learning is allowed to become relational instead of cumulative. A second dimension is literally added to the unidimensional progression of the lecturing line: the plane surface encourages the invention of mapping.

Thus, Brown and Atkins point out that

many topics have networks of connections which might be exemplified better by diagrams or maps [and that] ideas which are linked through visual symbols are also likely to be retained in the long-term memory. It is therefore worth spending a little time [they continue] thinking out a visual presentation for key concepts, relationships, and processes. *The effort may well deepen your own understanding of a topic . . .*' (Brown and Atkins, 1988, p.26, emphasis added).

The reversal of the hierarchy which privileged the 'lecture' is completed in this moment. Not only will lecturing be essentially improved by the preparation of material designed to be *read*, but teachers themselves will actually learn something they did not know beforehand. It is clear by now that teaching, rather than being something prior and superior to learning, interpenetrates with it, and is to some extent at least dependent upon it.

The introduction by Brown and Atkins of the idea of long-term memory tends to deconstruct the assumption of simultaneity of learning in the lecture theatre and begins to suggest that distance in time and space might actually be functional in the context of contiguous teaching. Where and when does learning actually take place: at the moment of receiving the teaching message? In anticipation of receiving it (remembering the function of the 'advance organiser' [Ausubel, 1968])? At the moment when the lecture ends, as the last element of the whole picture is put into place? Shortly afterwards in discussion with the lecturer or with other students, in the lecture theatre or social club? When the student's lecture notes are reviewed that night or the next day – or the following year, when the crucial context for *really* understanding the point of the lecture is only just then available? Or possibly all of these? And is not distance in time demonstrably functional in the kind of concept mapping which it is suggested is required for learning?

Furthermore, is the lecturer really in contiguity with the learner? It is hard to resist anecdotal evidence in dealing with this question. I have sat in the back of a lecture theatre towards the end of a course on which I was tutoring and observed students doing anything but learning from the words being uttered at the front. One student was writing a letter, which I could see began with the situational: she wrote that she was in another boring lecture (although she could actually not have been bored with the given lecture, as she did not pause in her writing for the duration). Another student was reading a 'women's' magazine; two others were completely engaged in conversation for the whole hour, and so on. None of the students within my observational range was apparently listening to the lecturer at all.

Distance, it is claimed, is a reality in non-distance teaching, and can be either beneficial or dysfunctional.

Another key Derridean idea is the *trace*: internal teaching always already contains the trace of external teaching. From the time that the first teacher drew in the sand a representation of the territory of the tribe, the teaching became iterable: it was immediately alienable from the originary drawing hand, and reproducible in another patch of sand, or on a rock or on a cave wall. From the time that the first singer (such as the one we call 'Homer') composed the first verses of the first inchoate epic narrative, the story – and the technique – became physiologically memorable and capable of repetition.[3]

Lecturers typically read from their written notes (and may supplement the reading with 'handouts', 'overheads', audiotapes). This year's lecture ('on DNA', for example) is an approximation of last year's, being performed in relation to the same set of notes, but this year's lecture may be only a pale imitation of the last one, if the lecturer is not well and delivers the lecture poorly (although, in another sense, the 'lecture' itself is thought to be the 'same', in its being as the idea of itself: it is the trace in the performance).

So this year's lecture is actually different from last year's, although it is 'the lecture on DNA'. In its textual nature as *this* performance it exists in its own right, and also in the sense of its reception by *this* (year's) class, by *this* individual, and by *this* aggregation of students. It may differ from what the lecturer *intended* to say, because she has a cold, because her voice is not working well and could not convey what she meant. So the listeners, the students, do not get the idea too well, the meaning of what the lecturer was getting at will have to be supplemented, will be *deferred*, until the students can check with each other's notes, study the lecturer's handout, ask supplementary questions, look the concept up in the textbook, track it down. (But, as Derrida writes: 'Whoever believes that one tracks down some thing? One tracks down tracks', 1973, p.158.)

Derrida has a term for what he sees as this undecidability of meaning: by using the term 'différance', which combines the meaning of two verbs meaning 'differ' and 'defer', he is able to refer to the idea that the meaning always differs from itself and is always deferred. To use our own key term: it is always *at a distance*.

Note the forms some of the supplements take: they are written, and they pre-exist the lecture; the lecturer's notes, handouts, and the textbook are all in existence prior to the coming into being of the lecture event; they are there during it, and they will be there afterwards, to supplement and to disseminate the teaching.

Why then is there such importance placed on the *oral* delivery of the lecture, on the *voice* of the lecturer? It is because of that particular prejudgement which Derrida calls *logocentrism*, that preference not only for the uttered word, 'the inward rational principle of verbal texts', in that sense of *logos*, but also a prerequisite belief in 'the inward rational principle of human beings, and the inward rational principle of the natural universe' (Harland, 1987, p.146). The advantages of such a belief obviously reside in the security which any such a metaphysics brings, and which is its *raison d'être*.[4]

As I have pointed out, lecturers may in many cases, and for much of the time, actually be *reading* their own texts, or those of others, in the act of lecturing. In terms of its etymology the word 'lecture' in fact means 'reading', and refers to the origins of lecturing in the medieval university, where the reading was of a standard text by someone such as Aristotle, accompanied by an exegesis of it. This procedure is of course still carried out, though the majority of lecturers would think of most of their lecture material as being 'original', as the degree of intertextuality of any given text is for the most part actually not available to the consciousness of the person involved.

Having been written down, these lecturers' texts are then available for reproduction, and conscientious, or 'technologiate' lecturers – to coin a phrase by analogy with 'literate' and 'computerate' – will make use of the textuality of their material, of its commodification – by making use of technologies of writing. These may take various forms of 'handouts': of lecture notes, lecture outlines, even of the whole lecture transcribed. In the process of delivery they will take the form of overhead transparencies, diagrams, summaries and exemplars on various kinds of boards and display apparatuses. These are all, in the broad sense, technologies of writing.

I now want to consider very briefly those aspects of distance education which are of potential or actual great value to reforming contiguous education. I turn to those technologies (in the broadest sense of the word) of distance education which I believe may usefully be regarded as having priority in a fully extended range of pedagogies.

Firstly, there is design *per se*. Detailed planning is intrinsic to distance education, but not to conventional teaching where *ad hoc* decisions are more characteristic. Curricula in the two modes are designed in completely different ways. On-campus education is only designed at the most global and most particular levels, while distance education is characterized by an even and intensive design process throughout the development of its curriculum design. Let me try to show what I mean by this.

In my experience at least, programmes of study, and units within them, are designed with the reproduction of the institution as one of their primary aims. A university decides at the highest level that it is to teach a certain discipline and it appoints staff who profess appropriate expertise. They then design a programme to cover the salient moments in that discipline, break the curriculum up into components of convenient size (units, subjects, courses), assign lecturers to each of these component units, and they in their turn prepare – usually 'write' – a set of lectures to cover that ground. Inasmuch as objectives are conceived of, they would be expressed, explicitly or not, in terms of the needs of the institution. They would characteristically be couched in terms of 'the aims of the unit' being to 'introduce students to', or some such locution indicating an operation to be performed on students, rather than something that students either do themselves or that they acquire. It is typically not their needs that are expressed, but the 'unit's', that is, the staff's or the institution's or both.

The field of distance education, on the other hand, is characterized by explicit principles relating primarily to the organization of learning. In mixed-mode institutions at least, there is a flow-on effect of this pedagogical planning which in the long term is having an effect on conventional education, not only because independent study materials designed for distant students are being used by conventional educators as part of the on-campus, but also because conventional educators are learning – by osmosis – the benefits of good design.

To support this industrialized process, then, there are normally manuals of instructional design which characteristically make explicit, bring to consciousness, the processes of course design in a way, or at levels, that is not done with contiguous education. Such manuals typically begin by inviting unit writers to consider the kinds of people for whom their units are to be designed. Community needs are addressed before those of the university, individuals' before institutions'. I am not arguing that disciplines and institutions should not continue their self-reproductive practices: this is probably in the nature of all institutions. I am, however, suggesting that contiguous education teachers should do as distance educators do and, in the best interests of their students, consider who they are, where they are coming from and what *their* needs might be.

Distance education is also characterized by technical aspects of its pedagogy which are not normally attended to consciously by practitioners of contiguous education. Concepts such as advance organizers, concept maps, sequencing and so on, usually play little part in the design of contiguous education, but form parts of the staple diet of instructional design in distance education. I am not of course saying that contiguous education lecturers do not consider the sequence in which they present material and may not attempt to map the network of concepts that they are teaching on overhead transparencies or whatever; what I am arguing is that thinking in these terms is *foregrounded* in the theory and practice of distance education in a way that it is not in contiguous education. In addition, I am suggesting that there is no *intrinsic* reason why this should be the case; the reasons are historical and contextual.

Under this rubric I first want to discuss print technologies which are specifically associated with distance education, including verbal text, graphics, illustrations, maps, diagrams and the like. We are on familiar ground here, in that contiguous educators usually have no difficulty in including these elements in their daily teaching. This will normally occur, however, on a casual basis, as each particular need is perceived. What I want to address is the incorporation of distance education materials as ready-made wholes into contiguous education. This has always been standard practice at some mixed-mode Australian institutions like Murdoch and Deakin Universities, but has recently been the subject of a study at the University College of Southern Queensland, where it is apparently a revolutionary practice (Taylor and White, 1991).

The cases of other communications technologies are a little more complicated in that media such as audiotape and videotape are not as yet as taken-for-granted as print, though this is changing. Some other

193

media, such as broadcast radio and TV, electronic mail, tele(phone)conferencing, and videoconferencing at present are not part of the range of techniques considered under the rubric of contiguous education. What might be the effect of contiguous educators reflecting on these practices? In what ways might existing forms of communication using these media benefit contiguous practices?

First, and obviously, audio and video material may be used as ancillary material in the lecture theatre. More profoundly, lecturers may come to think in terms of a range of sensory availability, in that hearing is not the only sense able to be employed in learning, and listening not the only mode of mental activity. In the realm of the visual, a range of kinds of seeing/viewing/reading may be mobilized in the presentation of texts (by which I do not only mean those constructed of words) which are stationary, or serial, or in motion. In the auditory realm, it need not be taken for granted that listening always produces orderly concept acquisition. Not only may different kinds of listening, not-listening and partly-listening produce different kinds of learning effects (changes in the organism) but it might be possible for students to *talk back*.

Then there are: project work, independent study contracts and other categories of learning which are predominantly learner-initiated and directed, perhaps even assessed. These are the *echt* distance education activities, but they may also have a place in mainstream contiguous education. Last, I might mention student networks – self-help groups and the like. In the distance education situation these may be epistolary or telephone networks, as well as meetings in study centres or homes. They correspond to small-group work in the contiguous education situation.

To sum up this argument we might adopt as our slogan a phrase such as 'Contextualised Independent Learning'. Learning in distance education is supervised but not invigilated, organized but not controlled, student-centred but not anarchic. The context referred to in the slogan is provided by the course, the unit, the programme of study, the book, the study guide, but it is also capable of gesturing towards the situation of independent learners – whether they sit in classrooms or not. As Cook (1989) asks: 'Is there liberation in distance?'

Notes

1. In this chapter I will often use the term 'contiguous education' to refer to the most typical kind of 'face-to-face' teaching, that is, the kind of education which

is conventionally carried on in lecture theatres; other terms which may be used include 'proximal' and 'conventional'.

2. C. S. Peirce was actually the first to state this proposition.

3. See, for example, Lord (1965) *The Singer of Tales*, for an account of oral composition, and a deconstruction of the Homeric legend.

4. Moodie points out that this situation also prevails in 'what in our culture is the most authoritative institution for determining truth, the law. In our courts oral testimony is always preferred over written (indeed, only relatively recently has non-oral evidence been accepted as other than an exception to the normal rules of evidence), and oral argument by lawyers is always preferred over written arguments' (personal correspondence).

12 Educational Technologies: reforming open and distance education

Terry Evans and Daryl Nation

This book began with an attempt to understand distance education and open learning in the context of the turbulent economic, political and social changes that are sweeping our world. Its contributors are committed to the vitality which is born of the confluence between practice, research and theory in open and distance education. All contributions suggest, in a variety of ways, that enduring vitality within these fields rests upon an outward gaze which connects with theory, research and practice in other educational endeavours and in society more generally. Workers within open and distance education have much to contribute to wider educational reform and much to learn from their colleagues in closely related fields and beyond.

In 1987, when first venturing into public debate in the field, we attempted to answer the question: Which future for distance education? We challenged the tendency for practitioners, research-ers and theorists to conceptualize distance education as an 'instructional industry'(Evans and Nation, 1987). These ideas have been extended in a number of published works since then (for example, Evans and Nation, 1989a; 1989c). To summarize severely: on one hand, there is a possibility that open and distance education will remain captive to 'educational technologists' with behaviourist orientations and become mass-produced forms of programmed learning in which students are essentially alienated from their teachers and fellow students or, on the other, there is the possibility of educators using technologies to create systems of teaching and learning which sustain dialogue between teachers and students who are separated in both space and time.

Five years later we remain convinced of the basic validity of both our critique of instructional industrialism and the approaches to practice, research and theory in distance education which inform it. However, in a variety of endeavours we have been involved in jointly and separately in recent years, we have come to rethink this original critique, especially in terms of educational technology. These recent endeavours have included: a postgraduate course in distance education taught by Deakin University and the University of South Australia (discussed in Chapter 3); development of two sociology courses employing texts which are radically dialogic; policy work on the reformation of an institution's system of teaching in the context of a massive reorganization of distance education nationally in Australian universities (discussed in Chapter 8); several evaluation and research projects and a sustained attempt to broaden our theoretical understanding. As is typically the case in open and distance education, much of this work has involved extensive collaboration with colleagues in our own and other institutions, some of whom are amongst the contributors to this book.

In this chapter we wish to deal critically with our own conceptions of educational technology and those of other practitioners, researchers and theorists as they relate to possible reforms within and from open and distance education. Our critique of instructional industrialism relied heavily upon a critical analysis of educational technology, especially as it had been employed in the UK Open University (OU) (Evans and Nation, 1989c, pp. 240–252). Recently, we have offered an extension of this thinking which also includes a basic shift in our understanding of educational technology, its role within distance education and the place of each within education more generally (Evans and Nation, 1992, pp. 3–13). This chapter takes these lines of analysis further with the purpose of exploring the relationship between educational technology and the nature of educational reform.

An important objective of the chapter is a continuation of the critical debate across the paradigmatic divide between instructional industrialists and their critics. Many potential contributors to the debate have yet to engage with it and there are many instances of unawareness of logically related ideas. Our reading in the literature suggests there are substantial bodies of relevant ideas, which could either complement or contradict each other, which exist in benign ignorance of each other. It is arguable that the complexities and diversities of late modernity are such that people are forever unable to make all the potential connections of intellectual life. Certainly, the more we look the more there is to find. Here we have focused on contributions which accord with our strategic purposes for practice, research and theory in reforming open and distance education.

There is compelling evidence that such debate produces shifts in theoretical and practical approaches which will encourage constructive changes within open and distance education and also foster exchanges between practitioners, researchers and theoreticians from other educational domains. Broader economic, political and social changes are creating demands for reform within education to both curricula and pedagogies. 'Educational technology' can be rescued from instructional industrialism, renovated and employed as a central concept in reforms of education in 'post-industrial societies' which are aimed at sustaining dialogue and democracy.

Centring educational technologies

In moving educational technology to the centre of our understanding of open and distance education, we regard educational technology not simply as sets of machines or peripheral processes, but as a fundamental aspect of the education process. Education is at the basis of human and social development. Since the evolution of the human species its members have learned about the physical, human and spiritual worlds which surround them; they have also played their parts in creating, recreating, damaging and destroying those worlds. Human cultures are built on the gradual and selective accumulation of knowledge as each generation communicates with its members and offspring. Education represents systematic procedures for teaching and learning aspects of the culture developed by present and preceding generations. Therefore, it is possible through historical and other analyses to trace the antecedent knowledges which constitute elements of contemporary cultures. It is also possible to uncover the pedagogies and technologies used throughout educational history.

It is important that we recognize that pedagogy and technology are – and have always been – fundamental and inseparable elements of education. Too often it seems, especially with the advent of the 'new' communications technologies, people understand technology as if it were a recent addition to education and/or separate from it. It is true that some technologies are constructed outside of education and then are adapted and incorporated into its fabric later; however, technologies of different kinds have informed and/or been produced by the pedagogies obtaining in particular educational contexts.

Educational technologies are not simply the tools of educators – although this is a popular misconception. Rather, they are the knowledge, values and practices which constitute the development and use of those tools. Wajcman (1991) explains this in terms of technology more generally:

> ... 'technology' is a form of knowledge.... Technological 'things' are meaningless without the 'know-how' to use them, repair them, design them and make them. That know-how often cannot be captured in words. It is visual, even tactile, rather than simply verbal or mathematical. But it can also be systematized and taught, as in the various disciplines of engineering.
>
> Few authors would be content with this definition of technology as a form of knowledge. 'Technology' also refers to what people do as well as what they know. An object such as a car or a vacuum cleaner is a technology, rather than an arbitrary lump of matter, because it forms part of a set of human activities. A computer without programs and programmers is simply a useless collection of bits of metal, plastic and silicon (pp. 14–15).

A piece of chalk and a blackboard, or even a stick and a patch of sandy ground are educational technologies in the hands of 'educators'. Such educators may be primary school teachers, army instructors, tribal elders or outdoor educators using their tools to communicate an aspect of their culture to the learners. Likewise, videoconferencing equipment or personal computers can be used as educational technologies by educators who know how to employ them for pedagogical purposes. Technologies are so fundamental to education that it is difficult to imagine educational contexts devoid of them. Certainly, any such contexts would need to be beyond forms of architecture, furniture and other physical products of human endeavour.

This understanding of educational technology does not accord with that used by many colleagues who are known as 'educational technologists'. Their approach concentrates on the technical use of electronic and audio-visual media and eschews considerations of the broader social and political contexts of their work. However, it is vital that such broader contextual factors are taken into account when shaping educational reforms – reforms which inevitably are imbued with educational technology. Ironically, understanding open and distance education as technological processes will be anathema to others of our colleagues who prefer to keep educational technology and technologists at arm's length. Some years ago we would have agreed with them; however, by understanding educational technology as a fundamental aspect of all teaching and learning, all educators are educational technologists!

One important influence in our rethinking of educational technology and our endeavour to give it a central place in educational practice has been the work of David Hamilton (1977;

1987; 1989a; 1989b; 1990a; 1990b). Hamilton has been engaged in distance education as a practitioner and has referred to the field in his theoretical work, but his central focus has been on research, theory and practice in the development of classroom education. Our engagement with his ideas is an instructive story in this context.

In 1989 we became interested in the course, *Classroom Processes*, developed by Rob Walker and his colleagues at Deakin University (Evans, 1991; Nation and Walker, 1992). The course is a reflection of Walker's long-standing interest in visual and other media which is something he explores further in this book (see Chapter 2). Visual representations of classroom life were a central feature of the course. A video took its students to a variety of classrooms and still photographs were used extensively in the printed teaching materials for similar purposes. Its students were expected to respond in kind. It is a compelling example of the centrality of educational technology to educational reform at the course level (Morgan, 1991).

Hamilton was commissioned to create a piece on the history of classrooms for the *Classroom Processes* video. He works at the University of Liverpool and was formerly at the University of Glasgow, and had been a visiting scholar at Deakin University (see, for example, 1990a). Walker was aware of Hamilton's long-term research project on classroom development. He had been able to report on this research in print but was able to use only 11 examples from an extensive collection of pictures and diagrams of classrooms in two substantial books (Hamilton, 1989a; 1990b). Yet his lectures and other presentations were replete with these images and the audio-visual technology embedded in the video allowed Hamilton to present a 'guest lecture' to students across the miles and years. The piece was commissioned, planned and written using e-mail, telephone and fax across the globe. The recording was made in Glasgow and edited in Geelong for integration into the course video as *The changing schoolroom*.

Readers may be forgiven for thinking that it is the discussion of the proficient use of both communications and educational technology by educators that is the purpose here – and this is partly the case. However, the major import of *The changing schoolroom* is the perspective it provides on the history of educational technology. The changing schoolroom makes no reference to 'distance education' but it offers a cogent synopsis of the various pedagogies which had been practised in European classrooms from the Middle Ages to the twentieth century. It relates these to the economic, ideological, political and social circumstances within which they had developed. Above all, it adopts the broader view of technology articulated by Wajcman above. Hamilton's book, *Learning about Education* (1990b), offers complementary ideas. It emerged from a series of lectures in which he discusses the fruits of his own research in the context of introducing aspiring teachers to the development of the principles and practices of teaching. Its references to distance education are brief but incisive.

Hamilton's discussion of the relationships between the development of production technologies and pedagogies are central to our purposes. He employs a typology of pedagogies analogous to technological changes in the economy: 'handicraft, domestic, batch and continuous production' (Hamilton, 1990b; pp. 67–71). Handicraft pedagogies were used by 'a specialist servant (tutor, nanny, governess)' who was employed within a family to teach various learned and polite accomplishments. Domestic pedagogies were practised by specialist teachers who conducted schools from their homes or in other private contexts which were analogous to the small workshops of the 'domestic system' of production. Batch production was the basis of the larger workshops which were integral to the emergence of industrialism and the early factory system. It was the principle underpinning 'the batch mode of mass production', Hamilton contends, which created systems of standardized schooling in the nineteenth century founded on class teaching and within which 'children were moved through the curriculum in batches' (p. 69).

According to Hamilton, the twentieth century has seen the emergence of mass schooling akin to a Fordist production line within which students 'work through a sequential and linear curriculum – itself a production line – at their own pace' (1990b, p. 70). In more recent versions, a modular curriculum is provided which allows learners to 'find a personalized pathway through the curriculum' following their 'own interests through the storehouse of humane experience' (p. 70). He cites the OU as a significant example and offers the following telling summary of its instructional industrialism:

Historically, one of the most important manifestations of continuous educational production was the establishment of the Open University, a distance-learning institution started in Britain in the late 1960s. The organization of the Open University is based on the assumption that students work at home (i.e. individually); that they follow a pre-packaged modular curriculum largely at their own pace; and that their learning activities are regulated largely through a policy of continuous assessment. As in the factory system, there is an elaborate division of labour in the Open University between, for instance, those who encode the curricula (course teams); those who distribute the curricula (course managers), and those who decode the curricula (course tutors). Indeed, the machinery of the Open University also includes counsellors who, rather like personnel managers, tackle the industrial relations (or learning relations) problems that are thrown up by the workings of the entire system.

The Open University is, therefore, a very sophisticated machine. As a production line, it needs constant fine tuning, maintenance and renewal. When working it is an enormous, efficient and accessible knowledge factory. But the systemization built into the machinery of the Open University is also its Achilles' heel. There is very little tolerance of error in the system. As in any moving production line, one small disruption (e.g. a postal strike) brings chaos. Moreover, Open University learners have little control over the workings of the system. At times, no doubt, they feel the smallest of cogs in the largest of machines. In times of crisis, techno-defence – passivity and patience in the face of mechanical malfunction – is probably the only thing that they learn (Hamilton, 1990b, p. 71).

With a view to post-Fordist futures, Hamilton suggests that recent developments in information technology may have revolutionary effects upon pedagogies in the twenty-first century which are just as significant as those made by 'Gutenberg's innovative system of production' from the fifteenth century (1990b, pp. 72–73). Hamilton cautions against the use of his typology as an evolutionary prescription because, for example, wealthy institutions, such as Oxbridge, can still practise versions of handicraft production.

Hamilton's work represents the type of analysis which assists in understanding educational technologies against the background of the social circumstances which influence their development. He has not attempted to provide a substantial discussion of open and distance education, although his brief analysis of the significance of the OU rings true to us as outsiders, but is contested by some of the contributors who are insiders. Certainly, the OU contributions in this book can be seen as critical engagements with instructional industrialist aspects of the University; it is a matter of conjecture as to whether they represent oppositional or marginal forms of OU life or are just part of a diverse post-industrialist university.

Hamilton's work is of considerable assistance in any attempt to broaden horizons when theorizing and researching educational technology. His insights are often contained in brief observations and summaries of specialist scholarship and, like Bolton (1986), they offer a complement to our attempts to harness Giddens's social theory for work in our field (Evans and Nation, 1992, pp. 8–10).

Many contributors to the literature in open and distance education have analysed aspects of educational technology. Garrison (1985) and Nipper (1989) have offered similar but independently developed models for understanding the 'three generations of technological innovations in distance education' (Nipper, 1989). Both Garrison and Nipper are interested specifically in 'interactive' forms of teaching at a distance which are based upon telecommunications and computer technologies. We shall consider Nipper's analysis here because it has been employed recently as the basis for two further discussions of technological change in distance education to which we wish to refer.

For Nipper the three generations of distance education are each based on the 'development of production, distribution, and communications technologies' (Nipper, 1989). The first generation, 'correspondence teaching', was engendered towards the end of the nineteenth century by the developments in printing and railways which 'made possible the production and distribution of teaching materials in large quantities to geographically dispersed learner groups'. Interaction between teachers and students was 'slow, sparse and limited to the periods when learners submit scheduled assignments' (p. 63).

'Multi-media distance teaching', the second generation, 'has been developed since the late 1960s, integrating the use of print with broadcast media, cassettes, and – to some degree – computers'. These approaches employ similar interaction between teachers and students as correspondence teaching, 'but include telephone counselling and some face-to-face tutorials' (p. 63).

The 'production and distribution of teaching/learning material to learners', Nipper suggests, are the fundamental features of both generations; there is minimal 'interactivity' between teachers and students and 'communication amongst learners has been more or less non-existent' (p. 63). In their efforts to provide education for students unable to attend traditional classrooms, the creators of these systems of distance education have made learning 'into an individual rather than a social process' (p. 64). It has been the development of 'interactive communication facilities' such as computer conferencing, Nipper contends, which has created the possibilities for a 'third generation' of distance education (p. 64–65).

Nipper's model has proved appealing as a basis for two recent examinations of the impact of electronic information technologies on distance education. Bates (1991) has provided a sobering review of Pelton's (1991) call for a global system of tele-education. Taylor (1992) has discussed the prospect of the adoption of telecommunications technologies in Australian universities.

The OU, Bates (1991) contends, is the paradigm case of the institutions which adopt the 'industrial model' and offer multi-media distance education. It invests heavily in highly produced courses delivered by 'one-way' media and it provides 'two-way' communication with students through correspondence tuition and limited face-to-face tutorials and summer schools (see Chapter 5). The efficiency of such institutions rests upon high enrolments and the consequent economies of scale which are possible in course production and delivery. Bates is interested in the challenges and opportunities of the new interactive technologies, particularly computer conferencing. Yet there are many organizational, political and financial impediments to their adoption, especially where institutions provide mass education. The instructional industrialist structures and practices of such organizations prove both self-perpetuating and virtually unshakeable in the face of educational approaches and technologies which advocate dialogue.

Models such as those of Garrison and Nipper make compelling common sense to practitioners in distance education. Much of the theorizing and researching which have dominated the field in the last two decades has striven to explain and justify the transition from correspondence to distance education. The interplay between the emergence of new forms of educational and communications technologies is often discussed but rarely critically analysed in terms of its broader social and political contexts. Some individuals and institutions are eager to adopt new media for educational purposes, yet others resist their intrusion.

A consideration of the above ideas suggests that a useful theoretical model can be employed which regards changes in educational technology as a central evolutionary process related to wider technological developments in societies. This is not to suggest evolution in some 'natural' sense, but rather to understand educational technologies as developments from, and contributors to, other technological processes extant in societies.

Bridging the educational technology chasm

By creating the Institute of Educational Technology (IET) in 1970, the OU had a significant influence in institutionalizing educational technology within distance education (Evans and Nation, 1989c, pp. 239–45). It is clear that for all its achievements the IET has struggled to create any clear conception for itself of educational technology in theory and practice. Detailed public accounts of this 'crisis of identity', as MacKenzie (1976) expressed it, are very instructive.[1]

David Hawkridge became the foundation director of the IET and Professor of Applied Educational Sciences in 1970. David Harris worked as a junior academic in the IET for three years from 1970.

Subsequently, he left the OU for a position in sociology and media studies but, as he mentions in Chapter 4, he has continued to work as a tutor on various OU courses. Along with another OU staff member, David Sewart (1981), Harris (1987) is one of the most cited critics of 'packaged learning'. In his contribution to the 'crisis of identity' debate he suggested:

> ... educational technology at the OU has not produced answers to the questions involved in designing meaningful curricula and pedagogies. Instead it has been diverted into answering far less important questions concerned with the smooth running of a given teaching system. This teaching system was shaped as much by administrative and political pressures as by any particular educational goals, and in three short years it had already become institutionalized, reified and unmodifiable in essence. Educational technology not only failed to prevent this happening, but actually permitted and even legitimized it, even if unknowingly, since educational technology became an important part of the process whereby educational aims and processes became defined in purely operational terms. . . . Education at the OU has been reduced to a basically administrative process involving the production and distribution of educational commodities – such as packets of knowledge and educational certificates. . . . The progressives at the OU – including the progressive educational technologists – have succeeded in creating only a progressive appearance for what is the old educational domination (Harris, 1976, pp. 44–5).

At the time, Harris recognized his views as 'personal, subjective and controversial' and that they were shared by few of his colleagues. His subsequent research changed his views in terms of details, but not in terms of theoretical substance which is framed by the critical theory of Habermas and his colleagues. He demonstrates how the 'rational practice' of educational technology creates a teaching system which attempts to control or programme students' learning (Harris, 1987). He recognizes that students and staff have the capacity to challenge and resist the system, although he expresses pessimism about the likelihood of thoroughgoing change (Harris and Holmes, 1976, pp. 84–85).

Including his own contribution to the 'crisis of identity' debate, Hawkridge has offered three detailed discussions of the nature, development and future of educational technology (1976; 1981; 1991). He has also published two substantial volumes relating to new information technology and education (Hawkridge, 1983; Hawkridge et al., 1988). Hawkridge defines educational technology 'as the systematic application of scientific or other organised knowledge to the practical tasks of education' (1976, pp. 8–9). He derives this definition from that used by Saettler in his *A History of Instructional Technology* and from Galbraith's definition of technology 'as the systematic application of scientific or other organised knowledge to practical tasks' (p. 8). Following Saettler he locates educational technology against the development of various educational methodologies, including those created by the Ancient Greeks, Abelard, Comenius, Bell and Lancaster and the significant contributors to modern educational psychology (pp. 9–14). Yet, as he wrote, he regarded programmed learning – of the Skinnerian and post-Skinnerian varieties – as the essential basis of educational technology. It was an applied science which eschewed 'theoretical-deductive' in favour of 'empirical-inductive modes of thought' (p. 27). He emphasized the need for practical approaches providing for the needs of learners. However, his discussion of the institutionalization of educational technology, through various private and public agencies, suggests that learners' needs would usually be understood through the filters of institutional requirements (pp. 21–26). All his references to science at this juncture suggest a commitment to pre-Popperian and pre-Kuhnian method and little appreciation of the competing understandings espoused by Harris.

Five years later Hawkridge (1981) offered another synthesis of 'the evolution of a theoretical foundation' for the field under the title: 'The telesis of educational technology'. Confirming his faith in positivistic social science he began with a dictionary definition of ' "telesis" as "progress intelligently planned and directed; the attainment of desired ends by the application of intelligent human effort" ' (p. 4). A cogent and sharply critical summary of the theoretical principles and key thinkers of behaviourist programmed learning, instructional technology and educational technology signalled a significant shift in his thinking. In part he was responding to critiques such as Harris's (1976) which he portrayed as follows:

I believe he listed, in a somewhat hostile fashion that many resented at the time, some of the weaknesses of educational technology based upon behaviourist assumptions. He was unable to provide solutions but at least he drew attention to problems that could not be solved within the intellectual framework of many educational technologists at that time (Hawkridge, 1981, p. 11).

Hawkridge completed the article with a thorough review of work by critics from within educational technology who drew from theory, research and practice outside behavioural psychology and thus established the foundations for a new educational technology. A decade later he returned to this theme.

By 1991 he could identify four challenges which had been made to educational technology throughout the previous two decades: the theoretical challenge from cognitive science; the technological challenge from information technology, the political challenge from the left; and the moral challenge from radical critics. Cognitive science, especially through the ideas of Bruner, Piaget and Vygotsky, has challenged behaviourist theories of learning in psychology; educational technology, he suggests, should 'reject these failed theories and adopt those that appear more likely to find support from research!' (Hawkridge, 1991, p.104). Information technology overlaps significantly with educational technology and he endorses the thoroughgoing interchange between the two fields. He urges an alliance with critics of information technology and commends Chandler (1990) for his critique of computing and the research agenda he proposed.

According to Hawkridge, the field has survived attacks by 'left wing' critics (such as Harris) who 'seek to reveal educational technology for what it is, to unmask its essence and mode of operation and to lay the foundation for learners' emancipation through rooting it out' (Hawkridge, 1991, p. 105). He mentions Robins and Webster as making the point, also made by Harris, that educational technologists 'pretend that technology is a neutral force' (p. 105). Robins and Webster, and Fox (1989) draw upon Lyotard's post-modern theory of commodified knowledge which can be used to understand distance education as part of a 'knowledge industry' from which students purchase packages of knowledge. Without fully endorsing such views, Hawkridge rejects Holmberg's critique of their approach as political rather than scholarly and argues that educational technologists must take up the political challenge.

Responding to the critique of 'educational design' by Mansfield and Nunan (1978), Hawkridge identifies radical critics who challenge the moral basis of his field. He concludes his synthesis of these views with the observation:

Two key values are held by educational designers: insistence upon knowledge derived from 'rational' or theoretical sources rather than practice or intuition, and upon dividing teaching into design and execution phases. Both conceal the intent to manage or control other people ... (Hawkridge, 1991, p. 107).

Hawkridge's purpose is to encourage educational technologists to meet these challenges by identifying the 'scientific *and* philosophical underpinnings' of their discipline. He calls for debate with the critics and further research. He has summarized the views of critics fairly and offered constructive criticism of them, but the above statement demonstrates that paradigmatic differences remain and will be difficult to overcome. Critical theorists such as Fox and Harris, for example, are regarded as making a 'political challenge', when their work is as demonstrably empirical and theoretical as that of 'cognitive scientists'.

The majority of researchers and theorists who have worked within fields such as cognitive science, which draw upon psychology, have considerable difficulty in regarding 'political issues' as inherent in the problems requiring explanation. This is exemplified in the recent debate relating to 'constructivism' and 'objectivism' in the journal *Educational Technology* (May and September, 1991; February, 1992). Hawkridge (1991, p. 104) has discussed the work of Jonassen (1991a; 1991b), who is a key person in the debate (see also Duffy and Jonassen, 1991a; 1991b). Put simply, constructivism recognizes that any scientific study of learning must understand the meanings which individuals bring to and create within the social situations they occupy. It is yet another version of a theoretical and methodological debate which is familiar to most students of disciplines such as history, philosophy and sociology. These issues have been raised within psychology before, to little positive effect (see, for example, Gergen, 1982; Harré, 1979, 1984; Harré and Secord, 1972). While these thinkers take account of the importance of power in human affairs, there is little consideration of this important issue in the debates among the educational technologists. Yet, with reformation as much a political as a rational process, and with educational technology being central in current educational reformations, it seems axiomatic that educational technology is as much a focus of and instrument for political ends as anything else.

Our own theoretical inclination has been informed by a critical appraisal of Giddens's social theory and its applications to distance education (Evans and Nation, 1987). This book and its predecessor worked to a more practical agenda in general sympathy with this approach. Issues from the broader ideological and political agenda have not been avoided, but there has been a concentration on the effects of government policies on systems of open and distance education and on power relations at institutional level. For example, the choice of the teaching strategies for a course is as much an ideological as it is a rational-scientific choice. It could even be a choice between approaches based upon constructivism or objectivism or an attempt to provide students with understanding of both, in an attempt to empower them as learners (Nation, 1987; 1989; 1991).

Morgan suggests that there is a 'new educational technology' at work in the IET which has fostered research and evaluation dealing with:

group processes in course teams, ideological critiques of the teaching of courses in information technology, studies in the qualitative-phenomenological tradition and social historical analyses of course development (Morgan, 1990, p. 14).

Many of these developments, Morgan suggests, have stemmed from responses to critiques from 'critical theorists'.

Harris has continued a constructive engagement with the OU teaching system, working as a tutor on a variety of courses. Harris suggests in Chapter 4 that the MA in Education courses he tutors for the OU were based on a critical approach with which he had considerable sympathy. He recognizes the irony that similar courses were abandoned in his own college during the Thatcher government's attacks on teacher education. His pessimism has softened in the practical circumstances of tutoring and his engagement with developments in critical theory and associated fields has given him fresh insights into teaching OU students. His practice of multi-media teaching within a conventional college context draws both upon his experience and research at the OU and his reading of media theory (Harris, 1992). He willingly accepted the opportunity to provide a revised critique of educational technology within the MDEd course discussed in Chapter 3. While he remains constructively pessimistic, demonstrably he has been able to put his theories into practice (Harris, 1991, pp. 218–225).

While many deep divisions exist between those who are struggling towards understandings of, and practical involvement with, 'new educational technologies', there are reasonable grounds for suggesting that the various competing parties are interested in constructive exchanges of ideas in terms of theory, research and practice. A search for complete consensus in this regard would seem at odds with the facts. The adherents of the competing approaches have learned much from their disputes, both from their opponents and intellectual fellow-travellers. The fundamental issue is not the survival of some defined parts of academic territories but the need to keep reforming our educational practices. Distance education, educational technology and open learning are all important overlapping fields in these endeavours; those who currently occupy them must continue to look outwards to provide ideas developed within them to colleagues in related fields and to search for new ideas in other contexts.

Educational reformations

Thus far we have explored the nature and divisions within educational technology and have located it centrally within education and, therefore, educational reform. We wish to conclude by referring to some practical issues and speculating about future educational reformations. The purpose, however, is not only to inform about interesting practices, but also to set the agenda for research and theoretical work.

Paul Levinson, a philosopher with strong practical credentials in distance education, 'is president of Connected Education, Inc., a not-for-profit organization that offers courses via computer tele-conferencing for graduate and undergraduate academic credit in conjunction with the New School for Social Research' (1989, p. 253). He has taught many courses, mostly in the areas of media studies and technological development. Much of his teaching is truly international as 'Connect Ed' has students in Central, North and South America, England, Japan, the Middle East and Singapore (Levinson, 1988, pp. 205, 216–17).[2]

In harmony with the model of three generations of educational technology offered by Garrison and Nipper, Levinson (1989) argues that computer-mediated communication is as important to the development of 'the cognitive media' as 'the alphabet and the printing press' (p. 48). Text-based media have cognitive superiority over the 'literal audio-visual media that replicate the content of human communications': they allow their readers to have 'contact with any idea ever thought, any person anywhere, and at any time'. Books were the first breakthrough of this kind and computer-mediated communication takes the same processes further, especially in terms of speed of communications and efficiency of information storage (pp. 45–8). This view seems to privilege unjustifiably printed alphabetic texts and to ignore the importance of the visual arts. Representations of visual art and those arts themselves employing the audio-visual media are surely very effective forms of communication (see, for example, Hughes, 1980; Waters, 1990).

Levinson's approach provides a substantial basis for researchers and practitioners who are interested in understanding the mediated nature of education and using this to develop their own teaching and research. The restructuring of the media as providers of 'infotain-ment' and their relationship with education, as explored by Walker in Chapter 2, would benefit from his ideas. Walker and Levinson are both interested in the deconstruction of the conventional classroom and the nature of its possible replacements. These approaches eschew behavioural psychology and instructional design but they do not ignore psychological theory and research; they regard cognitive psychology as a most fruitful theoretical domain. They draw more heavily upon the philosophy of science, media studies, artificial intelligence and literary theory. Feenberg (1989) and Harisim (1989) also range very productively across these territories. An excellent synthesis by Davie and Wells (1991) explores existing research on teaching in both classrooms and computer-mediated communications to demonstrate that the latter can be superior in empowering students to participate more often and more critically.

A broader conception of educational technology allows for a more thorough understanding of the challenges, difficulties and opportunities offered by the newer technologies which are becoming available progressively in open and distance education. Furthermore, it assists us to understand that these technologies are developments from previous pedagogies, including the classroom, and that these are the roots of the reformations which are occurring at present. This is especially the case in open and distance education as they struggle with reforming their various historically-rooted institutional forms to cope with contemporary circumstances.

For decades, distance educators, especially those who have worked in conjunction with campus-based institutions, have practised, researched and theorized about the synergy which can occur in 'mixed-mode' or 'dual-mode institutions' (for example, see Campion and Kelly, 1988; Jevons, 1984; Smith and Kelly, 1987; Taylor and White, 1991). Recently, Rumble (1992) has raised this issue from the perspective of the distance teaching universities, in a broad ranging discussion based upon the strategic principles of business planning. Despite their capacity to develop and deliver high quality courses in a cost-effective manner and to concentrate exclusively upon the needs of part-time students, distance teaching universities (DTUs) cannot compete effectively against dual-mode universities (DMUs). The latter have advantages in the flexibility of their teaching strategies and the wider range of courses they can offer (Rumble, 1992, pp. 33–5). To the surprise of some, no doubt, Rumble's detailed economic analysis suggests that the DMUs can achieve more cost-efficiencies than their distance teaching counterparts (pp. 35–40). His conclusions have stark implications for the latter:

While there are a number of strategies which DTUs can adopt, nearly all of them can also be copied by a CBU [campus based university] once it has adopted distance teaching. Thus the most effective response for a DTU may well be to turn itself into a DMU, either by establishing an on-campus program, or by merging with a CBU (Rumble, 1992, p. 43).

Rumble's analysis confirms the need for the breadth of vision both

211

practically and theoretically which this project has attempted to encourage. Harris's experiences at the 'centre' and on the 'margins' of a distance teaching university, coupled with his rigorous theoretical perspective, could prove valuable in the systemic change which Rumble has in mind. In Chapter 6, Burge and Haughey have provided a manifesto for those who aspire to transformative learning, whether they be in conventional institutions which decide to adopt distance teaching or distance teaching institutions which commence campus-based programmes. However, we need to remain aware of the interrelationships between such systemic, curricular and pedagogical changes and the broader contexts in which they are located.

The processes of educational reform we are currently engaged with are not only interrelated with one another but also are part of the broader interconnections which constitute what has been termed 'post', 'late' or 'high modernity' (see, for examples, Giddens, 1991; Giroux, 1990; Lather, 1991). Giddens argues that:

> In high modernity, the influence of distant happenings on proximate events, and on intimacies of the self, becomes more and more commonplace. The media, printed and electronic, obviously play a central role in this respect. Mediated experience, since the first experience of writing, has long influenced both self-identity and the basic organisation of social relations. With the development of mass communication, particularly electronic communication, the interpenetration of self development and social systems, up to and including global systems, becomes ever more pronounced (1991, p. 4).

Open and distance education have emerged as powerful examples of 'high modernity'. Their practitioners operate at a distance, both spatially and temporally, from a dispersed array of proximate teaching and learning events. As we have emphasized, these practices are mediated through print, audio-visual and electronic media. These media affect the self-identities of students and their teachers, and the social relations which surround them, both individually and jointly. Distance education projects across the landscape educational choices and options for people who may otherwise have had limited or no such choices previously. As Evans (1989b) suggests, this means that time-space relations are reconstructed into new forms which institutions and their students, together with their families, friends, colleagues, etc, manage in their own interests. As these forms of choices are exercised by people there are challenges presented to traditional educational institutions which seek to perpetuate their own interests. As learning through post-industrial forms of education takes place in the home, workplace, community centre, etc, so the academies find their traditions eroded and seek to incorporate contemporary educational practices in order to preserve their own interests.

These educational challenges are not confined by national or other boundaries. Globalization is a feature of late modernity which has been embraced by distance education, especially as educational institutions and their political bosses and business allies in developed nations seek to extend their influence and sources of revenue into developing nations. In the case of distance education this globalization operates at different levels. Courses are 'marketed' in developing nations, consultants and others help national governments establish open universities, etc, in the image of developed nations' institutions. Bureaucrats and administrators from developing nations circle the globe visiting institutions and conferences in pursuit of ideas, systems, course materials, etc, which they can implement at home. The colonization of the developing world can be seen as continuing under the benign guise of educational development (see Guy, 1991).

Let us conclude with some speculation. Is it possible to create a truly global university (or school)? How could it be achieved? Would it be a force for colonization or empowerment? Many would retort with the sensible question: why create a global university at all? There is a simple response to that: there is a demand from students for education which is based in universities thousands of kilometres from their homes. This demand has been satisfied for centuries by students travelling overseas to study. There are other ways of satisfying these needs. For a century the University of London has been prepared to examine students for its degrees, but the students have been expected to organize their own tuition, except in some limited circumstances. The University of London and the International Extension College are now collaborating to offer distance education courses, principally in Africa. As we have seen above, Levinson teaches globally and his successful students obtain prestigious degrees. Most of the Distance Education Centres of the Australian universities offer courses to students in the Asia-Pacific region. Despite these examples, at present most students wanting education at a prestigious university journey overseas.

In any market place there are always those who are interested in supplying goods and services where a demand exists. An Australian resident with a need for books published overseas can often obtain them more efficiently and cheaply from a British or US supplier than from an Australian bookshop or publishers' agent. The particular services which create speedy transactions are fax ordering and international credit card payments.

If Rumble is right, there may be many distance teaching universities throughout the world looking for collaborative business with dual-mode and campus-based universities (1992, pp. 40–43). A prospective combination to serve a global market may be as follows: a prestigious campus-based university, which has major control of the curriculum and examination; a distance teaching university which has international recognition for high quality course development and delivery; and smaller dual mode or distance teaching universities in markets with large numbers of potential enrolments. Such a combination would use communications and information technology to both administer and teach its courses and would do well in (and require) a mass market. Operations such as Levinson's would remain competitive in niche markets.

Are prospects like these really on the agenda in distance education? It is not necessary to go beyond the case studies in this book to confirm a positive answer. The same general principles from the 'quality movement in management' which have been manifested at Athabasca University and the OU are relevant here. Granger's reflections on the curricular collaboration between Empire State College and the OU provide practical knowledge for those engaged in such ventures. It may not be quite as easy as the chief executive officers and their advisers suggest! The trauma of adapting a system which works regionally to national and international contexts has been dealt with by Moodie and Nation. Following Walker's argument, is it possible to avoid a 'Fordist' model in a mass global university?

Notes

1. These are available in special numbers of the *British Journal of Educational Technology* (vol 7, no. 1, 1976) and *Programmed Learning and Educational Technology* (vol 13, no. 4, 1976) and, especially, Northcott (1976).
2. Levinson's contributions published in 1989 and 1990 are the best known within distance education. They succinctly summarize the relevant aspects for our field of his wide-ranging work on the evolution of knowledge and technology and the relationships between them. It is not possible to do any critical justice to his theoretical work in the present context. Levinson subscribes to a view of technology similar to the one we have espoused in this chapter. However, it must be said that although our own work draws upon many theoretical sources in common with Levinson, his approach is founded on wider sources of knowledge and is critical of sociologists' tendencies to ignore natural influences upon human behaviour (for example, 1989, pp. 200–203).

References

Academic Audit Unit, Committee of Vice-Chancellors and Principals (1991) *Quality Assurance in Universities*, (May) London: Committee of Vice-Chancellors and Principals.

Allen, P (1991) Black and Ethnic Minority Access at Wolverhampton Polytechnic, unpublished PhD thesis, Wolverhampton: Wolverhampton Polytechnic.

Althusser, L (1971) *Lenin and Philosophy and Other Essays*, trs. Brewster B, New York: Monthly Review Press, from *Lénine et la philosophie*, Paris: Maspéro, 1969.

Altrichter, H, Evans, T D and Morgan, A R (1991) *Windows: research and evaluation on a distance education course*, Geelong: Deakin University.

American Association of Colleges (1991) *The Challenge of Connected Learning*, Washington, DC: American Association of Colleges.

Ausubel, D (1968) *Educational Psychology: a cognitive view*, New York: Holt, Rinehart & Winston.

Bååth, J (1981) 'On the nature of distance education', *Distance Education*, 2, 2, pp. 212–19.

Bååth, J (1982) 'Distance students' learning – empirical findings and theoretical deliberations', *Distance Education*, 3, 1, pp. 6–27.

Badaracco, J L and Ellsworth, R R (1989) *Leadership and the Quest for Integrity*, Boston: Harvard Business School Press.

Ball, S and Goodson, I (1985a) 'Understanding teachers: concepts and careers', in Ball, S and Goodson, I (eds) pp. 1–26.

Ball, S and Goodson, I (eds) (1985b) *Teachers' Lives and Careers*, London: Falmer Press.

Bartlett, L (1989a) 'Images of reflection: a look and a review', *Qualitative Studies in Education*, 2, 4, pp. 351–7.

Bartlett, L (1989b) In the Beginning: text, context and pupil attention in initial classroom encounters, unpublished PhD thesis, Brisbane: University of Queensland.

Bates, A (1991) 'Third generation distance education', *Research in Distance Education*, 3, 2, pp. 10–15.

Beauchamp, L, Haughey, M and Jacknicke, K (in press) *Coming Back to the Question*.

Becker, H (1963) *Outsiders: studies in the sociology of deviance*, New York: Free Press.

Bennett, N (1976) *Teacher Styles and Pupil Progress*, London: Open Books.

Bennett, T and Woollacott, J (1987) *Bond and Beyond*, London: Macmillan.

Berg, L (1969) *Risinghill: the death of a comprehensive school*, Harmondsworth: Penguin.

Bernstein, B B (1977) *Class, Codes & Control Vol. 3*, 2nd edn, London: Routledge.

Berthoff, A E (1987) 'Foreword' in Freire, P and Macedo, D. (eds).

Bolton, G (1986) 'The opportunity of distance', *Distance Education*, 7, 1, pp. 5–22.

Boud, D and Griffin, V (eds) (1987) *Appreciating Adults Learning*, London: Kogan Page.

Bowles, S and Gintis, H (1976) *Schooling in Capitalist America: educational reform and the contradictions of economic life*, Philadelphia: Temple University Press.

Boyd, R D and Meyers, J G (1988) 'Transformative education', *International Journal of Lifelong Education*, 7, 4, pp. 261–84.

Brand, S (1988) *The Media Lab*, New York: Viking Penguin.

Brookfield, S (1983) *Adult Learners, Adult Education, and the Community*, Milton Keynes: Open University Press.

Brookfield, S (1986) *Understanding and Facilitating Adult Learning*, San Francisco: Jossey Bass.

Brookfield, S (1987) *Developing Critical Thinkers: challenging adults to explore alternative ways of thinking and acting*, San Francisco: Jossey Bass.

Brown, G and Atkins, M (1988) *Effective Teaching in Higher Education*, London: Methuen.

Brundage, D H and MacKeracher, D (1980) *Adult Learning Principles and their Application to Program Planning*, Toronto: Ontario Ministry of Education.

Buber, M (1970) *I and Thou*, New York: Scribners.

Buckingham, D (1990) 'What are words worth?', *Cultural Studies*, 5, 2, pp. 228–47.

Bunch, C (1987) *Passionate Politics: essays 1968–1986 – feminist theory in action*, New York: St Martin's Press.

Bunch, C and Pollack, S (eds) (1983) *Learning Our Way: essays in feminist education*, Trumansburg, NY: Crossing Press.

Burge, E J (1988) 'Beyond andragogy: some explorations for distance learning design', *Journal of Distance Education*, 3, 1, pp. 5–23.

Burge, E J and Lenskyj, H (1990) 'Women studying in distance education: issues and principles', *Journal of Distance Education*, 4, 2, pp. 20–37.

Burge, E J and Snow, J E (1990) 'Interactive audio classrooms: key principles for effective practice', *Education for Information*, 8, pp. 299–

312.

Calvert, J, Evans, T D and King B (in press) 'Inter-institutional collaboration in Australia: constructing a Master of Distance Education course', in Moran, L and Mugridge, I, (eds) *Collaboration in Distance Education*, London: Routledge.

Campion, M. (1991) 'Critical essay on technology in distance education', in Evans, T D and King, B (eds) pp. 183–203.

Campion, M and Guiton, P (1991) 'Economic instrumentalism and integration in Australian external studies', *Open Learning*, **6**, 2, pp. 12–20.

Campion, M and Kelly, M (1988) 'Integration of external studies and campus-based education in Australian higher education: the myth and the promise', *Distance Education*, **9**, 2, pp. 171–201.

Campion, M. and Renner, B. (1992) 'The supposed demise of Fordism: implications for distance education and higher education', *Distance Education*, **13**, 1, pp. 7–28.

Carr, W and Kemmis, S (1986) *Becoming Critical: knowing through action research*, Geelong: Deakin University Press and London: Falmer Press.

Chandler, D (1990) 'The educational ideology of the computer', *British Journal of Educational Technology*, **21**, 3, pp. 165–74.

Cockburn, C (1989) 'Equal Opportunities: the short and long agenda', *Industrial Relations Journal*, **20**, 3, pp. 213–25.

Connell, R W, Ashenden, D J, Kessler, S and Dowsett, G W (1982) *Making the Difference*, Sydney: Allen & Unwin.

Connelly, F M and Clandinin, D J (1988) *Teachers as Curriculum Planners: narratives of experience*, Toronto: Ontario Institute for Studies in Education and New York: Teachers' College Press.

Cook, J (1989) 'The liberation of distance: teaching women's studies from China', in Evans, T D and Nation, D E (eds) 1989b, pp. 23–37.

Culler, J (1983) *On Deconstruction: theory and criticism after structuralism*, London: Routledge and Kegan Paul.

Culley, M and Portuges, C (1985) *Gendered Subjects: the dynamics of feminist teaching*, Boston: Routledge.

Cziko, G (1989) 'Unpredictability and indeterminism in human behaviour: arguments and implications for educational research', *Educational Researcher*, April, pp. 17–25.

Dale, R (1981) 'Control, accountability and William Tyndale', in Dale, R et al. (eds) *Schooling and the National Interest*, Vol. 2, London: Falmer Press.

Dale, R, Esland, G and MacDonald, M (eds) (1976) *Schooling and Capitalism*, London: Routledge.

Daloz, L A (1986) *Effective Teaching and Mentoring*, San Francisco: Jossey Bass.

Daniel, J (1991) 'The Open University in a changing world', *Open Learning*, **6**, 1, pp. 3–8.

Davie, L E and Wells, R (1991) 'Empowering the learner through computer-mediated communication', *American Journal of Distance Education*, **5**, 1, pp. 15–23.

Dean, I (1975) 'Report of the external studies sub-committee', (ES75/1, 17.3.75) Interim Council, Deakin University.

DEC Working Party (1989a) *Distance Education Discussion and Direction Papers*, Churchill: Gippsland Institute of Advanced Education.

DEC Working Party (1989b) *Proposed Schedule for National Course to be Offered Through the Monash Gippsland DEC*, Churchill: Gippsland Institute of Advanced Education.

DEC Working Party (1989c) *Report of Meeting Held 29 June 1989*, Churchill: Gippsland Institute of Advanced Education.

DEC Working Party (1989d) *Weekend Schools and National Distance Education Provision*, Churchill: Gippsland Institute of Advanced Education.

DEC Working Party (1990) *Towards a New Approach to Distance Education: a discussion paper*, Churchill: Monash University College Gippsland.

DEC Working Party (1991) *Diverse Forms of Complementary Tuition*, Churchill: Monash University College Gippsland.

Delgado-Gaitan, C and Trueba, H (1991) *Crossing Cultural Borders: education for immigrant families in America*, London: Falmer Press.

Derrida, J (1973) *Speech & Phenomena & Other Essays on Husserl's Theory of Signs*, trs. D. B. Allison, Evanston: Northwestern University Press.

Derrida, J (1976) *Of Grammatology*, Baltimore, Md: Johns Hopkins University Press, trs. Gayatri Chakravorty Spivak from *De la grammatologie*, Paris: Minuit, 1967.

Derrida, J (1981) *Positions*, University of Chicago Press, trs. Alan Bass from *Positions*, Paris: Minuit, 1972.

Duffy, T M and Jonassen, D H (1991a) 'Continuing the dialogue: an introduction to this special issue', *Educational Technology*, **31**, 9, pp. 9–11.

Duffy, T M and Jonassen, D H (1991b) 'Constructivism: new implications for instructional technology', *Educational Technology*, **31**, 5, pp. 7–12.

Edwards, R (1991) 'The inevitable future? Post-Fordism and open learning', *Open Learning*, **6**, 2, pp. 36–41.

Eliot, T S (1944) *The Four Quartets*: 'Burnt Norton', London: Faber & Faber.

Ellsworth, E (1989) 'Why doesn't this feel empowering? Working through the repressive myths of critical pedagogy', *Harvard Educational Review*, **59**, 3, pp. 297–324.

Empire State College (1988) *Handbook for Tutors*, Saratoga Springs, NY: Empire State College.

Empire State College (1991) *1989–91 Bulletin*, Saratoga Springs, NY: Empire State College.

Evans, T D (1982) 'Being and becoming: teachers' perceptions of sex-roles and actions towards their male and female pupils', *British Journal of Sociology of Education*, **3**, 2, pp. 127–34.

Evans, T D (1988) *A Gender Agenda*, Sydney: Allen & Unwin.

Evans, T D (1989a) *Gender* (Unit SSS123/223 *Pathways in Sociology*) Geelong: Deakin University.

Evans, T D (1989b) 'Taking place: the social construction of place, time and space, and the (re)making of distances in distance education,' *Distance Education*, **10**, 2, pp.170–83.

Evans, T D (1990) (ed.) *Research in Distance Education 1*, Geelong: Deakin University.

Evans, T D (1991) 'An epistemological orientation to critical reflection in distance education' in Evans, T D and King, B (eds), pp. 7–18.

Evans, T D and Bonning, F (1989) 'Democratic curriculum development at a distance', in Evans, T D and Nation, D E (eds) 1989b, pp. 179–95.

Evans, T D and King, B (eds) (1991) *Beyond The Text: contemporary writing on distance education*, Geelong: Deakin University Press.

Evans, T D and Nation, D E (1987) 'Which future for distance education?', *International Council For Distance Education*, Bulletin **14**, pp. 48–53.

Evans, T D and Nation, D E (1989a) 'Dialogue in practice, research and theory in distance education', *Open Learning*, **4**, 2, pp. 37–43.

Evans, T D and Nation, D E (eds) (1989b) *Critical Reflections on Distance Education*, London: Falmer Press.

Evans, T D and Nation, D E (1989c) 'Critical reflections in distance education', in Evans, T D and Nation, D E (eds) 1989b, pp. 237–52.

Evans, T D and Nation, D E (1992) 'Theorising open and distance education', *Open Learning*, **7**, 2, pp.3–13.

Eyland, A, Elder, L and Noesjirwan, J (1983) *Equal Opportunity Project Staff Report*, Sydney: Macquarie University.

Faith, K (ed.) (1988) *Toward New Horizons for Women in Distance Education: international perspectives*, London: Routledge.

Feenberg, A (1989) 'The written world', in Mason, R and Kaye, A (eds) pp. 22–39.

Feyerabend, P (1975) *Against Method*, London: New Left Books.

Feynman, R (1990) *What do You Care what Other People Think?*, London: Unwin Paperbacks.

Fitzclarence, L and Kemmis S (1989) 'A distance education curriculum for curriculum theory', in Evans, T D and Nation, D E (eds) 1989b, pp. 147–77.

Foucault, M (1972) *The Archaeology of Knowledge*, London: Tavistock.

Foucault, M (1979) *Discipline and Punish: the birth of the prison*, London: Penguin, trs. Alan Sheridan from *Surveiller et Punir: naissance de la prison*, Paris: Gallimard, 1975.

Fox, S (1989) 'The production and distribution of knowledge through open and distance learning', *Educational Training and Technology International*, **26**, 3, pp. 269–80.

Freire, P (1970) *Pedagogy of the Oppressed*, New York: Seabury Press.

Freire, P and Macedo, D (1987) *Literacy: reading the word and the world*, South Hadley, MA: Bergin & Garvey.

Gardner, H (1985) *Frames of Mind*, New York: Basic Books.

Gardner, H (1991) *The Unschooled Mind*, New York: Basic Books.

Garrison, D R (1985) 'Three generations of technological innovation in distance education', *Distance Education*, 6, 2, pp. 235–41.

George, J (1990) 'Audio conferencing: just another small group activity', *Educational Training and Technology International*, 27, 3, pp. 244–48.

Gergen, K J (1982) *Toward Transformation in Social Knowledge*, New York: Spring-Verlag.

Giddens, A (1987) *Social Theory and Modern Sociology*, Cambridge: Polity Press.

Giddens, A (1991) *Modernity and Self-Identity*, Cambridge: Polity Press.

Gillard, G (1981) 'The implied teacher-learner relationship in distance education', *Australian & South Pacific External Studies Association Forum*, Suva, September.

Giroux, H (1986) 'Radical pedagogy and the politics of student voice', *Interchange*, 17, pp. 48–69.

Giroux, H (1987) 'Introduction' to Freire, P and Macedo, D (eds) pp. 1-28.

Giroux, H (1990) *Curriculum Discourse as Postmodernist Practice*, Geelong: Deakin University.

Godzich, W (1986) 'Foreword' to de Certeau, M *Heterologies: discourse on the Other*, trs. Brian Massumi, Minneapolis: University of Minnesota Press.

Gorbutt, D, Harris, D and Harris, M. (1991) 'Quality assurance: measurement and myth', *Evaluation and Assessment in Higher Education*, March.

Gore, J M (1989) 'Agency, structure and the rhetoric of teacher empowerment', paper presented at the Annual Meeting of the American Educational Research Association, San Francisco, March.

Gottlieb, E (1989) 'The discursive construction of knowledge: the case of radical education discourse', *Qualitative Studies in Education*, 2, 2, pp. 131–44.

Gouldner, A (1968) 'The sociologist as partisan: sociology and the welfare state', *American Sociologist*, 3, 2, pp. 103–16.

Grace, G (1987) 'Teachers and the state: a changing relation', in Lawn, M and Grace, G (eds) *Teachers: the culture and politics of work*, London: Falmer Press.

Grace, M (1989) ' "Is the University awful?": political activism and consciousness raising among external students', in Evans, T D and Nation, D E (eds) 1989b, pp. 55–71.

Green, M F (1989) *Minorities on Campus: a handbook for enhancing diversity*, Washington, DC: American Council on Education.

Groundwater-Smith, S (1990) *Perspectives on Schools Broadcasting*, Sydney: Curriculum Support Unit, NSW Department of School Education.

Grundy, S (1987) *Curriculum: product or praxis*, London: Falmer Press.

Guy, R (1991) 'Distance education and the developing work', in Evans and King (eds) pp. 152–75.

Habermas, J (1984) *The Theory of Communicative Action, vol 1: reason and the rationalization of society*, Boston: Beacon Press.

Hall, J W (1991) *Access through Innovation*, New York: American Council on Education & MacMillan Publishing Company.

Hamilton, D (1977) *In Search of Structure*, London: Hodder and Stoughton.

Hamilton, D (1987) 'The pedagogical juggernaut', *British Journal of Educational Studies*, 30, 1, pp. 18–29.

Hamilton, D (1989a) *Towards a Theory of Schooling*, London: Falmer Press.

Hamilton, D (1989b) 'The changing schoolroom' in Walker, R and Lewis, R, *Classroom Processes: the video* (typescript) Geelong: Deakin University.

Hamilton, D (1990a) *Curriculum History*, Geelong: Deakin University.

Hamilton, D (1990b) *Learning about Education: the unfinished curriculum*, Buckingham: Open University Press.

Hammersley, M. (1986) 'Measurement in ethnography: the case of Pollard on teaching style', in Hammersley, M. (ed.) *Case Studies in Classroom Research*, Milton Keynes: Open University Press.

Harisim, L (1989) 'On-line education: a new domain', in Mason, R and Kaye, A (eds) pp. 50–62.

Harland, R (1987) *Superstructuralism: the philosophy of structuralism and post-structuralism*, London: Methuen.

Harré, R (1979) *Social Being*, Oxford: Blackwell.

Harré, R (1984) *Personal Being*, Cambridge: Harvard University Press.

Harré, R and Secord, P F (1972) *The Explanation of Social Behaviour*, Oxford: Blackwell.

Harris, D (1976) 'Educational technology at the Open University: a short history of achievement and cancellation', *British Journal of Educational Technology*, 7, 1, pp. 43–53.

Harris, D (1987) *Openness and Closure in Distance Education*, London: Falmer Press.

Harris, D (1989) 'Emancipatory potential and micropolitical practice', paper presented to the British Sociological Association Annual Conference, March.

Harris, D (1991) 'Towards a critical educational technology in distance education', in Evans, T D and King, B (eds) pp. 204–25.

Harris, D (1992) 'Distance education: researching formations', in Evans, T and Juler, P (eds) *Research in Distance Education 2*, Geelong: Deakin University Press.

Harris, D and Holmes, J (1976) 'Open-ness and control in higher education: towards a critique of the Open University', in Dale, R, Esland, G and MacDonald, M (eds) *Schooling and Capitalism*, London: Routledge and Kegan Paul.

Hart, M (1985) 'Thematization of power, the search for common interests, and self-reflection: towards a comprehensive concept of emancipatory education', *International Journal of Lifelong Education*, 4, 2, pp. 119–34.

Hart, M (1990) 'Critical theory and beyond: further perspectives on emancipatory education', *Adult Education Quarterly*, **40**, 3, pp. 125–38.

Haughey, M (1989) 'The critical role of the educational developer', in Parer, M (ed.) *Development, Design and Distance Education*, Churchill, Victoria: Gippsland Institute, pp. 51–6.

Haughey, M (1991) 'Confronting the pedagogical issues', *Open Learning*, **6**, 3, pp. 14–23.

Hawkridge, D (1976) 'Next year Jerusalem! The rise of educational technology', *British Journal of Educational Technology*, **7**, 1, pp. 7–30.

Hawkridge, D (1981) 'The telesis of educational technology', *British Journal of Educational Technology*, **12**, 1, pp. 4-18.

Hawkridge, D (1983) *New Information Technology in Education*, Beckenham: Croom Helm.

Hawkridge, D (1991) 'Challenging educational technology', *Educational Training and Technology International*, **28**, 2, pp. 102–10.

Hawkridge, D, Newton, W and Hall, C (1988) *Computers in Company Training*, Beckenham: Croom Helm.

Hocking, H (1990) 'Educational research in chaos: new paradigms for the changing era', *Australian Educational Researcher*, **17**, 1, pp. 1–22.

Hooks, B (1988) *Talking Back: thinking feminist, thinking black*, Boston: South End Press.

Hopper, M W (1971) 'Proposal to offer subjects for the Diploma of General Studies externally in 1972', Churchill: Gippsland Institute of Advanced Education.

Hopper, M W (1974) 'The college and the external student' in Kent, P and Dooley, J (eds) *Whither Advanced Education?*, Melbourne: National Press, pp. 103–12.

Hopper, M W (1976) 'The Institute and the community', Churchill: Gippsland Institute of Advanced Education.

Hopper, M W (1979) 'The regional CAE: its potential as an Australian community college' in Anwyl, J E (ed.) *Australian Community Colleges*, Melbourne: Centre for the Study of Higher Education, University of Melbourne.

Horlock, J H (1987) 'Academic Standards' (internal Open University paper).

Hughes, R (1980) *The Shock of the New*, London: British Broadcasting Corporation (book and television series).

Hunt, R A (1991) 'Foreword' to Newman, J M (1991) *Interwoven Conversations: learning and teaching through critical reflection*, Toronto: OISE Press and London: Heinemann.

Illich, I (1970) *Deschooling Society*, Harmondsworth: Penguin.

Jevons, F (1984) 'Distance education in a mixed institution: working towards parity', *Distance Education*, **5**, 1, pp. 24–37.

Jewson, N and Mason, D (1986) 'The theory and practice of equal oppportunities policies: liberal and radical approaches', *Sociological Review*, **34**, 2, pp. 307–34.

Johnson, R (Chair) (1989) 'Report of the joint Department of Employment, Education and Training/Higher Education Council assessment team on the designation of Distance Education Centres for Australia', Canberra.

Johnson, R (1991a) 'Developments in distance higher education in Australia', *International Council of Distance Education Bulletin*, **26**, pp. 11–22.

Johnson, R (1991b) 'The reorganization of Australian distance education: some comments', *Open Learning*, **6**, 3, pp. 52–3.

Jonassen, D H (1991a) 'Evaluating constructivist learning', *Educational Technology*, **31**, 9, pp. 28–33.

Jonassen, D H (1991b) 'Objectivism versus constructivism: do we need a new philosophical paradigm?', *Educational Technology Research and Development*, **39**, 3, pp. 5–14.

Keegan, D (1980) 'On defining distance education', *Distance Education*, **1**, 1, pp. 13–36.

Keegan, D. (1986) *Foundations of Distance Education*, Beckenham: Croom Helm.

Kelly, M (1987) 'The high cost of "efficiency and effectiveness" in Australia', *Open Learning*, **2**, 3, pp. 19–24.

Kelly, P (1991) (internal Open University correspondence).

Kennedy, T (1989) Distance Education Centre Developments, memo to all staff, 18 August, Churchill: Gippsland Institute of Advanced Education.

King, B (1989) 'Teaching distance education', in Evans, T D and Nation, D E (eds) 1989b, pp. 95–121.

Kuhn, T S (1970) *The Structure of Scientific Revolutions*, 2nd edn, Chicago: University of Chicago Press.

Labour Party (1966) *Time for Decision*, Manifesto for the 1966 general election.

Lakatos, I and Musgrave, A (1970) *Criticism and the Growth of Knowledge*, Cambridge: Cambridge University Press.

Lather, P (1991) *Getting Smart: feminist research and pedagogy with/in the post modern*, New York: Routledge.

Lee, J (1971) Speech to a public meeting in Cardiff, June 1971. Quoted in *Open University Admissions Committee*, paper AD/47/8.

Lee, J (1979) Interview, in *The First Ten Years*, Milton Keynes: Open University.

Lehmann, T (1978) *Independent Study Program – WNET Course 101: Final Report and Recommendations*, Saratoga Springs, New York: Empire State College.

Lehmann, T and Thorsland, M (1977) *Empire State College Field Test of British Open University Courses*, Saratoga Springs, NY: Empire State College.

Levinson, P (1988) *Mind at Large: knowing in the technological age*, Greenwich: JAI Press.

Levinson, P (1989) 'Media relations: integrating computer telecommunications with educational media', in Mason, R and Kaye, A (eds) pp. 40–49.

Levinson, P (1990) 'Computer conferencing in the context of the evolution of the media', in Harasim, L (ed.) *Online Education: perspectives on a new environment*, New York: Praeger.

Lévi-Strauss, C (1972) *Structural Anthropology Volume 1*, London: Penguin, trs. Jacobson, C and Grundfest Schoepf, B from *Anthropologie structurale*, Paris: Plon, 1958.

Liston, D P and Zeichner, K M (1987) 'Critical pedagogy and teacher education', *Journal of Education*, **169**, 3, pp. 117–37.

Livingston, K (1990) 'The shake-up in Australian higher education and its impact on distance education', *International Council of Distance Education Bulletin*, **24**, pp 52–9.

Lord, A (1965) *The Singer of Tales*, New York: Atheneum.

MacGregor, K (1991) 'Quality of teaching faces student test', *The Times Higher Education Supplement*, 13 September, p. 2.

MacKenzie, N (1976) 'A crisis of identity?', *British Journal of Educational Technology*, **7**, 1, pp. 4–6.

McTaggart, R (1989) 'Principles for participatory action research', paper presented at the Third World Encounter on Participatory Research, Managua, Nicaragua, September.

Mansfield, R and Nunan, E E (1978) 'Towards an alternative educational technology', *British Journal of Educational Technology*, **9**, 3, pp. 170–76.

Maranhao, T (1991) 'Reflection, dialogue and the subject', in Steier, F (ed.) *Research and Reflexivity*, London: Sage, pp. 235–50.

Marton, F and Säljö, R. (1984) 'Approaches to learning', in Marton, F, Hounsell, D and Entwistle, N (eds) pp. 36–55.

Marton, F, Hounsell, D and Entwistle, N (eds) (1984) *The Experience of Learning*, Edinburgh: Scottish Academic Press.

Mason, R and Kaye, A (eds) (1989) *Mindweave: communication, computers and distance education*, Oxford: Pergamon Press.

Meek, V L (1984) *Brown Coal or Plato? A study of the Gippsland Institute of Advanced Education*, Hawthorn: Australian Council of Educational Research.

Merriam, S B and Caffarella, R S (1991) *Learning in Adulthood*, San Francisco: Jossey Bass.

Mezirow, J (1981) 'A critical theory of adult learning and education', *Adult Education*, **32**, 1, pp. 3–24.

Mezirow, J (1989) 'Transformation theory and social action: a response to Collard and Law', *Adult Education Quarterly*, **39**, 3, 169–75.

Mezirow, J (1991) *Transformative Dimensions of Adult Learning*, San Francisco: Jossey Bass.

Mezirow, J and Associates (1990) *Fostering Critical Reflection in Adulthood: a guide to transformative and emancipatory learning*, San Francisco: Jossey Bass.

Minnich, E K (1990) *Transforming Knowledge*, Philadelphia: Temple University Press.

Modra, H (1989) 'Using journals to encourage critical thinking at a distance', in Evans, T D and Nation, D E (eds) 1989b, pp. 123–46.

Modra, H (1991) 'On the possibility of dialogue in distance education', in Evans, T D and King, B (eds), pp. 83–100.

Monash Distance Education Centre (1992) *Policy for Course Presentation in Distance Education*, Churchill: Monash Distance Education Centre.

Monash University (1959) *Council Minutes*, November, Appendix G.

Monash University College Gippsland (1990) *Academic Board Minutes*, A 90/5, 13 June, 2.2.1.

Monash University File (1970), CF/0/ 1.3 folio 18.

Moodie, G (1991a) 'Academics' resistance of external course pressures: attempts to establish external studies at Monash University 1958–70', *Distance Education*, 12, 2, pp. 191–208.

Moodie, G (1991b) 'The TV Open Learning project – differing notions of "quality" in a new distance education program', in *Australian & South Pacific External Studies Association Forum Papers*, Bathurst: Charles Sturt University.

Morgan, A (1990) 'What ever happened to the silent revolution? Research, theory and practice in distance education', in Evans, T D (ed.) pp. 9–20.

Morgan, A R (1991) '*Classroom Processes*: a case study of course production' in Altrichter, H, Evans, T D and Morgan, A R (eds) pp. 23–70.

Murgatroyd, S (1980) 'What actually happens in tutorials?', *Teaching at a Distance*, 18, pp. 44–53.

Nation, D E (1985) 'I'm sorry to bother you at home, but you said we could ring ...', paper presented at the Thirteenth World Conference, International Council for Distance Education, Melbourne, August.

Nation, D E (1987) 'Some reflections upon teaching sociology at a distance', *Distance Education*, 8, 2, pp. 524–35.

Nation, D E (1989) 'Personal reflections on an introductory sociology course', in Evans, T D and Nation, D E (eds), (1989b), pp. 39–54.

Nation, D E (1991) 'Teaching texts and independent learning' in Evans, T D and King, B (eds), pp. 101–29.

Nation, D E and Walker, R (1992) 'Course development without instructional design', in Parer, M (ed.) *Developing Open Learning Courses*, Churchill: Centre for Distance Learning, Monash University.

Neill, A S (1968) *Summerhill*, Harmondsworth: Penguin.

Newman, J M (1991) *Interwoven Conversations: Learning and teaching through critical reflection*, Toronto: OISE; London: Heinemann.

Nipper, S (1989) 'Third generation distance learning and computer conferencing', in Mason, R and Kaye, A (eds) pp. 63–73.

Northcott, P (1976) 'The Institute of Educational Technology, the Open University, 1969–1975', *British Journal of Educational Technology*, 13, 4, 11–23.

Northedge, A (1991) *The Good Study Guide*, Milton Keynes: Open University Press.

Nunan, E (1983) *Countering Educational Design*, Beckenham: Croom Helm.

Olsen, G (1978) 'Servitude and inequality in spatial planning: ideology and methodology in conflict' in Peet, R (ed.) *Radical Geography*, London: Methuen, pp. 353–61.

Open University (1973) *Education, Economy and Politics* (E352), Milton Keynes: Open University.

Open University (1984) *Long Term Review Group*, Milton Keynes: Open University.

Open University (1987a) *Classroom Studies* (E812), Milton Keynes: Open University.

Open University (1987b) *Gender and Education* (E813), Milton Keynes: Open University.

Open University (1988a) *Educational Organisations and Professionals* (E814), Milton Keynes: Open University.

Open University (1988b) *Language and Literacy* (E815), Milton Keynes: Open University.

Open University (1989) *Strategic Academic Review*, Milton Keynes: Open University.

Open University (1990) *Report of the Equal Opportunities Team*, Milton Keynes: Open University.

Open University (1991) *1991 Residential Schools Three Year Plan*, Academic Board Paper, AcB/50/11 Milton Keynes: Open University.

Palmer, P (Gillard) (1986) *The Lively Audience*, Sydney: Allen & Unwin.

Parkin, F (1974) 'Strategies of social closure in class formation' in Parkin, F (ed.) *The Social Analysis of Class Structure*, London: Tavistock Publications.

Paul, R H (1990) *Open Learning and Open Management: leadership and integrity in distance education*, London: Kogan Page.

Pelton, J (1991) 'Technology and education: friend or foe?', *Research in Distance Education*, **3**, 2, pp. 2–9.

Penrose, R (1991) 'Review of Quantum Profiles by Jeremy Bernstein', *New York Review of Books*, **38**, 6 (March 28), pp. 37–8.

Perry, P (1991) 'A view from quality street', *The Times Higher Education Supplement*, 12 July, p. 16.

Perry, W (1974) 'The Open University – another look', *Royal Television Society Journal*, July/August.

Perry, W (1976) *Open University: A Personal Account by the First Vice-Chancellor*, Milton Keynes: Open University Press.

Perry, W (1986) 'Distance education, trends Worldwide', in van Enckevort, G et al. (eds) *Distance Education and the Adult Learner*, Heerlen: Open Universiteit, pp. 15–20.

Perry, W G (1968) *Forms of Intellectual and Ethical Development in the College Years*, New York: Holt, Rinehart & Winston.

Philo, G, Hewitt, J, Beharrell, P and Davis, H (The Glasgow Media Group) (1976) *Bad News*, London: Writers and Readers.

Philo, G, Hewitt, J, Beharrell, P and Davis, H (The Glasgow Media Group) (1982) *Really Bad News*, London: Writers and Readers.

Philo, G, Hewitt, J, Beharrell, P and Davis, H (The Glasgow Media Group) (1985) *More Bad News*, London: Writers and Readers.

Polanyi, M (1960) *Personal Knowledge: towards a post critical philosophy*, 3rd edn, London: Routledge.

Popper, K (1968) *The Logic of Scientific Discovery*, London: Hutchinson.

Pratt, J (1971) 'Open, University!', *Higher Education Review*, Spring, pp. 6–24.

Rappaport, J (1986) 'Collaborating for empowerment: creating the language of mutual help', in Boyte, H C and Riessman, F (eds) *The New Populism: the politics of empowerment*, Philadelphia: Temple University Press, pp. 64–79.

Rehm, M (1989) 'Emancipatory vocational education: pedagogy for the work of individuals and society', *Journal of Education*, **171**, 3, pp. 109–23.

Riseborough, G (1985) 'Pupils, teachers' careers and schooling: an empirical study', in Ball, S and Goodson, I (eds).

Rogers, C (1983) *Freedom to Learn for the 80s*, Columbus, OH: Merrill.

Rubin, G (1975) 'The traffic in women: notes on the "political economy" of sex', in Reiter, R (ed.) *Toward an Anthropology of Women*, New York: Monthly Review Press.

Rubinstein, D and Stoneman, C (eds) (1970) *Education for Democracy*, Harmondsworth: Penguin.

Rumble, G (1992) 'The competitive vulnerability of distance teaching universities', *Open Learning*, 7, 2, pp. 31–45.

de Saussure, F (1959) *Course in General Linguistics*, Bally, C and Sechehaye, A, edited in collaboration with Reidlinger, A, NY: Philosophical Library, trs. Baskin, W, from *Cours de linguistique générale*, Paris, 1915.

Schoenheimer, H P (1973) *Good Australian Schools and Their Communities*, Melbourne: Technical Teachers' Association of Victoria.

Schön, D A (1983) *The Reflective Practitioner: How Professionals Think in Action*, New York: Basic Books.

Schön, D A (1987) *Educating the Reflective Practitioner*, San Francisco: Jossey Bass.

Scott, P (1990) 'Postmodern challenge I', *Continuing Higher Education Review*, **54**, 3, (reprinted from *The Times Higher Education Supplement*, Aug–Sept, 1990).

Scriven, B (1990) 'Australia restructures distance higher education', *International Council of Distance Education Bulletin*, **22**, pp. 21–3.

Senge, P M (1990) *The Fifth Discipline: the art and the practice of the learning organization*, New York: Doubleday.

Sewart, D (1981) 'Distance teaching: a contradiction in terms?' in *Teaching at a Distance*, **19**, pp. 8–18; also in Sewart, D, Keegan, D and Holmberg, B (eds.) (1983) *Distance Education: international perspectives*, London: Croom Helm.

Shor, I (1989) 'Developing student autonomy in the classroom', *Equity and Excellence*, **24**, 3, pp. 35–7.

Shor, I and Freire, P (1987) *A Pedagogy for Liberation: dialogues on transforming education*, South Hadley: Bergin and Harvey.

Shrewsbury, C (1987) 'What is feminist pedagogy?', *Women's Studies Quarterly*, **15**, 3–4, pp. 6–14.

Simon, R (1987) 'Empowerment as a pedagogy of possibility', *Language Arts*, **64**, pp. 370–82.

Skidelsky, R (1969) *English Progressive Schools*, Harmondsworth: Penguin.

Smith, P and Kelly, M (eds) (1987) *Distance Education and the Mainstream*, Beckenham: Croom Helm.

Smyth, J (1989a) 'A critical pedagogy of classroom practice', *Journal of Curriculum Studies*, **21**, 6, pp. 483–502.

Smyth, J (1989b) 'When teachers theorize their practice: a reflexive approach to a distance education course', in Evans, T D and Nation, D E (eds) 1989b, pp. 197–223.

Student Research Centre (1986) 'The human dimension in OU study', *Open Learning*, **1**, 2, pp. 14–21.

Tait, A (ed.) (1991) *Proceedings of an International Conference on The Student, Community and Curriculum*, 10–13 Sept 1991, Cambridge, UK.

Taylor, E and Kaye, T (1986) 'Andragogy by design? Control and self-direction in the design of an Open University course', *Programmed Learning and Educational Technology*, **23**, 1, pp. 62–9.

Taylor, J C (1992) 'Distance education and technology in Australia', *International Council of Distance Education Bulletin*, **28**, pp. 22–30.

Taylor, J C and White, V J (1991) *The Evaluation of the Cost Effectiveness of Multi-Media Mixed-Mode Teaching and Learning*, Canberra: Australian Government Publishing Service.

Taylor, M (1986) 'Learning for self-direction in the classroom: the pattern of a transition process', *Studies in Higher Education*, **11**, 1, pp. 55–72.

Tight, M (1989) 'The ideology of higher education', in Fulton, O (ed.) *Access and Institutional Change*, Bletchley: SRHE/Open University Press.

Tobias, S. (1990) 'They're not dumb, they're different: a new tier of talent for science', *Change*, **22**, 4 (July/August), pp. 10–30.

Travis, A and Hencke, D (1991) 'Major's charter negotiates Whitehall obstacle course', *The Guardian*, July 12.

Van Manen, M (1991) *The Tact of Teaching: the meaning of pedagogical thoughtfulness*, London: Althouse Press.

Wajcman, J (1991) *Feminism Confronts Technology*, Cambridge: Polity Press.

Waller, W (1965) *The Sociology of Teaching*, New York: Wiley.

Waters, R (1990) *The Wall: live in Berlin*, Compact Disc 846 612–2, The Netherlands: International Music.

Wearne, H (1989) 'The development of the colleges of advanced education with special reference to the course development of the Gippsland Institute of Advanced Education', Master of Arts research paper, Faculty of Arts, Monash University.

White Paper (1991) *Higher Education: a new framework*, May, cm.1541, London: HMSO.

Williams, G (1991) 'Identifying and developing a quality ethos for teaching in higher education', unpublished report, Centre for Higher Education Studies, University of London.

Williams, J, Cocking, J and Davies, L (1989) *Words or Deeds: a review of equal opportunity policies in higher education,* London: Commission for Racial Equality.

Willis, P (1977) *Learning to Labour,* Farnborough: Saxon House.

Winston, B (1986) *Misunderstanding Media,* Cambridge, MA: Harvard University Press.

Wishart, D (Chair) (1981) 'Report of the advisory committee on off-campus studies to the Victorian post-secondary commission', Melbourne: Victorian Post-Secondary Commission.

Woodley, A. (1981) *Implementation of Higher Education Reforms: the Open University of the United Kingdom,* Paris: European Cultural Foundation, Institute of Education.

Young, K (1989) 'The space between words: Local Authorities and the concept of Equal Opportunities', in Jenkins, R and Salamos, J (eds) *Racism and Equal Opportunity Policies in the 1980s,* Cambridge: Cambridge University Press.

Young, M F D (ed.) (1971) *Knowledge and Control: new directions for the sociology of education,* London: Collier Macmillan.

Young, P L (1972) 'Report to council concerning the external studies operation of the Gippsland Institute of Advanced Education', Gippsland Institute of Advanced Education Council, 72/4, 2.3.

Notes on Contributors

Elizabeth E Burge is the Distance Learning Coordinator at the Ontario Institute for Studies in Education, affiliated with the University of Toronto. She is interested in how learners and teachers work in interactive contexts in relation to models of teaching.

Bernadette Butcher is Equal Opportunities Adviser for Manchester Central Hospitals, Community Care (NHS Trust) and Course Coordinator and Lecturer on the 'Access into the Health Professions' course at South Manchester College.

Garry Gillard is a Lecturer in Distance Education in the External Studies Unit at Murdoch University in Western Australia. He also teaches in Murdoch's Communication Studies programme. He is committed to minimizing the distance between students and teachers in all forms of education.

Daniel Granger is the Director of the Center for Distance Learning at Empire State College of the State University of New York. He has written and spoken extensively on adult and distance learning and continues to explore the development of educational modes responsive to individual and social needs.

David Harris is a Senior Lecturer in Sociology and Media at the College of St Mark and St John in Plymouth, England. He has researched and published widely on educational technology, distance education and the media. His book *From Class Struggles to the Politics of Pleasure* was published in 1992.

Margaret Haughey is an Associate Professor in the Department of Educational Administration at the University of Alberta and President of the Canadian Association for Distance Education. Besides distance education, her research interests include alternative research philosophies, and school-based practice.

Bruce King is an Associate Professor and Director of the Distance Education Centre at the University of South Australia. He has written on aspects of curriculum development and policy initiatives in open and distance education.

Roger Mills is Pro-Vice-Chancellor (Presentation and Student Support) at the UK Open University. He has been closely involved in the devolution of decision-making from the centre of the University to its regions and returns in 1993 to be Director of the East Anglian Region of the University based in Cambridge.

Alistair Morgan is a Lecturer in Educational Technology in the Institute of Educational Technology at the UK Open University. His research and publication concern project-based learning and student-centred approaches to pedagogy in open and distance learning.

Gavin Moodie is an Assistant Registrar at Monash University in Victoria, Australia. His interest in distance education commenced during his employment at Deakin University. Currently, he is Manager of the Australian TV Open Learning Project. His main interest is in university administration.

Ted Nunan is an Associate Professor in the Distance Education Centre of the University of South Australia. He has written on the critical analysis of distance education and educational design.

Ross Paul is President of the Laurentian University, Sudbury, Ontario, Canada, a middle-sized regional university serving north-eastern Ontario, with a strong distance education programme. He is best known as the author of *Open Learning and Open Management* and as a writer and performer of satirical musical reviews.

Lee Taylor is the Director of Equal Opportunities at the UK Open University.

Mary Thorpe is a Senior Lecturer in the Institute of Educational Technology at the UK Open University. She has written on tuition and learner support, and on practitioner evaluation of open and distance learning, and has worked on continuing education and third world studies courses.

Rob Walker is Associate Professor of Education at Deakin University, having previously worked at the Centre for Applied Research in Education at the University of East Anglia (UK). A lapsed pharmacologist and lapsed sociologist, he is currently actively involved in distance education (in Education), in evaluating science education programmes and in drug education.

Alan Woodley is a Senior Research Fellow in the Institute of Educational Technology at the UK Open University.

Index